RUSSIA
AFTER THE WAR

The New Russian History

Series Editor: Donald J. Raleigh,
University of North Carolina, Chapel Hill

This series makes examples of the finest work of the most eminent historians in Russia today available to English-language readers. Each volume has been specially prepared with an international audience in mind, and each is introduced by an outstanding Western scholar in the same field.

RUSSIA
AFTER THE WAR

HOPES, ILLUSIONS, AND
DISAPPOINTMENTS, 1945–1957

Elena Zubkova

Translated and edited by
Hugh Ragsdale

M.E. Sharpe
Armonk, New York
London, England

Library of Congress Cataloging-in-Publication Data

Zubkova, E. IU. (Elena IUr'evna)
Russia after the war: hopes, illusions, and disappointments, 1945–1957 / by Elena
Zubkova; translated and edited by Hugh Ragsdale.
p. cm. — (New Russian history)
Includes bibliographical references and index.
ISBN 0–7656–0227–X (cloth : alk. paper)
ISBN 0–7656–0228-8 (pbk : alk. paper)
1. Soviet Union—Social conditions—1945–1991. 2. Soviet Union—Economic
conditions—1945–1955. 3. Reconstruction (1939–1951)—Soviet Union.
I. Title. II. Series.
HN523.5.Z8   1998
306'.0947—dc21
98–17042
CIP

Printed in the United States of America

The paper used in this publication meets the minimum requirements of
American National Standard for Information Sciences—
Permanence of Paper for Printed Library Materials,
ANSI Z 39.48-1984.

∞

BM (c)   10   9   8   7   6   5   4   3   2
BM (p)   10   9   8   7   6   5   4   3   2

Contents

Photographs follow page 98

Translator's Introduction

In contrast to the enormous literature on that most controversial of all subjects of the early postwar period, the Cold War, Soviet internal affairs have received relatively meager attention. What we know of them is little more than a litany of several chiefly ominous events: the forced repatriation of reluctant Soviet military and civilian personnel from Central Europe at the end of the Second World War, the infamous Leningrad Affair (purge) of 1949, the Nineteenth Party Congress of November 1952, and the even more infamous Doctors' Plot of early 1953.[1] As Alexander Werth (who was there) observed, it is "the most unexplored period in the whole history of the Soviet Union."[2] In one of the few respectable, if dated, textbooks of the period, Roger Pethybridge agrees: "The last stage of Stalin's rule is as difficult to interpret as any period in the Middle Ages."[3] These two authors were long among the leading authorities on the subject, yet both were compelled to devote the bulk of their accounts to foreign affairs, as there was simply insufficient information on Soviet internal affairs.

If any part of this opaque picture has been more obscure than the whole, it is public opinion. When I told colleagues and Russian émigrés that I was translating a book on Soviet public opinion, their nearly invariable response was incredulous: Was there such a thing? they asked.

Fortunately, we now have a substantial remedy for this sad state of affairs. The work of Elena Zubkova is, in the literal sense of an oft-abused word, unique. She is bold enough to attack these two difficult facets—public opinion and the high tide of Stalinism—of this doubly obscure subject at once. If some of her discoveries confirm our expectations, most of them are new and informative. The merest sampler of her subject matter illustrates the point:

viii TRANSLATOR'S INTRODUCTION

- Given the brutal male mortality rate during the Second World War, what did young Russian women do for a family life in the postwar generation?
- If the government perceived the moral solidarity of veterans (*shalmannaia demokratiia*) as a threat to its stability, what kind of policy did it deliberately utilize to divide them against each other?
- Why did the nearly half million amputees among the veterans have to be re-certified as disabled by a new medical examination every year?
- What prompted children to ask parents why Stalin did not order God to send better weather, and what prompted good members of the Communist Party to attend church services to pray for rain?
- Why did the government ship grain abroad while tens of millions of Russians suffered malnutrition at home (and 2 million died of it)?
- What led the Russian peasants to expect President Harry Truman and Prime Minister Winston Churchill to declare war on the Soviet Union for the sake of abolishing the collective farm?
- In the face of the daunting difficulties of their life at home, why did the Russians of this generation take such a lively interest in foreign affairs—more perhaps than we did—especially in such hot spots as Greece and China?
- What prompted some Russians to anticipate real democracy and a free-market economy after the war?
- How do we account for the juxtaposition after the war of both pious adulation and visceral hatred of Stalin?
- What kind of literary discussion evoked such vital interest as to have people climbing the pipes outside the Writers' Union in order to listen through a second-story window?
- When the doors of the GULAG Archipelago were thrown open in 1953, what impact did the massive release of many brutalized prisoners have on conventional society?
- How are we to appreciate the pathos of those prisoners, falsely accused and convicted, later released in the great post-Stalinist amnesty presumably conferring legal rehabilitation, only to find that the stigma of Stalinist suspicion would never leave them?

One of them found bittersweet relief in what might reduce a Western citizen to abject despair.

When will we former convicts, not guilty of anything, ever be fully rehabilitated? I have resolved the question for myself: Never. My fate?

My future? It has already been determined. In words: trust. In fact: suspicion. In the hearts of the powers that be: eternal suspicion. But that no longer bothers me. The more important problem is settled: my children can respond without fear on that line in the questionnaires: "Who is your father?" They can write boldly and honestly: "reserve officer, soldier in the Great Patriotic War, communist since 1931."

In the aftermath of the Cold War, the fortunes of history in the former Soviet Union are ambivalent, to say the least.[4] In the immediate wake of glasnost, there were dramatic revelations addressed to the so-called blank spots (*belye piatna*) of Soviet history. It was an exciting time. As distinguished Soviet historian Natan Eidelman (now deceased) told me, for a while it was more interesting to read than to live. As time passed, however, the profession of scholarship had to adjust to the new conditions of the marketplace, and the problems of material life sometimes took precedence over the taste for the academic and aesthetic way of life. At that point, something of a dissolution of the old historical establishment took place. It was in part because old dogs did not easily learn new tricks, in part because historians (humanists in general) did not produce the material items most in demand in the new conditions of uncivil capitalism and lost their livelihood as a consequence. I know of one academic department of the premier Institute of History (Academy of Sciences) in which the staff is less than half its former size, a department whose prominent research and writing waits for years to be published—if it is published at all.

In spite of such problems, some of the old guard has refashioned itself in a glasnost spirit. Yet most of this style of history is being done by a new generation of historians, and Elena Zubkova's book is a striking example of it. Much of the work in this genre, however, has appeared in the short and relatively transient form of journalism, what the Russians call *publitsistika*, less in the form of sustained and systematic research and writing at book length—this is part of Zubkova's achievement and distinction—and less yet in English translation.

Zubkova's work is seminal. There is undoubtedly more to be done in the provincial archives, in Politburo records, and perhaps—who knows?—in the still rarely accessible Presidential Archive; but the first step has been taken. The way has been shown. It is not to be expected, of course, that in the last years of Stalin's life opinion polling by scientific sampling was practiced in the Soviet Union. Zubkova is able to demonstrate, however, a considerable interaction of government policy and public mood. It may surprise the reader how sensitive the Soviet government was to public opinion—in fact, how responsive it was—especially, for example, in the question of price reductions or in reaction to the most innocent and harmless adolescent discussion groups.

With enviable skill Zubkova has used her factual findings to recreate the psychological atmosphere of the time. Here is a by no means unemotional study of the drama and tragedy of the end of the Stalinist epic, and the author's depiction of it exemplifies the best traditions of the humanism of the Russian intelligentsia.

This is distinguished work, and the publisher, the editor of the series, and I are pleased and proud to be able to offer it to the American public.

I am grateful to the author, Elena Zubkova, for offering us the second (first English) edition of this study for translation and for her prompt responses to multiple queries; to Patricia Kolb of M.E. Sharpe for commissioning the translation; to Donald J. Raleigh for inviting me to do the translation and for editorial advice in the course of it; to Elizabeth Granda and Ana Erlic of M.E. Sharpe for professional handling of the production process; to Galina Levina of the Kennan Moscow Project in Moscow for facilitating my communications with the author; to Kate Ragsdale, Jonathan Wallace, and Martha Ragsdale for critical readings; and to Andrei Korobkov and Alexander Frenkel for responding to my queries about difficult Russian expressions. We all know whose responsibility the final result is.

Hugh Ragsdale

RUSSIA
AFTER THE WAR

Introduction

For some people Russia has been a mysterious sphinx, for others an improbable monster. Their interest has always been characterized by a certain pragmatic consideration, whether prompted by the novels of Dostoevskii or nourished by fears of the Evil Empire. Few eras in the history of Russia, however, have been as obscure and enigmatic as the high-water mark of Stalinism, the period between the victory of 1945 and Khrushchev's famous denunciation of the tyrant in 1956. Fortunately, thanks to the blessings of glasnost, we are now in a position to assess this grim and dramatic subject on the basis of authentic historical records.

We must not imagine that Soviet history can be confined to the chronological boundaries 1917–1991. In fact, we Russians still labor psychologically under the legacy of the Soviet past. The majority of living Russians were born and acquired their social consciousness in the Soviet period. The older people among us lived through the war and the eras of Stalin and Khrushchev and have their own conception of those times. Their personal impressions and experience represent an enormous fund of social memory crucial to an understanding of both our past and present, and the serious historian is hardly entitled to sacrifice this living, contemporary history to subjects more abstract and farther afield.

After the great expansion of interest in social history during the past few years, the importance of mind-sets and public opinion is no longer an unfamiliar idea. Still, research in the social psychology and cultural anthropology of the Soviet period is only now beginning to take shape. Until recently our entrenched historiographic tradition was dominated by political research. Soviet history was represented chiefly as the record of isolated decisions made on high, while the attitudes and the perceptions of ordinary citizens were confined to diaries, travelogues, and memoirs.

Of course, we have seen attempts to fathom the phenomenon of Soviet man and the nature of his interaction with authority. Alexander Zinoviev developed the idea of "homo sovieticus,"[1] and Mikhail Geller reflected on the evolution of ideas that contributed to the formation of Soviet man;[2] but there has been no concrete research devoted to public opinion of the period, patterns of thinking, and the behavior of Soviet people. The mass movements and the public outlook of the era of the Revolution and of the 1920s have been studied, but those of the period after the Second World War have been completely neglected. One of the principal reasons for this state of affairs was the limited access to sources of information on attitudes and opinions. From the late 1920s to the late 1950s there were no institutes of sociology and public opinion in the USSR. Those who wanted to study Soviet society of that period had no data from sociological surveys or opinion polls. Data of this kind were held in secret by state security organs and were entirely inaccessible until the beginning of the 1990s.

This circumstance, however, did not deter Vera Dunham, who researched the subject using a source that was never secret, Soviet fiction.[3] The target of Dunham's work was the socio-political outlook—and the system of values—of the Soviet middle class, the chief social buttress of the Stalinist regime, and the interaction of this class with the supreme authority. In spite of divergent opinion on the comprehensively repressive system of fear and terror in the USSR, Dunham defined the broad functional spectrum of values and dynamics of behavior on which the Soviet regime rested. She called this relationship between the middle class and the government, the source of the system's stability, the "Big Deal."

The problem of achieving a working relationship between state and society was present at every level of the social pyramid, and it is this approach of Vera Dunham to the study of postwar Soviet society that we must not only continue but amplify. Such work, however, demands the exploitation of a new and larger scale of source materials to reflect the public attitudes of different social constituencies, those that together form that elusive abstraction, the people. That is precisely the goal of this study.

The postwar period, especially its first two to three years, represents one of the key phases in the development of Soviet government and society. While the political and economic structures of the USSR remained practically unchanged, a complex of hopes and expectations prompted by the sacrifices of the great victory led to major changes in Soviet society. These expectations formed the special character of the postwar years, the unique temper of the time. Many of these expectations, above all the hope for liberalization of the Stalinist regime, turned out to be purely illusory; but these very illusions were an essential feature of the postwar spirit, one of the components of the public's strategy of survival. For the majority of Soviet people, the question of survival in the new peacetime was no less complicated than it had been during the war itself. The postwar situation brought adjustments in the values and expectations left over from the war and prewar years, rearranged priorities of different categories of society in pursuit of their interests, and influenced the relationship between the people and the state.

The relationship of the public to the government and its policies, as well as to the political figures carrying them out, is one of the central themes of this book. It concentrates especially on those questions that either agitated Soviet society as a whole or affected the interests of large segments of society (the peasantry, the urban population, the intelligentsia). The structure of the book reflects what the people in the postwar years regarded as their most essential problems. It is based chiefly on the Russian experience and does not deal with developments in the non-Russian republics, a diverse and complex subject worthy of its own independent treatment rather than a superficial survey.

The chronological scope of the book is bounded by the developments of two critical years, 1945 and 1957. These dates are significant not only from the viewpoint of internal political developments, the end of the war, and the crisis which delivered preponderant power to Khrushchev. The years 1945 and 1957 are crucial especially as turning points in the evolution of the public mood, of the people's hopes. This is how they are represented in this book, the greater part of which is devoted to the period 1945–1953, the period that social historians are just beginning to explore.

The post-Stalinist period, the Thaw, is much better represented in scholarly research and documentary publications. The bulk of these works continue to exhibit a predominantly political focus, but they analyze political developments in a broad social context.[4] Similarly, historians of the period 1945–1953 are interested chiefly in the activity of the power structure as a whole or in individual Soviet leaders.[5] A special chapter of N.V. Romanovskii's 1995 book, *Liki stalinizma,*

1945–1953 (The Faces of Stalinism, 1945–1953)[6] is devoted to analyzing the dynamics of Soviet society after the war. Other researchers have examined the influence of the war on different aspects of Soviet life.[7] These works are dedicated, however, principally to those changes that took place in the demographic and social composition of the Soviet population after the war, and they deal only indirectly with the subject of public opinion. Research dealing specifically with this question in the post-Stalinist period is still rare.[8]

Admittedly, scholars have done studies of different social groups of postwar Soviet society. They have given us monographs on the workers,[9] and they have studied the peasantry and the development of agrarian policy especially intensively.[10] They have seriously examined the intelligentsia from several perspectives, including differences and changes in its outlook, its role in the dissident movement, and the way in which it fits into Soviet cultural policy as a whole.[11] Yet even those scholars gathering the large quantity of factual material necessary for this kind of research were as a rule not explicitly interested in the attitudes and the behavioral norms of the population.

The study of public opinion in this book has required a special complex of source materials. First are those of a private nature, diaries and memoirs, the greater part of which are published, and correspondence.[12] The correspondence consists chiefly of archival documents of three kinds: letters to the Central Committee of the Communist Party, 1945–1957; letters addressed to the editorial office of the journal *Novyi mir* (New World), 1953–1957; and correspondence intercepted and examined by the military censorship division of the state security apparatus, 1945–1946. This last category may not be considered fully private, as it consists of excerpts from correspondence forwarded by the organs of state security to the Central Committee in order to portray public opinion.

The memoirs, diaries, and letters are supplemented by another large group of sources that are still more informative. These are studies of public opinion conducted by the organs of government. The most important set of these materials is from the Central Committee archive and consists of the following varieties of documents: résumés of the political outlook of the population; reports of Central Committee inspectors on local conditions and opinion at the local level; lists of questions asked by audiences during lectures and meetings; résumés of citizens' observations and proposals during discussions of government projects or decrees; accounts of discussions of party or government decisions in party organizations and production units.

This second category of sources has all the peculiarities inherent in its bureaucratic origins, a factor that must be considered in interpreting its contents. First, the evidence has usually already been selected and edited. Sometimes the compilers of such documents recorded the most typical features of the public mood (commonly encountered expressions or questions), but sometimes they emphasized above all examples that deviated from consensual opinion. In these circumstances, it is impossible to determine the principles of selection of evidence, as the original data have not been preserved. Second, these documents are organized either by subject matter—for example, a particular political campaign—or by regions (usually *oblasts*, provinces). For this reason, with the exception of the broadest categories of the public—for example, the urban or rural population—it is practically impossible to identify the different social groups represented in the collection of opinion. Finally, these materials bear an ideological imprimatur and consequently reflect corresponding judgments and evaluations. Criticism of the regime is almost universally characterized as "unwholesome," "hostile," or even "anti-Soviet."

In order to get a reliable perspective on the public outlook, to describe the priorities of social expectations, and to determine the range of problems on which postwar society focused, we must employ a comparative analysis of the data in each category of official sources as well as in private sources. It is not possible to deal confidently with any kind of quantitative variables. There is not the remotest approximation here of scientific sampling by sociological opinion polls. What we may speak of with a great degree of assurance, however, are trends in the evolution of postwar opinion, the social distribution of the people's mix of expectations, and the more salient mind-sets at a given time.

Among the multiple source materials, literary fiction must also be mentioned. Its presence on the pages of this book is by no means incidental: fiction reflects (as does journalism) the nuances of social life that may escape other categories of sources. In the peculiar historical circumstances of Russian—even more of Soviet—political life, the role of literature was never confined to aesthetic creativity alone. It expressed the public mood and served as a medium of rapport among people—a function of literature especially conspicuous after the death of Stalin. Of course, from the viewpoint of historical inquiry, the use of literary works of a particular epoch can only be selective, but the interest of contemporaries in these works was also selective. In this instance, we are interested in those literary monuments eliciting the greatest public resonance, those serving peculiarly as trademarks of their time. For the postwar period these works include Ilia Ehrenburg's *Ottepel* (The Thaw), Vladimir Dudintsev's *Ne khlebom edinym* (Not by Bread Alone), and Valentin Ovechkin's *Raionnye budni* (District Routine, everyday life in the provinces). These books, in the opinion both of contemporaries and of their descendants, take their place in the ranks of significant social landmarks not so much by virtue of their artistic merit, which is debatable, as by their influence on the formation of public opinion in the country.

One other kind of source material especially dear to me is a series of interviews with people who lived through the postwar period and who now offer their testimony on the events of that time. Among my interview subjects were journalist Iurii Apenchenko, historian Pavel Volobuev, journalist and literary critic Igor Dedkov, journalist and economist Otto Latsis, writer Viacheslav Kondratiev, historian Iurii Sharapov, and dozens of people who wished to remain anonymous but whose assessments, opinions, judgments, or life stories helped me to understand, and, especially, to *feel* that dramatic and far from simple time. These living witnesses have enriched and enlivened the material of this book substantially.

The subject and the contents of this book require one essential caveat. Much of the story told here deals with the experience of people still living. It is possible that the personal experience and observations of the reader will partly or wholly differ from the assessment and conclusions presented by the author. This is unavoidable; everyone's experience is unique. Nevertheless there is in the fates of individuals something common that describes the fate of the era. That is what I wish to present.

The publication of this book has been facilitated by the assistance of many people whose professionalism, personal experience, and practical advice helped me to realize my conception. The project has benefited from the financial support of the Moscow Social Science Fund. I would like to express my gratitude to my colleagues at the Institute of Russian History of the Russian Academy of Sciences, the Russian Center for the Preservation and Study of Documents of Recent History (RTsKhIDNI), and the Center for the Preservation of Contemporary Documentation (TsKhSD) for their assistance.

PART I

STRATEGIES OF SURVIVAL

Chapter 1

The Social Psychology of the War

The literature on the Great Patriotic War, as the Armageddon of the eastern front during World War II is known in Russia, is so large that it has generated a historiography of historiography. Hundreds, even thousands of books are devoted to military operations, to command staff proceedings, to the reasons for the early defeats and the subsequent victories, and to the study of defense industry and the organization of support in the rear. The history of the war, based on precise reports of the production of tanks and planes, comparative body counts, inventories of cities taken and lost, and assessments of strategic trumps and mistakes—all of this is, of course, a necessary part of history. It is, however, military history of a limited perspective. War has an additional face, the social dimension, which epic deeds at the front and labor heroism in the rear do not describe. The social history of the Great Patriotic War is often overlooked, it seems, because war is perceived as an interruption of normal life, or at least as a deviation from an imaginary norm. But conflict, tragedy, and disaster are part of Russian life, if not of life itself. More important, the wartime experience was the foundation for the outlook of many in the postwar generation, and the source of their expectations.

The social history of the war is still weakly represented in scholarship although it is abundantly recorded in letters from the front, diaries, soldiers' memoirs, in the documentary publications of Ales Adamovich, Daniil Granin, and Svetlana Aleksievich;[1] in the letters, interviews, and documentary films collected by Konstantin Simonov; and in the wartime prose of soldier-authors Viktor Nekrasov, Viktor

Astafiev, Vasil Bykov, Boris Vasiliev, Grigorii Baklanov, and Viacheslav Kondratiev.[2] These sources, although well known, have not yet been exploited systematically for research in social history.

The war itself is not the subject of this book. It is the reference point, the first chronological landmark. But not chronological only: the social psychology of the war years shaped all of postwar life. Without an understanding of the phenomenon of the war as it entered the flesh and blood of that generation, postwar history and social behavior are incomprehensible. We must therefore consider several social features of the war that subsequently influenced the formation of the postwar atmosphere.

Stalin prepared his people for the impending war, but it was a peculiar preparation. Peculiar not only in that on the very eve of the war he destroyed the leaders of the officers' corps and bled the army white. The greater peculiarity was the particular concept of war that was stubbornly drilled into the minds of the people. In the first place, the war was represented as a counter-stroke, that is, as a defensive war, an act of retribution against the aggressor. Second, the people were persuaded that if war were unavoidable, it would be of short duration and would take place on enemy territory. No one thought that the war would spill over into the Soviet border districts. "With little loss of blood and a powerful blow, we will rout and destroy the enemy." These words of a popular song were the leitmotiv of all the propaganda of the prewar period. Official propaganda inspired faith in the invincibility of Soviet arms. The war was portrayed not only as victorious and short but as inevitable. "If there is war, if there is a campaign tomorrow, let's get ready today." Such songs corresponded to the outlook of the people. Konstantin Simonov, reflecting on the characteristics of peacetime that formed the people's expectations of war, described the popular attitude.

> Above all, the psychological, ideological preparedness for sacrifices, the highest form of which was the sacrifice of life in battle, was learned from the Five-Year Plans. . . . The tempo of construction in the conditions of capitalist encirclement—either we become an industrial power or they will not respect us—was a tempo demanding sacrifice under great pressure, preparation for a sharp decline in living standards, for the interruption of ordinary life, for family separations, for so much of what war in various circumstances brings to people.[3]

People continued to live as usual, but in the back of their minds they were ready at a moment's notice to unite with and to fight unreservedly with the army. The prewar atmosphere was saturated with a martial spirit reinforced by the militarization of all ranks of society: everyone belonged to at least one organization with a prescribed agenda of duties, be it a youth organization or a collective farm. Soviet society of the 1930s is commonly described as a grand barracks. If the description is in some respects apt, it is not so in all. From the viewpoint of its mentality, prewar society does not fully correspond to the barracks model, as many contemporaries did not feel themselves to be in a barracks atmosphere. Sergei Alekseev, now a corresponding member of the Russian Academy of Sciences, captured the difference in his own words.

> In the face of all of the tragic features of life in those days, in the hearts and souls of us boys and girls a romantic spirit, a sense of joy and brotherhood, lived on . . . , and expressed itself, moreover, in moral matters. . . . Perhaps I am idealizing. . . . But it is dreadful for me to think of life now—or then either—without the clean, clear, civic romanticism of my youth that somehow served as a saving grace at the very height of the terrorist madness of Stalin's dictatorship.[4]

We cannot, of course, attribute feelings characteristic especially of the younger generation to the society as a whole, but they give us an example of a social consciousness in prewar society close to that of the army. Notwithstanding the likeness of their outward appearance and the particulars of their internal organization (strict discipline, strong hierarchy, subordination to command, etc.), the army and the barracks are not one and the same. Intrinsic to the social psychology of the army is a spirit of militant morale not necessarily at home in the barracks. Practically all psychologists have observed this characteristic of the army. They disagree only in their various approaches: if Lev Voitolovskii identified such concepts as army and crowd, calling the former an "inspired crowd,"[5] Gabriel Tard ranked the army in psychological organization higher than the crowd, emphasizing the principle of psychic unity characteristic of the army.[6]

Both army and barracks, as models of public organization subordinated to strong discipline, are ideally manageable units of administration. Moreover, the greater leveling of factors of personality in the barracks makes it even more submissive. Why, then, did the Stalinist regime deliberately cultivate the spirit of the army, never allowing society to retire completely into itself and stand apart as one gigantic barracks?

In fact, the explanation is clear: the psychology of the regime was to design a model administrative unit endowed with a clearly stipulated element of initiative, easily defined and easily revised—not for the sake of generosity but in order to establish a kind of collateral dedication to duty. The limited freedom of the unit of administration allowed it to execute the decision made on high in an optimal fashion, which it could not do if it were supervised heavy-handedly from above. The Stalinist personality in power was, on the one hand, "a mere executant," as historian Mikhail Gefter wrote. On the other hand, "was not this same person all-powerful within the bounds of the authority granted him? This strange blend of plenary power and accountability conferred a kind of shock-brigade mentality."[7]

Side by side with this shock-brigade mentality, however, was an entirely commonplace psychology of the barracks, and it was this contradictory state of affairs that explains the well-known paradox of the early period of the war. Society, so long and so fully prepared psychologically and ideologically for the impending attack, was simply shocked, was for a time paralyzed and incapable of the necessary response. How could this happen?

The shock of the first days and months of the war was produced not so much by the surprise attack as by the news of the Red Army's retreat. No one was prepared for this news—not the army, the society as a whole, or Stalin himself. A difficult period of readjustment began as the disparate elements of society formulated something like the concept of "a people at war." It was not an instantaneous process. The idea that everyone rose up as one man is, according to historian Gennadii Bordiugov, just another myth: "Some fought for socialism. Others thought not of socialism but of the Fatherland. Yet others, the bureaucratic time-servers, were paralyzed. Still others in the first days, weeks, and months simply joined the common cause of the people."[8]

The first reaction of the leadership was to use the principles of barracks life to establish maximum administrative control of the army. This effort failed.[9] It is not hard to understand why: the barracks had not even had time to mobilize. To undertake an attack on tanks with a .30-caliber rifle, a political commissar ahead and a machine gun behind, was hopeless. Something altogether different was needed, something coming purely from the human spirit, the spirit of self-sacrifice. The initiative of the people compensated for the paralysis of authority and the incapacity of the military command, though it cost, of course, millions of lives. Such was the price of the incompetence of the Stalinist system.

But this is a retrospective assessment. It does not reflect what took place in the hearts and minds of the people who voluntarily or otherwise departed for the front, fought, suffered defeat, and eventually triumphed. Understandably, many veterans reject the charge that their whole war effort was directed to the defense and support of the regime, which, without their stubborn commitment, would have simply disintegrated. Such charges are not only morally offensive; they are incompatible with the facts, as they overlook the chief consideration, the outlook of the front-line soldiers themselves. This outlook was not, of course, perfectly uniform and stable. The war was viewed differently from different vantage points—the trenches, the staff headquarters, the penal battalions, and the guards' corps. But there were in the various perceptions of the war common factors shared by all. The soldiers' letters and diaries often represent the experience of the front not in the usual halo of heroism but simply as an ordinary, stressful kind of life, the most terrible part of which was death. As people gradually grew accustomed to this new life, it was not the new but the old prewar life that seemed strange and unimaginable.

Thus the wishes of the soldier, as one of them, Mansur Abdulin, relates, "were most often the simplest: to have a good sleep, to bathe, to spend perhaps a week under a roof, to receive a letter from home. The grandest dream was to remain alive and to see what would become of life."[10] These were the thoughts of the soldiers at war. As the dream receded into the past, the very perception of the war years was transformed. As veteran Viacheslav Kondratiev put it, the war "was remembered fondly by those fighting it, because all that was physically terrible and dreadful was forgotten, and what remained was the inspiring side of it, that is, the bright and pure elements, the features of justice and liberation." In sum, "the war was the most important experience of our generation."[11] Viktor Astafiev voiced similar reflections: "In the course of time you suddenly discover what your life has consisted of, what you are proud of, what you are sad about—and that is the war."[12] This acknowledgment reflects not only the experience of the war but the background of postwar life against which the war stands out as incomparably more vivid, and especially, more inspiring. The emotional temper of the war years was in many respects unique, not only by virtue of its extreme stress but above all because it required a reordering of previous priorities both in political and in human relations.

As paradoxical as it seems, the value of the individual rose just as whole armies were being lost, as the life of the soldier seemed to grow

cheap. The psychological turning point, unrelated to the military turning point, grew out of the triumph over this paradox. For the war
brought a rare opportunity for the spontaneous development among
the people of a civic spirit, which for decades had been cultivated only
as duties—often impractical and abstract—handed out by the regime.
And suddenly this spirit acquired the flesh and blood of a concrete
purpose, the defense of the Fatherland, in tandem with the historical
traditions of the past. A person began to feel the sentiment of citizen-
ship. "In the war I was indispensably necessary," recalled the hero of
Viacheslav Kondratiev's story, "Znamenatelnaia data" (A Red-Letter
Day). "Not just anyone could replace me. Let's suppose that instead of
me on this left flank was another soldier with the same weapon. And
without the confidence that he could hold off the Germans, with a
different gaze, different wits, and a weaker nature. . . . At the front you
had the feeling that the fate of Russia lay in your hands alone."[13]

The character of civic spirit is conveyed here surprisingly accu-
rately: an inner overestimation of one's self that acquires the imprimatur of society's sanction ("I was indispensably necessary"). In
this circumstance, the quality of personal spontaneity grows accordingly. It was no accident that many veterans remembered that in the
war they felt freer than during peacetime. But free from what?

The well-known veterans' saying that "the war cancels the past" is
especially true of freedom. Thus in conditions in which the function
and jurisdiction of formal controls over social behavior were re-
stricted, the boundaries between such concepts as liberty and license
were easily crossed. The place of formal control, which was earlier
preemptive, was taken by self-control or informal control exercised by
the informal social units that took shape in dugouts or common
trenches. As a rule this informal outward and inward control was
considerably more effective than the state system of comprehensive
surveillance. In any event, as Konstantin Simonov wrote, the saying
"the war cancels the past" did not acquire general currency at that
time. "For all of its seductiveness, it was rarely spoken with a sense of
justification, frankly and proudly. It did not become an element of
belief; more often in the conditions at the front it was subjected to
heavy criticism. As a result it was not typical of our life, it was simply a
superfluous froth of opinion."[14]

The "spirit of freedom" that veterans of the war still recall is entirely different from a wartime "freedom as a way of life" and incomparably more important for the evaluation of the postwar situation.
"As an eyewitness and as a historian I can attest," wrote Mikhail Gef-

ter, "that many of the developments of 1941 and 1942 constituted an *elemental de-Stalinization*."[15] He elaborated this thought elsewhere: "The tough trials of the war gave birth—along with a feeling of personal responsibility for the fate of the Fatherland—to a personal view, or rather to the embryo of a personal view, of what the nation should become now and in the future."[16]

The formation of a new view of oneself, of the world, and of the fate of the country was stimulated not only by the growing feeling of personal responsibility but by reflection on new information that war brought in its wake. The war created its own special mode of association of people whose paths during peacetime rarely crossed. The village and the city came together, as did university students and recently released convicts. By decrees of the Presidium of the Supreme Soviet of 12 July and 24 November 1941 more than 600,000 people were liberated from the GULAG, and 175,000 of them were inducted at once into the army.[17] In comparison with the size of the army, this was not many people; but as a source of new information previously hidden from the majority, they had a great impact. Some people, especially intellectuals, for example, discovered things that they had not imagined: the reality of the camps, the villages that lived on the verge of hunger, the collective farmers who were forced to surrender their own vital necessities in order to feed the cities.

To carry on candid conversations, especially on political subjects, was dangerous even during the war. As the poet David Samoilov recalled: "The Stalinist bacillus of suspicion and surveillance was widespread at the front. It spoiled the quality of personal relations and perhaps diminished the alertness of the nation."[18] Nevertheless, according to the veterans, conversations at the front were remarkably candid in spite of the presence of agents of SMERSH[19] and other "observers." It is true that political subjects as a rule remained beyond the bounds of these conversations. So what did they talk about? "We cursed the leadership, as always. Why were there no planes, why were there not enough artillery rounds, and what was the source of all the chaos? But we were patient and understanding; what we lacked would probably soon be supplied."[20]

What did the soldiers think of Stalin, of the leadership of the country? "They thought little about it. Were they afraid? No, soldiers in the face of death were as if at confession, they were not afraid of anything. We believed Stalin and the high command more than we believed our own officers."[21] The process of the "elemental de-Stalinization" initiated by the war is not related in the memory of the soldiers to the name of Stalin. The upper limit of criticism rarely rose higher than the divisional level and only exceptionally turned from personal assessments to political generalizations. Therefore, to suggest that the war opened the eyes of the people to the reality of the regime is unwarranted. The war alone did not on the whole change people's relationship to the regime. Those who believed in it earlier just came to believe in it even more, especially after the victory. Those who had no illusions remained unconverted. The psychological impact of the war took a different form. The war awoke in people the capacity to think in unaccustomed ways, to evaluate a situation critically, and never again to accept uncritically any exclusive version of the truth. It was precisely this capacity that represented a potential threat to the regime, which was designed for a subject thinking within the limited bounds of what was permitted. Another kind of person emerged from the war, however—one who looked upon many things through different eyes, saw what formerly was overlooked, and doubted what not so long ago was considered quite reasonable. A process of psychological reorientation was catalyzed by the last stage of the war when the Soviet soldier crossed the frontier and encountered another society, politically, culturally, and economically. As a result soldiers returned from the war in possession of a comparative experience and knowledge of considerable significance.

"The contrast between the standard of living in Europe and among us, a contrast which millions of military people encountered, was an emotional and psychological shock," recalled Konstantin Simonov.[22] In his play, *Pod kashtanami Pragi* (Under the Chestnuts of Prague), written in the heat of the new impressions in 1945, there is a scene in which a Czech woman is speaking to a Russian colonel: "You cannot love Europe. These estates, these villas, these houses with iron roofs will only irritate you. Do you deny it?" To which he replies, "Ideas may be denied, but an iron roof cannot be denied. Iron is iron."[23] The acceptance of this metallic truth, notwithstanding its obviousness, was a kind of Herculean labor. The psychic shock should have been gradually supplanted by a new view of life based not on ideological blinders but on reality and facts. In such a world outlook any situation represents an opportunity for a variety of views and depends to some degree on individual choice.

Along with the awareness of the multiplicity of ways of life and the value of personal choice, the war brought to peacetime life another principle intrinsic to army life: the custom of command and submission, strong discipline, the unquestioned authority of a command.

"And yet another vice came from the front," as the war correspondent Valentin Ovechkin writes. "A command had to be obeyed, to hell with what subordinates think of the commander."[24] The state structures and the political institutions reinforced this tradition, and the postwar atmosphere of victory itself favored it. The spirit of freedom fostered by the war could not, however, simply dissolve and disappear without a trace, and that fact formed a distinct counterweight to the attempt of the authorities to return to an unqualified form of the prewar political order. How serious an obstacle was it?

In fact, the public attitude toward human confrontation was influenced by the war. Of course, in the war the confrontation was one of pure mutual enmity, of "us" versus "them." The imperative of killing was the basic principle of the science of hate. *They* were perceived not simply as another society but a society hostile without qualification. Each member of this hostile camp was depersonalized, that is, was perceived not as an individual person but only as a part of *them,* and natural human relations simply were not possible in this reciprocally lethal confrontation. *They* had nothing in common with *us. We* proceeded from the assumption of this absolute antagonism and consequently included within our ranks absolutely all members of our society, enlisted personnel or officers, both front and rear. The border between *us* and *them* did not pass within the societies but around *their* exteriors. The assumption of the psychological unity and harmony of society (in which there were no internal enemies) among many of our countrymen gave birth to the distinct hope that this feature of the military world would transfer to the civilian world.

In reality the psychological situation after the war took on a somewhat different form: *They* were beaten and ceased to exist as an object of confrontation. But the habit of thinking in terms of *us-them* persisted. In place of *them* was a vacuum. The concealed agenda of postwar developments may only be perceived to the extent that this vacuum was filled. This process was played out in a sufficiently complex fashion as postwar attitudes took shape and formed the demands and pretensions of different social groups. The habit of thinking in terms of *us-them,* however, made a public confrontation with the government more plausible than seemed likely at the time.

Chapter 2

The Victory and the Victors

The war naturally left a dreadful legacy across the country. An extraordinary state commission, charged with calculating the material losses resulting from combat operations and defense expenditures more generally, assessed the cost at 2,569 billion rubles.[1] This figure took into account the destruction of cities and towns, industrial enterprises, and railroad bridges; the loss of output of pig iron and steel; the contraction of the motor vehicle fleet and the livestock population; and so on. Nowhere, however, was there mention of the number of lives lost (if we ignore the figure of 7 million announced by Stalin in 1946).

The magnitude of human losses in the Soviet Union during the Second World War is still disputed among historians. One reason for the disagreement is the lack of a complete statistical base and authoritative figures on birth and death rates, the natural rate of growth of the population, and other demographic indicators.[2] Research based on the methodology of demographic balance[3] indicates total human losses in the USSR during the war of 26.6 million people.[4] Approximately 76 percent, that is, about 20 million, were men, the greater part of whom had been born between 1901 and 1931—the most capable contingent of the male population.[5] This circumstance alone suggests the seriousness of the demographic problems of postwar society. In 1940 the Soviet population numbered 100.3 million females and 92.3 million males. The primary source of the imbalance was the superior life expectancy of women, especially after age 60. In 1946 the Soviet population numbered 96.2 million females and 74.4 million males; and in comparison with the prewar situation, the substantially greater number of women was already conspicuous in the age cohort of 20- to 44-year-olds. In 1940, there were 37.6 million women and 34.8 million men between the ages of 20 and 44, whereas in 1946 there were an equal number of women and 10 million fewer men of the same age cohort.[6] In the countryside the situation was even worse. Whereas in 1940 the ratio of women to men on collective farms was approximately 1.1:1, in 1945 it was 2.7:1![7]

Women thus constituted the great majority of the postwar Soviet population. This situation brought on serious problems, not only demographic but psychological as well, eventuating in social pathology and the lonely solitude of women. The postwar fatherlessness of so many children engendered a striking vogue of adolescent vagabondage and crime. Nevertheless, all the losses and deprivations notwithstanding, it was precisely the initiative of women that made postwar society so prolific. Bereft of husbands, left without the hope of having a conventional family, and in the most difficult of material conditions, many women continued to bear children. In 1946, for example, 752,000 children were born to unmarried mothers; in 1947, 747,000; in 1948, 665,000; in 1949, 985,000; in 1950, 944,000; in 1951, 930,000; in 1952, 849,000.[8]

The children of wartime were a special problem, the least secure part of the population. During the war, children suffered side by side with adults and sometimes more than adults. They died in bombing raids, of hunger and disease, or they were forcibly deported abroad. The war years depressed the birth rate of the population palpably. In 1946 there were 53 million children below age 14—14 million fewer than in 1940.[9] Many teenagers had to go into industrial production during the war, both in order to take the place of adult workers leaving for the front and in order to secure the means of subsistence for themselves and their families. Teenagers worked as if they were adults, sometimes ten to twelve hours a day. Stressful work and constant undernourishment unavoidably damaged the health of the younger generation.

In June 1945 the party Central Committee ordered an official inspection of the industrial enterprises of Gorkii Oblast (province) for the purpose of evaluating teenagers' working conditions and the state of their health. The commission's conclusions were disturbing: "In the majority of the industries examined, normal living conditions for teenagers were not available, and these circumstances lead to sickliness and retardation of their physical development."[10] In the Molotov Factory a medical examination of 1,070 teenagers was carried out. It found 379 (35 percent) of them clinically ill: sixty-four suffered from diseases of the digestive tract; fifty-one, skin rashes and other dermatological disorders; six, tuberculosis; and four, muscular dystrophy. Of 670 youths between ages 15 and 17, 340 (50.6 percent) suffered from a retardation of growth (height) of one to two years, and 413 (61.6 percent) were underweight. The majority were anemic.[11]

Psychologists observed that the children of wartime matured early—that is, they developed an outlook on life more sophisticated than that of their peers growing up in peaceful conditions. Such precocity exacted an inevitable psychological price. The child's psyche suffered aggravated trauma from the loss of loved ones, the fear of death, and the dread of being orphaned. A whole generation of children grew up without fathers in Russia, children without a home in the full sense of the word. They grew up in a truncated family or without any family, in schools, kindergartens, or urban shelters designed to ameliorate this deprivation. And the postwar shelter was a special world with its own norms of behavior and forms of social control. It was an institution that in many respects formed the psyche of a whole generation. Its children learned to live by the unwritten rules of shelter society, and it was no accident that in their subsequent adult life the social relations formed in the shelter played no less a role than those of blood relations. These people were team players, disdaining individualism; and yet, ironically, it was especially in their midst that striking forms of individualism took root.

The society emerging from the war differed from conventional society not only in its demographic structure but also in its social composition. It was no longer made up of the traditional categories— the urban and rural, industrial workers and civil servants, youth and pensioners—but rather of a mentality born of the war. In this sense the most prominent face of postwar society was that of the man in uniform, the veteran. Toward the end of the war, the Soviet army numbered 11 million people.[12] According to the law of 23 June 1945 on demobilization, the first to be discharged from the army were the thirteen most senior age-groups, and by 1948 the process of demobilization was fundamentally complete. A total of 8.5 million men were demobilized.[13]

In various ways, everybody faced the problem of transition from war to peace, economically, socially, and psychologically. Of course, the process affected most the interests of those now completely alienated from civilian society, those who had lived four years in a different environment, the soldiers. The gravity of the losses, the material deprivations experienced with minor exceptions by everyone, were aggravated for the veterans by the additional psychological problems inherent in the transition to civilian life. For many, therefore, the mobilization that had been so much anticipated at the front turned into a serious problem in itself—especially for the youngest soldiers, those born in the years 1923–1927, who had gone to the front straight from the schoolroom without the chance to acquire any occupational experience at all. War was their only profession, their only competence the capacity to wield weapons and fight. Moreover, this generation had suffered losses greater than any other, especially in the first year of combat. The war to a remarkable degree washed away the boundaries between age-groups. The various generations, their human losses mounting, virtually merged into one—the generation of victors—forming thereby a new mentality that united them in a shared community of problems, attitudes, wishes, and aspirations. Of course, this community of concerns was relative—even in the war there was no perfect unity among soldiers—but the spirit of front-line brotherhood continued for a long time to influence the postwar atmosphere.

The majority of demobilized veterans sought work almost at once. Thus, according to the figures of some forty regional party committees, of 2.7 million recently demobilized persons in January 1946, 2.1 million (71.1 percent) were employed. Of the number of veterans employed at that time, more than half (55 percent) worked on collective farms or state farms.[14] The figures on veterans' employment varied significantly by different regions. In Irkutsk Province, for example, in January 1946 more than half of the able-bodied returning veterans had not found work; in the city of Tiumen, 59 percent were unemployed; in Astrakhan Province, 64 percent.[15] The reasons for this situation varied. Sometimes there was no work for the particular specialty in which the demobilized were qualified; sometimes they were offered unskilled work and pay not commensurate with their qualifications. Thus of forty-seven demobilized veterans returning to the factory Red Chemist in Vladimir Province, only sixteen received work in their field of qualification, while the remainder were directed to wood-cutting.[16] This state of affairs was similar in other regions.

In addition to the problem of finding work was the problem of finding living space, a matter especially acute in areas that had suffered heavy combat damage. In such places many families of the demobilized had to live in dugouts or in other poor substitutes for homes. It was not only the demobilized who lived in such conditions, however, and the mastery of primitive circumstances was only one of the strategies of survival in postwar society.

The war, it seemed, had exhausted the last reserves of human strength. The Soviet army, alone among those engaged in the war, did not follow the practice of granting rest-and-recreation furloughs (with the exception of short-term leaves for the wounded). Czech historian Boguslav Shnaider [Czech Bohuslav Šnajder—H.R.] observed that human losses in the Soviet army could have been fewer had it not suffered unremitting psychological overload. "Soldiers of the Red Army were under constant psychological pressure, which was unprecedented in the history of warfare. Fatigue and psychic exhaustion exceeded all imaginable limits."[17] This fatigue made itself felt after the war as well. The veterans noticed with surprise that during the war, constantly shuttling between life and death, people did not suffer from conventional "peacetime" illnesses. When the war ended, on the other hand, such illnesses quickly reappeared: their reserves of physical resistance had run out. By no means everyone returned from the front in good health. While we have statistics, however imprecise, on the wartime losses, until this day we lack figures on those who died of wounds and illnesses after the war. Toward the end, among those demobilized on grounds of health, there were 2 million invalids; and among them, around 450,000 with one amputated limb and around 350,000 with a diagnosis of osteomyelitis (inflammation of bone marrow).[18] The invalids, more even than the other veterans, were in need not only of surgery or medication but of psychological treatment as well. Toward the end of the war, however, only a third of the infirmaries for invalids had a physician attached, not to speak of full medical services.[19] Much more complicated for the invalids than for the other veterans was the search for work, and the situation of those who had lost their sight was practically hopeless. Without supplementary income, it was very difficult, almost impossible, to live on a single invalid's pension. The begging of cripples around bazaars and railroad stations became a characteristic feature of the time. Invalids were required to undergo an annual medical examination—to confirm the continuation of their disability—a procedure exacted even of those who had lost a limb at the front ("as if it would grow back," in the grim joke of the veterans). The majority of invalids left thus on the sidelines of life were young people; and their consciousness of not being needed, their superfluousness in the new postwar life, for the sake of which they had sacrificed themselves, was especially painful.

Other veterans were able to get good work or prestigious duties and to enter institutes of higher education or continue studies interrupted by the war. Their acquisition of a higher social status, however much it was deserved, nevertheless introduced a notorious difference of interests into this social community formerly so closely knit. It prompted a process that Mikhail Gefter denominated "the fracturing of the generation of victors,"[20] and it was not in the least spontaneous but was deliberately orchestrated from above.[21]

The veterans returning from the war were sometimes considered potential neo-Decembrists, suggesting an analogy with the developments in Russia after the War of 1812, in particular the uprising of several regiments in St. Petersburg in December 1825.[22] This potential was not, of course, realized, in any event not directly, in the early postwar years, as it was suppressed by the regime. Thus the question is almost never raised: were the veterans capable of forming an active force for political (*obshchestvennyi*) change immediately after the war? I pose this question quite seriously, not merely to assess the potential strength of the forces committed to freedom but in order to identify a moment when progressive reforms might have found sufficiently broad social support. If we continue the analogy with the Decembrists, then the factor of timing appears to be a key consideration: the Decembrist uprising occurred more than twelve years after the end of the war of 1812—again, not accidentally. The war alone did not engender political positions, not to speak of forming organizations for the pursuit of political activity, because war assigns other duties. But war also modifies the bases of cultural life, stimulates a reexamination of conventional assumptions, and forms a moral-psychological foundation for the future. What comes of it all depends on the particular conditions of the postwar years. It must be obvious, however, that the first years after the end of a successful war are not the most favorable time to engage in a struggle with the victorious government. The poor prospects of such an open confrontation in the Soviet Union in 1945 may be explained by the influence of several factors.

First, the very character of the war—patriotic, liberating, just—presupposes the unity of the society—people and government—in the commitment to a national cause, the expulsion of the enemy. Victory in such a war was envisioned as a triumph of the entire nation. Linked by a common interest, the common challenge of survival, the community of government and people was gradually forged as they jointly laid aside the assumptions of civilian life and brought together the deceived hopes below and the crisis of command above.

Second, we must consider the psychological factor of the overload of stress on the people, of four years spent in the trenches and the consequent need for emotional release, for liberation from the endurance test. The people, having long borne the burdens of demolition, naturally grasped the opportunity for peaceful construction. At this juncture, the enjoyment of peace was of premium value and excluded any consideration of violence. "The massive homelessness of millions of people, which is to say, the war, is sickening," Emmanuil Kazakevich wrote from the front; "more than the danger and the risk, it is really the homelessness. . . ."[23] Speaking in May 1945 to a group of writers, her colleagues, Vera Ketlinskaia summoned them to envision in all of its complexity "not only the pride of the victors but the enormous grief of the long-suffering people."[24]

A period of convalescence, both physical and emotional, was inevitable after the war, a complex and painful period of restoration of civilian life in which conventional problems, such as housing, might have to remain unresolved for a time. The problem of housing was not only one of living space: one of the most serious problems after the war was the establishment of a family life. The leading challenge for the veterans of the time was to readjust to such a life, to enroll themselves in it, to learn to live in such an unaccustomed way. "Everybody wanted to organize some kind of life," Viacheslav Kondratiev recalls. "We had to live. Some married. Others entered the party. . . . We had to adjust to a new life. There was no alternative."[25] Perhaps some people had alternatives, but for the majority of veterans the problem of reintegrating into civilian life was depressingly simple. They had to take life as they found it.

Third, loyal to the Soviet order though they were, not all veterans looked upon it as ideal, or even as just. The facts of the prewar years, the experience of the war, and observations during the campaign in Europe forced them to reflect, to wonder about the justice of elements of the regime, if not of the regime as a whole. There was not necessarily a direct link, however, between dissatisfaction with the structure of life at home and action aimed at changing it. The establishment of such a link depended upon the evolution of a concrete program of future action, a conception of goals and a mechanism for their realization; but no such instrument existed. "There was much in the system that we did not accept, but we could not imagine any other kind," Viacheslav Kondratiev admitted.[26] This statement may seem surprising, but it reflects a contradiction characteristic of people's thinking in the postwar years. The regime was perceived as an inflexible given, irremediable and independent of human will, of one's own aspirations and wishes.

All of these factors allow us to affirm the impossibility during the first days after the victory of open popular opposition to authority.

Such was the peculiarity of the moment. Yet the potential for the development of a mature and dynamic political opposition was present. That is, there was a fully possible prospect that the veterans themselves—the liberal fraction of them—could become a potential support and one of the principal moving forces of a future process of reform. Reform is usually preceded by an emotionally critical stage characterized by a mental ferment and the consolidation of active political forces. The war initiated this stage, which continued long after the war had ended. Although its development proceeded by increments, obscured by the many mundane problems, the process produced distinct forms of expression.

It was sustained particularly by the channels of communications among the veterans, who after the war remained in contact with each other, destined to be a part of an invisible network, a combat community with its attendant legacy of common postwar problems. Life in the communal huts and apartments so typical of the time was an awkward medium for this kind of intercourse. Therefore it took place as a rule away from home, either in the student dormitories to which many veterans returned, or, more typically, in newly opened cafés, snack bars, and beer halls—"blue Danubes," as they were called. These latter places became the refuges of veterans' social life and gave rise to an altogether peculiar phenomenon of the time, "tavern" (*shalmannaia*) democracy.

> How many of these holes-in-the-wall, snack bars, pavilions, and taverns (*shalmany*), these blue Danubes, were opened by the wrecked and half-destitute country in order to comfort and warm the returning soldiers, in order to provide them the glow of an evening's uninhibited company, to help them speak out, to soften their hardened souls, to enable them to look one another in the eye unhurriedly and to realize that a seemingly unimaginable peace and quiet had really come? In the inconceivably close spaces between shell-scarred houses, in the open fields, among huts and fences, in rustic groves these evening retreats sprang up, and here popular parlance, ignoring the street address, fixed to each establishment a distinct and indelible name, which is not to be found in the guidebooks.[27]

This modest portrait from Viktor Smirnov's story "Zaulki" (Back Streets) tells us what the blue Danubes were in the life of people returning from the war. They were merely everyday life, yet they were so much more.

Led by their own problems in separate ways, the veterans came together again where the nostalgia of the front reigned. And the more commonplace or desperate postwar life became, the more sharply and distinctly were the values of the warrior imprinted in their consciousness, especially those making him "indispensably necessary." The peaceful life was already structured on other principles: the soldier who experienced during wartime the feeling that "he alone held the fate of the country in his hands" was driven after the war to the sad admission that "with me, without me, everything goes on anyway."[28] The former values persisted only among a narrow circle of friends, really only in the little retreats of blue Danubes. "9 May, 1950," Emmanuil Kazakevich noted in his diary, "the Day of Victory . . . I went to a beer bar. Two invalids and a plumber . . . were drinking beer and reminiscing about the war. One of them wept and said: If there were another war, I would go. . . ."[29]

Nostalgia for the front inspired the tone of camaraderie in the blue Danubes, where candor in conversation and sentiment was habitual, notwithstanding the presence of spies. There society was constituted as formerly by the laws of war, and the openness with which people shared their experience contrasted with the completely different spirit saturating the atmosphere outside. Whatever we may think of these blue Danubes, they came to embody by force of circumstance the last refuge of the spirit of freedom brought from the front. All the other channels were simply closed; and it was not the fault of the veterans that, in place of genuine freedom, all that was left them was the freedom to talk over a glass of beer, or that this freedom, too, was soon taken away, putting the finishing touches on a deliberate campaign to wipe out the potential benefits inherent in the victory.

This campaign began in fact on the day after the victory, the credit for which was immediately divided and apportioned. On the day when the war ended, *Pravda* distributed the credit for the victory in the following fashion: "The victory did not come of itself. *It was won* by the self-sacrifice, the heroism, the military mastery of the Red Army and of the whole Soviet people. *It was organized* by our invincible Bolshevik Party, the party of Lenin and Stalin, *it was led* by our great Stalin. . . . Long live *our great Stalinist victory!*"[30] [Author's emphasis—E.Z.] And so the victory was called "ours" and "Stalin's" simultaneously, but the subtext was obvious: "our" victory occurred only because it was primordially "Stalin's." In the same issue of *Pravda,* in the column entitled "News from Abroad," the victory was characterized as "a day forecast by Comrade Stalin."[31]

In his "Address to the People" Stalin himself distributed the emphasis somewhat differently. The *vozhd'* (leader) addressed himself to "compatriots, fellow countrymen and countrywomen," giving the obligatory credit to the victorious people: "The great sacrifices that we have borne in the name of the freedom and independence of our Fatherland, the innumerable deprivations and losses suffered by our people in the course of the war, the intensive labor in the rear and at the front, offered on the altar of the country, have not been made in vain and eventuated in the complete victory over the enemy."[32] The address contained not a word of the party and its role in the organization of victory. Stalin simply excluded this intermediary link between himself and the people.

On 24 May Stalin pronounced his famous toast "to the health of the Russian people," naming the Russian people "the leading force of the Soviet Union among all the people of our country." Speaking of it as the "leading people," he again remained silent on the "leading party."[33] A month later, on 25 June, at a reception in the Kremlin in honor of the participants in the victory parade, a fresh nuance appeared in Stalin's interpretation, the so-called "proposition of the screws." In spite of the frequency of the citation of this toast, taken out of context it offers only a limited opportunity for analysis. In any event, the context of the occasion is no less important than the content of the toast. Stalin spoke toward the end of the reception, after the tributes in honor of the military commanders, the scientific and technical advisers, and the industrial leaders had already been made. The keynote of his speech was clear. He proposed a toast "to the health of the people of modest rank and obscure station. To the people who may be considered the screws in the great machine of state, without whom we, the marshals and commanders of the front armies, to put it crudely, are not worth a farthing. These are the people who sustain us, as a foundation supports a summit."[34] Stalin thus revised his former thesis on the union of leader and people, sketching their relationship as one of summit and base, thereby necessarily diminishing the status of the latter from that of "great people" to people as screws—cogs—in the machine. The toast contained an additional thought: Stalin not only established the hierarchical principle in the community of leader and people; he also set the simple people against their superiors, their bosses—beneath his own level, of course—preserving for himself the function of supreme arbiter at the nexus where the lines of the management of the masses and the management of the bosses came together.

Even before the importation from the war of the grim dichotomy of *us* and *them* began to change the nature of personal relations, Stalin tried consciously or unconsciously to direct the process into the channel that he needed. He removed himself from the society of *we*, moved into a kind of solitude, preserving for himself the right of orchestrating the process of marking sociopolitical boundaries, among which was the definition of "ours," "not ours," "theirs," and "the enemies'." This was in reality a return to the prewar system of power relations, reestablishing the absolute power of the leader and ignoring those who genuinely deserved the credit for the victory. It was not surprising that many veterans felt offended and bitter to be assigned to the ranks of mere "screws." And although propaganda affirmed that the words of the leader about the screws were affectionate and fatherly and that they "exalt all our people," these illusions did not prevail. Life itself left few hopes and illusions. The veterans, by their own admissions, felt less and less needed, and some of them, the invalids, felt entirely superfluous.

Chapter 3

"How to Live After the War?":
The Conflict of Expectation and
Reality

The war changed the face of world politics. The common threat brought nations together, postponed their usual quarrels, and turned national pride and ethnic antagonisms into unwanted handicaps. The worldwide cataclysm diverted the nations from the usual posturing about the superiority of one political system or another and encouraged them to embrace the priority of common human values and the idea of global unity. At the end of the war this idea seemed about to materialize, conciliating the conflicts among recent allies and damping the ardor of the diehard revanchists. Even the genesis of the Cold War, followed by the atomic psychosis, could not entirely scotch the idea of a Common European Home. Of course, merely beginning to turn this idea into political reality required the passage of several decades and the change of several political generations. The postwar leaders continued to think in terms of the old categories of confrontation: one side feared the spread of communist contagion, and the other guarded itself against bourgeois influence. The iron curtain descended between East and West Europe. Thereafter Soviet citizens could only guess at what was going on in the world, until they realized with bitter surprise that the defeated enemy had quickly regained his feet and laid the foundations of a new and vigorous life, while they themselves were subsisting on meager rations and blaming their misery on the consequences of the war.

But it did not have to be so. The victory offered Russia the opportunity to choose whether to develop itself together with the civilized world or to go its own way as formerly in the tradition of socialist messianism. There was without doubt an alternative to the policy of isolation.

The victory raised to an unprecedented height not only the international prestige of the Soviet Union but the authority of the regime inside the country as well. "Drunk with the conceit of victory," wrote the veteran Fedor Abramov, "we decided that our system was ideal, . . . and we not only neglected to improve it, but, on the contrary, we grew ever more dogmatic about it."[1] The Russian philosopher Georgii Fedotov, reflecting on the influence of Stalin's soaring authority on the development of internal political processes, also came to a disturbing conclusion: "Our forebears, in the company of foreigners, felt compelled to blush for Russian autocracy and serfdom. If they had observed such worldwide servility before the tsar as Europe and America exhibited before Stalin, it would not have occurred to them to feel embarrassed about the behavior of their countrymen."[2]

The saying "victors are not to be judged" is not an acquittal but a cause for reflection, as illustrated by Viktor Nekrasov's comments:

> Alas! We excused Stalin for everything! Collectivization, the purges, the execution of his colleagues, the defeats of 1941. And he, of course, then understood all the power of the people believing in his genius, understood that there could no longer be any mistake about that, that only throwing the harsh truth [he was indispensable!—H.R.] in their face would unite them, that there could be no return to the rivers of blood, not of the war, but of the prewar period. And we, callow intelligentsia, having become soldiers, believed in this myth with our whole heart and entered the party of Lenin and Stalin.[3]

May 1945 was the high point of the authority of Stalin. His name was linked in the mind of the masses with the victory, and he was perceived as being virtually the bearer of divine providence. The war correspondent Alexander Avdeenko recalls going to the victory parade with his young son.

> I take my son in my arms, raise him up. The Lenin Mausoleum is ten meters or a little more away. The reviewing stand and everybody on it is as if in the palm of our hands.
> "Do you see him?"
> "Aha. Standing in the rain. The old man. Is he getting wet?"
> "Tempered steel does not fear rain."
> "Is he a man of steel? Is that why he is called Stalin?"
> "An ordinary man, but a will of steel."

"Papa, why is he not happy, is he mad at somebody?"
"At God, probably, who didn't send us good weather."
"So why didn't Stalin order God to send us good weather . . . ?"[4]

Stalin the man had by this time been so transformed into the idol of the *vozhd'* that he virtually acquired the image of a living icon. The mass consciousness, attributing mystical power to the icon, as it was supposed to do, canonized all that was identified with it, be it the authority of the system or the authority of the ideas on which the system was based. Such was the contradictory role of the victory, which brought both the spirit of freedom and the psychological instruments thwarting the further development of that spirit, the instruments that perpetuated the supremacy of the alleged architect of victory. The euphoria of victory was not the most receptive atmosphere for discussing social problems, and this fact constitutes an obstacle to our analysis of the situation, though it does not entirely spoil it.

Otherwise, Georgii Fedotov, imagining all the obstacles to a progressive transformation of the Soviet regime, could scarcely have written in 1945 that "there is now no more agonizing issue in Russia than that of freedom. Not in the sense, of course, of the question whether it exists in the USSR, something that only foreigners, the most ignorant of them, can contemplate. But rather whether its rebirth is possible after a victorious war. That is what we are all thinking now, we genuine democrats and semifascist fellow travelers alike."[5] As for the question whether it was possible, neither Fedotov nor other soberly thinking people inside or outside the country gave a single uniform answer. Certainly they did not imagine a sudden metamorphosis into democracy in the USSR. They simply evaluated the postwar situation as a chance for the development of freedom, although they did not consider it to be promising.

The democratic traditions in the internal life of the country were very weak. The structures of political and cultural life gravitated distinctly toward authoritarian forms and were not receptive to innovations of an alien kind. But the war, in opening a window onto the world at large, permitted a view of the democratic experience of Europe and America. Not by chance, Mikhail Gefter, considering the evolution of attitudes of people during the war, wrote that "we are, of course, Russian and Soviet, but we have seen the world, too."[6] The war expanded the scope of the Russian outlook and the perspective in which the individual could imagine his own potential. In spring 1945 "people not without grounds considered themselves giants," as

Emmanuil Kazakevich expressed it.[7]

The veterans entered an atmosphere of peacetime life without forgetting the most terrible and dreadful war. The reality of peacetime was more complex, however, than they had imagined, not at all what it had appeared from the vantage point of the trenches. "In the army we often spoke of what life would be like after the war," recalled the journalist Boris Galin, "how we would live on the day after the victory; and the nearer the end of the war came, the more we thought of it, and we pictured things in rainbow colors. We never imagined the scale of destruction or the scope of reconstruction required to heal the wounds inflicted by the Germans."[8] Konstantin Simonov largely agreed: "We imagined life after the war as a holiday that would begin when the last shot was fired."[9] It was difficult for people to entertain other expectations after four years of the extraordinary stress of combat. It was altogether understandable that a normal life, a simple life in which one was not subjected to constant danger, seemed during wartime to be a providential promise. The war led people, those at the front and those in the rear, to romanticize the prewar period and to a certain extent to idealize it. Enduring the deprivations of the war years, people often subconsciously revised their recollections of peacetime, remembering the good and forgetting the bad. The wish to restore time past prompted the simplest answer to the question, "How to live after the war?" "As before the war," of course.

Life as holiday, life as fairy tale: with the help of this image in the mass mind a special conception of postwar life was formed—without contradictions, without pressure—a tendency stimulated in reality by one factor, hope. Such a life existed, however, only in books and the theater. It is a fascinating fact that during the war the libraries experienced an increased demand for the literature of adventure and fairy tales.[10] On the one hand, this interest is explained in part by the change in the age of the people working in the libraries and using them. During the war 50 to 70 percent of teenagers went into industrial production. After the war the reading rooms of libraries were filled by young veterans whose intellectual growth had been interrupted by the war and who consequently returned from the front to the reading tastes of their youth. But there is another side of the question: the growth of interest in this genre of literature and films was a choice to reject the cruel reality of the war. It was a demand for compensation for psychic overload. Thus it was possible to observe during the war, as for example Mansur Abdulin tells us, "the enormous appetite for all that was not related to the war, for films with dancing and merrymaking, for performing artists and comedians."[11] The faith that life after the war would quickly improve continued for several years after it ended.

Kubanskie kazaki (Kuban Cossacks) was the most popular of all postwar films. It depicted the life of a village in the north Caucasus after the war as contented, abundant, and joyful. Reality was utterly different, of course, and the film was consequently subjected to severe and appropriate criticism. But the critics did not consider one circumstance: there was an element of truth in this film-fable that conveyed the spirit of the time. The journalist Tatiana Arkhangelskaia remembers an interview with one of the participants in the making of the film, who told how hungry the well-dressed boys and girls were, while in the film they happily gazed on a surfeit of fruits made of plaster and papier-mâché. "But we believed," she added, "that it would be that way and there would be plenty of everything . . . all one could wish. And we needed to think so in order to sing songs and make everything seem all right."[12]

Hope for the better and the optimism that it nourished imparted a kind of shock tempo to the first stages of postwar life, generating a special, victorious public atmosphere. "My whole generation, with the exception of just a few, experienced the difficulties," remembers the builder V.P. Serikov. "But our spirits didn't fall. The chief thing was that the war was behind us. There was the joy of work, of victory, a spirit of competition."[13] The emotional élan of the people, the aspiration actually to realize through work a peaceful life, enabled them quickly enough to resolve the basic tasks of reconstruction. This outlook, however, notwithstanding its great creative force, bore within itself a tendency of another kind: the need for a relatively painless transition to peace ("the worst is behind us") and the perception of this process as generally untroubled. The farther it proceeded, the greater was the intrusion of reality, which was in no hurry to turn into life as fairy tale.

The difficulties of life, unavoidable after such a destructive war, were accepted as normal by the majority of the population, with resignation. Far from all problems inherited from the war, however, belonged to the normal category. The plenipotentiaries of the Central Committee were forced to admit as much after examining the conditions of life in different regions of the country. In December 1945 a delegation from the Agitation and Propaganda Department of the Central Committee undertook an inspection of the coal-mining industry in Shchekinsk District of Tula Province in central Russia. The results were alarming. The living conditions of the workers were recognized as "very difficult," and the repatriated and demobilized workers lived especially poorly. Many of them lacked underwear, and the little that was available was worn out and dirty. They went for months without soap, the dormitories were very crowded, the inhabitants slept on wooden platforms or similar double-tiered bunks (for which they paid 10 percent of their monthly income). They received enough bread, 1200 grams a day, but its quality was poor. There was not enough butter, and petroleum products were used as butter substitutes.[14]

There were many signs of poor food supply in the localities. Groups of workers from Penza and Kuznetsk wrote letters to Politburo members V.M. Molotov, M.I. Kalinin, and A.I. Mikoyan, complaining of the difficult material conditions of life and the absence of the majority of necessary goods from the market.[15] In response to these letters a commission of the People's Commissariat of Trade investigated and determined that the workers' complaints were well-founded.[16] In Nizhnyi Lomov of Penza Province the workers of factory No. 255 spoke out against the delay in the issuance of bread cards, and the workers of the plywood and match factories complained of long delays in receiving their pay.[17] The difficult working conditions at the war's end persisted in restored enterprises. Many people continued to work without shelter, in the open air, and during the winter, knee-deep in snow. Workplaces were often not lighted or heated, and people were poorly clothed for winter conditions. For this reason the secretaries of many local party committees in Siberia turned to the Central Committee with an unprecedented request: to allow them to skip the annual revolutionary anniversary celebration of 7 November 1946 on account of the "inadequate clothing of the population."[18]

Poor living conditions were one of the chief sources of dissatisfaction and agitation among the workers of the Urals and Siberia, most of whom were evacuees from the combat zones farther west. At war's end these people naturally wanted to return home. A commission of the Central Committee reviewed the situation of a series of defense plants in September and October 1945. It found distressing conditions, particularly in a tank factory in Omsk.

> The insistent demands of the workers to return to their former places of residence are prompted by the difficult living conditions [and by] dissatisfaction with the supply of clothes and shoes as well as food products. . . . Houses and dormitories are poorly constructed and not suit-

able for Siberian wintertime conditions. . . . The workers and their families endure extremely acute shortages of clothing, shoes, and linens. Annual production of textile goods is about .38 items per worker and of shoes .7 pairs per worker. Some workers are so poorly clothed that they cannot show up at their place of work.[19]

The workers protested against such living conditions. They refused to work more than eight hours a day, expressed open displeasure at the administration of enterprises, demanded their immediate return to former places of residence (the majority of the workers in Omsk had been evacuated from Leningrad, Voroshilovgrad, and other such cities). The situation was similar in the factories of the Urals and Siberia.[20] In order to forestall the further development of such attitudes among evacuated workers, special orders were issued forbidding them to leave their place of work under threat of legal liability. Not even threatening measures, however, sufficed to stop the elemental movement to return home. In August 1945 the People's Commissariat of Military Censorship registered 135 letters from Omsk workers addressed to relatives and friends, complaining of bad living conditions. "Conditions of life in the factory are terrible," according to one of these letters. "People are putting together a pack of supplies and fleeing, especially Leningraders. About four hundred have left recently. The order of the Commissar Malyshev is to return all those fleeing to Omsk and to prosecute them. We'll see what develops."[21] The writers of some letters expressed themselves more decisively: "The workers have given all their strength to defeat the enemy, and they want to return home, to their own people, their own homes. And now it turns out we have been deceived. They've shipped us out of Leningrad, and they want to leave us in Siberia. In this case we workers should say that our government has betrayed us and our work. They might imagine what kind of humor this leaves us in."[22]

Workers' demonstrations took place in several defense plants of the Urals and Siberia from July to September 1945. The situation grew so acute that on 4 August 1945 the Secretariat of the Central Committee gave special attention to the question. It ordered the administration in three factories where working conditions were most distressing to take urgent measures for the satisfaction of the legal demands of their employees (that is, with the exception of their demand to return home).[23]

The situation was scarcely better in the villages, many of which, especially in the regions subjected during the war to German occupation, were virtually depopulated. The population of the collective farms (including persons demobilized) toward the end of 1945 comprised only 85 percent of that of 1940; and the able-bodied proportion, only 67.5 percent of the prewar level.[24] The number of able-bodied men was reduced from 16.9 million in 1940 to 6.5 million at the beginning of 1946.[25] In several regions, for example in northern Russia, there were villages to which no live adult male returned.[26] Sown acreage was naturally reduced during the war, which of course depressed the harvest yield. The productivity of the collective farm lands fell as a result of the deterioration of work in the fields and the decline of the level of scientific agronomy. Women constituted the basic element of the able-bodied population of the village. They had to do all of the heavy work, and the administrative responsibilities were handled after the war by men. Collective farm production at the end of the war was in a critical condition, the peasants living essentially from their own private plots.

Besides destruction and ruin the war left another singular legacy, the growth of crime. This problem was felt especially acutely by the inhabitants of cities and industrial centers. If we judge by the letters that people wrote to government organs and to the newspapers, the struggle against crime in many cities after the war turned into a struggle for survival. The workers of Saratov wrote to *Pravda* in fall 1945 that "since the beginning of fall Saratov has been terrorized by thieves and murderers. To be forced to undress on the street, to have watches snatched from the wrist has become an everyday occurrence. . . . The life of the city simply ceases as darkness approaches. The inhabitants have grown accustomed to walking in the streets rather than on the sidewalks, and they watch suspiciously everyone who approaches them."[27] "A day doesn't pass without someone in Saratov being murdered or robbed, often in the very center of the city in broad daylight. . . . It's gone so far that the only people who go to the theater or the movies are those who live next door [to the theater]. The Karl Marx Theater, located in the suburbs, is empty in the evenings."[28] The workers of the Moscow suburb Podolsk shared the same problems.

> Marauding bandits and thieves detain peaceful citizens . . . not only in the evening, but kill, undress, and rob them in broad daylight, and not only in the obscure alleyways but on the main streets as well . . . even around the local party headquarters and the city soviet. After work, people gather in groups in order to protect themselves on their way

home. Thus meetings after work are poorly attended, because workers are afraid to remain, afraid of being attacked on the way home. And it is no longer safe at home, either, because robberies take place there day and night.[29]

If it was unsafe to walk on the streets, it was equally unsafe to ride commuter trains, where special bands of criminals operated. People not only were afraid to remain for meetings after work but began to leave work before dark.[30] Such behavior reflected both the reality of crime and the spread of various kinds of rumors both in conversation as well as in spontaneously circulated leaflets describing alleged assaults and murders.[31] Some of these fears stemmed from elementary lack of information about the real state of affairs, and the authorities made no effort to share such information.

Statistical accounts of crime in the postwar years were incomplete and contradictory and, as a rule, included all categories of crime classified by Soviet legislation as liable to prosecution. Thus people committing minor offenses, those late to work or absent from work, were counted along with the real criminals. The figures of the Ministry of Internal Affairs are more accurate on the number of crimes investigated by the police. In 1946 there were 430,071 such cases; in 1947, 404,167; and in 1948, 191,720.[32] The figures prepared in 1948 by the Ministry of Internal Affairs on *all* crimes differ somewhat from those given above: 546,275 in 1946 and 453,165 in 1947.[33] By comparison, in 1940 a total of 1,253,947 crimes were recorded.[34] Thus even if we take into account the incomplete nature of the data, the postwar crime rate was on the whole significantly lower than the prewar rate. The popular perception, however, indicates that the criminal activity was considerably more serious than is suggested by the statistics. As we observed above, the people's fear of the criminal element stemmed not so much from reliable information as from the lack of it and the dependence on rumor instead. Robbery was in the circumstances more than conventionally threatening, as it often cost people their last meager possessions. It was poverty that explained the scale of fear, just as it explained the crime wave itself. This does not mean, of course, that the problem of crime after the war existed only in people's imaginations. The authorities also perceived it as one of their most serious problems, at least during the first two postwar years.[35] As the population confronted the problem, however, it began at once to recede. Hunger took its place. The hungry years, the worst of which were 1946 and 1947, scarcely spared anyone. Even those who did not literally go hungry recall these years as the worst.

Chapter 4

The Hungry Years: The Famine of 1946–1947

The food supply crisis reflected a problem that to one degree or another confronted nearly all the combatant countries. In the Soviet Union—in Russia, Moldavia, and Ukraine—people experienced not merely food shortages but genuine disaster, famine. The first signs of the problem appeared in summer 1946. Drought afflicted a number of regions of central Russia, the middle and lower Volga, Ukraine, and Moldavia and threatened to ruin the harvest in those areas. In Siberia, on the other hand, a good harvest of the grain crop was expected, which might have compensated to a certain extent for the losses to drought in European Russia. As the harvest in Siberia and Kazakhstan began, however, drenching rains occurred in the central and northern regions. Climatic conditions and the general wear and tear on the aging farm machinery forced the harvesting of the crop in many of these regions by hand. As a result, the 1946 grain crop of 39.6 million tons was 7.7 million tons smaller than that of 1945 and 2.4 times smaller than that of 1940.[1] The harvest losses, however, were not the principal cause of the problem. "Relatively speaking, the 1945 shortfall," according to V.F. Zima, "fell within acceptable bounds and gave no grounds for extreme measures in the conduct of the government's grain procurement campaign."[2] The authorities themselves contributed to the crisis. They strove to avoid any reduction in the state grain reserve and thus proceeded by traditional methods of the late 1920s; that is, they required supplementary procurements. They assigned surcharges to collective and state farms over and above the conventional grain taxes in kind. The majority of collective and state farms were consequently forced to surrender grain usually designated for division among the peasants as personal income. The state thus left the village on the verge of famine.

The cities suffered similar problems of food supply. People who lived in cities, and some in rural areas (not including collective farmers), were provisioned by a system of ration cards. In 1945, the rationing system incorporated 80.6 million people.[3] There were workers' ration cards of the first and second class as well as special cards for civil servants, children, and other dependents. The norms of distribution on ration cards and the prices of rationed products were strictly regulated. For example, a daily norm of bread on a worker's card of the first class was 800 grams, and of the second class, 600; other norms were lower. The prices of rationed products were substantially lower than market prices. Thus the ration price of rye bread, a staple for most of the population at the time, varied in the different regions of Russia from seventy-five kopecks to a ruble fifteen kopecks per kilogram, while its commercial market price was from eight to ten rubles a kilogram.[4]

In September 1946 the Council of Ministers and the Central Committee began the "campaign to economize on bread," the first step of which was to raise the ration prices. The Politburo issued the order on 6 September 1946, and several days later it was dispatched under the stamp "not for publication" to the various party organizations. According to this document, "The Council of Ministers of the USSR and the Central Committee of the Communist Party are taking into account the problems of raising ration prices and understand that it will require sacrifices on the part of workers, civil servants, and peasants for the sake of the common good. We must keep in mind that without serious sacrifices it is impossible to liquidate the grave legacy of the war."[5] In order to compensate the public for higher ration prices, commercial prices of food products were simultaneously lowered. While ration prices were raised by 2.5 to 3 times (on various products), however, commercial prices were not lowered proportionally—that is, they were only reduced by between 10 and 20 percent.[6] Neither was it possible to find sufficient compensation in the decision to supplement the pay scale of workers in the lower and middle levels of pay: those earning up to 300 rubles a month received an extra 110 rubles; those earning up to 500 rubles, 100 rubles; those earning up to 900 rubles, 80 rubles. Pensioners received an extra 60 rubles a month, and students, an extra 80.[7]

The new prices were scheduled to be introduced on 16 September, and the information was received by party and government organs between 10 and 14 September. The authorities had always considered the personnel of these organs the most politically conscious and loyal sector of the public, and therefore their reaction would serve as a kind of indicator, a prognosis of the reaction of the rest of the population. As the materials reaching the Central Committee from the party organizations demonstrate, the discussion of the order to raise ration prices proceeded relatively calmly, although not without expressions of bewilderment. Most of the questions concerned that part of the document on the necessity of new sacrifices in order to overcome postwar difficulties. "Define the word 'sacrifices,' " demanded one member of the Moscow party organization. "What does it mean? Death, filth, pauperage, and the like, or perhaps something not so hellish as we imagine?" "How much longer can the working people of our country bear such sacrifices and deprivations?" another asked, as if in response to the first question. "How can we continue like this?" wondered a third. "Sacrifices and sacrifices. Understand me, if a family of three now needs 600 to 700 rubles [to buy food on ration cards], that is not all that has to be bought. The government is not giving away soap, there is no butter or lard, only substitutes, there is no kerosene. We are at the last extremity. Wages hardly suffice to buy rations, and there is no money for rent, clothes, or soap."[8]

In sum, these people doubted both the justification and the advisability of resolving the provisions crisis at the expense of the people. "Our factory has thrown away millions of rubles on engines," said one party member, "and there are many such factories. The government has accepted these millions in expenses, yet it can't accept a little increment of price supports. So for some reason it lays the cost on the shoulders of the workers."[9] They proposed their own solutions to the provisions crisis—for example, a repetition of the New Economic Policy (NEP) of the 1920s.[10] A more common policy recommendation from the arsenal of the 1920s was to extract goods from the farms by force. A characteristic suggestion maintained that "the war enabled a large portion of the population (workers in commercial organizations, peasants in many regions) to accumulate big profits. Why not appropriate these funds for the needs of the country?"[11] This opinion about the workers in commercial organizations might have had some basis in fact (the rationing system and the absence of legal free trade in conditions of extreme dearth did generate great abuses in the market); but similar judgments about the peasantry were the product of traditional stereotypes and elementary ignorance of the real situation in the villages. Such opinion was actually the exception rather than the rule, and a different opinion was regularly heard: "What kind of measures can be taken to improve the work of the collective farms? Because of poor organization and the absence of experienced personnel, many collective farms operate at a loss and produce no grain year after year. Many of them are destitute."[12]

Information on the reaction of party personnel to the forthcoming rise in ration prices was gathered and studied in the Central Committee. On the basis of provincial committee reports, a list of sixty-one commonly posed questions was compiled. A special list of thirty-three of the more typical questions was presented to Stalin. The majority of the questions included in the summary list were of a specific character and had to do with clarifying elements of the orders of the Council of Ministers and the Central Committee. The participants in the discussion in the party organs were interested in the duration of the new price structure, whether prices would be raised on goods not covered by the new orders, whether prices in cafeterias and lunch bars would be raised, and so on.[13] The local party cadres were naturally concerned about the problem of explaining to the masses the necessity of such an unpopular measure. According to the official explanation, the chief causes of the deteriorating situation were the drought and the harvest failure. That was understandable. But another circumstance they found to be mysterious: while shortages prevailed at home, the Soviet government felt able to extend food aid to other countries, thus aggravating the hardship of its own citizens. In the course of 1946–1947 alone, 2.5 million tons of Soviet grain were shipped to France, Bulgaria, Romania, Poland, Czechoslovakia, Yugoslavia, and other countries.[14] This policy required an explanation. "How are we to understand that we sell grain abroad and raise prices on it at home?" "How are we to answer workers if they ask, Why do we aid France, Poland, and Finland with grain and raise prices on it here?"[15] Such questions demanded answers sooner than the government supposed.

A resolution on the raising of ration prices was prepared in secret, but rumors of it circulated among the people on the eve of the publication of the official decree. Such information came from responsible party personnel, who could scarcely refrain from discussing in the family circle this most alarming of all questions. It also was leaked by the presses that were preparing the new price lists. In any event, by 12 and 13 September, especially in large cities like Moscow and Leningrad, these rumors became the chief subject of conversation. Women working in industrial enterprises reacted especially emotionally. "If they raise prices and do not raise our pay, then we will die of hunger," said a woman in a garment factory. Many may have shared her feeling. "Life is already unbearable. If they raise prices, I'll croak." "Large families will suffer most from price increases. I am terrified, wondering how we'll make it. There is not enough bread as it is. If it becomes three times as expensive, we'll lie down and die."[16]

Some people did not believe that the rumors of a price increase, in a situation so difficult for most of the people, could be true. "There cannot be a price increase on staple products, as it wouldn't be in keeping with the policy of the Soviet government," one of the doubters argued. "A price increase would be a public scandal. It would be an unexpected blow to the people."[17] Others were less optimistic and tried to explain in their own way why the government had nevertheless decided upon such a step. They spoke of harvest failure, of the difficult situation in the country, of the consequences of the recent war. The chief cause of the new sacrifices was seen, however, in something else: "If our government decides to raise the price of food products, then it most likely means that the Soviet state is in danger. It must be threatened by a new war."[18] Such an explanation was encountered not only among workers. It was widespread among all sectors of the population, for example among the residents of Moscow: "I am convinced that the price increase is related not only to the shortage of grain in the country but to the necessity of forming a reserve on account of the tense international climate. England and America are threatening us with war." "The problem is not only that everything will be more expensive and inaccessible to the workers. The worst is that it is a sure sign of an impending war."[19] As the provisions crisis developed, rumors of a new war became widespread.

The people's ignorance of the authorities' real intentions not only generated various kinds of rumors and conjectures but provoked behavior that the authorities found difficult to control. On 14 September Central Committee Secretary N.S. Patolichev informed A.A. Zhdanov that "in many cities, especially in Moscow and Leningrad, the people know of the imminent ration price increases, and consequently lines have formed in the stores to buy food. The communists are not adequately prepared to explain matters to the people, and therefore it would be advisable to publish the decree on the price increase not later than 15 September, that is, tomorrow."[20] The decree was in fact published on 16 September in the form of a short communiqué from the Council of Ministers. It made no reference to "sacrifices" or to difficulties arising from the drought and harvest failure. Rather the price increase was represented as a measure introduced to prepare conditions for the abolition of the rationing system in 1947.[21] According to official reports, the bulk of the population accepted the news "with understanding." If we judge by characteristic expressions of opinion, the people's patience was based not so much on comprehension of the real reasons for the reform as on the conviction that "the party and Comrade Stalin wish the people no ill."[22] "Once Comrade Stalin has signed the decree," as one Leningrader put it, "we believe that it is the correct, the only way. There is no alternative."[23] It is difficult to judge the degree of consensus on this question, because opinion of this kind was usually expressed in official circles, at meetings probably well prepared in advance. There is evidence, however, that similar opinions were common in private conversations. "It will be hard for many people," as the workers of a chemical complex in Voskresensk expressed it, "but certainly it couldn't have been done without the knowledge of Comrade Stalin. So it's necessary, there is no other way."[24]

The conviction that there was no alternative was not, however, universal. On the contrary, people said in public that "the government has taken a wrong turn."[25] Of course, the conversations in the street, and especially in bread lines, were more candid. In the store at factory No. 620 in Moscow on 16 September fifteen to twenty consumers gathered. One woman complained, "What will I live on? My husband alone works, and I have nine children. We will have to steal." "But [you] will go to prison," another responded. According to yet another, "In prison they'll be fed free of charge."[26]

In many stores, there was not enough bread to meet demand even at the new prices. In response, several workers at a freight-car factory in Omsk refused to go to work.[27] There were serious interruptions of bread supply in retail stores. The principal problems of provisioning, however, were still ahead.

Part of the workers hoped to resolve the problems arising from the price increases by raising their production norms and pay scales. Workers' meetings addressed many such suggestions to the administration of enterprises: eliminate shutdowns, secure the necessary raw materials, and so on. Thus in place of the screws/cogs in the machine of the economy, the little guys usually held responsible for everything, the local authorities began to assert their role, which was natural if we recall the conviction that "the party and Comrade Stalin wish the people no ill." The workers were of course not informed that all ministries, administrative offices, and directors of enterprises had been categorically forbidden by a special order of the Council of Ministers and the Central Committee to raise salary scales or rates of pay.[28]

Ten days after the price increases, on 27 September 1946, the government and the Central Committee issued another joint decree, "On Economizing in the Consumption of Grain," which provoked a great deal more public expression of dissatisfaction than the previous one. This new decree, effective 1 October, reduced considerably the number of people entitled to provisioning by ration cards. The rural population suffered most of all: the workers and administrative personnel of the state farms, the Machine-Tractor Stations, and local industrial enterprises. A total of 23 million people in rural areas lost their ration cards, as did 3.5 million in the cities, chiefly unemployed adult dependents. On 30 October, the state planning agency (Gosplan) was ordered to present a proposal to reduce further the number of those on ration cards. In addition, the decision was made in October to reduce retail trade in bread by 70,000 tons.[29] In fact, the sale of bread in the stores was reduced by 35,000 tons in October and by another 25,000 tons in November.[30] At the same time the quality of bread declined: from 1 November 1946, the proportion of oats, barley, and corn (combined) in bread was raised to 40 percent, and for the cities of Moscow and Leningrad, to 25 percent.[31] All of these changes were soon evident in the mood of the population.

Unlike the 16 September price increase for rationed bread, this new government initiative weighed heavily on the living standards of many families and was nowhere regarded as reasonable and justified. It was even suggested that "Comrade Stalin does not know of the many outrages that are taking place in the country."[32] Some opinions were more categorical: "This is being done by wreckers. The Boss [Stalin] is vacationing in Sochi, and the wreckers have taken over."[33] Once again everything focused on the figure of the *vozhd'*. Reports circulated in Leningrad, for example, that "a group of workers went to Comrade Stalin in Moscow and told him how difficult life had become for the people, and Comrade Stalin had written: lower the price of bread to one ruble seventy-five kopecks a kilogram."[34] The name of Stalin in workers' circles was as usual spared all criticism; in any event, informers for the Central Committee omitted any reference to it. Critical comments, if they bypassed local authorities, were not addressed to anyone in particular or referred to vague third parties, though parties with undoubted authority. "They cannot tell us the truth." "Why do they not take us into their confidence?" "During the elections to the Supreme Soviet, they promised to lower prices and to abolish the rationing system. Now the elections are over . . . , and they have not abolished the rationing system, they have cut the bread quotas, and they have raised prices."[35]

After their dependents' ration cards were invalidated, workers began to move to enterprises in cities where they continued to receive cards. The industrial enterprises of Leningrad, for example, hired twice as many employees in October as in September. The situation was similar in the other Russian industrial centers.[36] Several enterprises had to turn down those looking for work on the grounds that they lacked sufficient ration cards. The factories of Kazan fired workers for the same reason, but some of those terminated continued to come to work. As they said, "We have nowhere else to turn."[37] In the villages, among the workers of the state farms, the Machine-Tractor Stations, and local industries—that is, in the categories deprived of ration cards—the opposite process took place: they left their former places of work and migrated to the cities. The local authorities were thrown into disarray. From 1 October they were occupied with one single question: to distribute bread cards and examine the multiple complaints of the people who had lost them.[38] All of these policies— the beginning of forced procurements, leaving the villages without grain, then the curtailment of rationing cards, the reduction of the bread supply, and the authorities' stubborn refusal to release grain from the state reserves in the face of the growing supply crisis— brought about the hungry winter of 1946–1947.

There are no precise data on the loss of life from the postwar famine. The very fact of it was assiduously hidden by the Soviet authorities, and medical statistics are both incomplete and partly falsified (for example, in the case of diagnoses of dystrophy as one of the causes of the high rate of illness and death in 1946–1947). The historian V.F. Zima, who did the first and most substantial research into the origins and consequences of the famine of 1946–1947, has estimated that in the USSR as a whole about 100 million people suffered malnutrition after the war and that from 1946 through 1948 it caused about 2 million deaths.[39] At least half a million people starved to death in the Russian Republic.[40]

Especially afflicted were the rural regions, the collective farms, where the farmers did not receive the grain that they themselves had raised. The first alarming signs began to appear in December 1946 and January 1947. In official documents, they were referred to as "provisioning problems" (the word "famine" was not used), and they took the following form: the Kaluga provincial party committee informed the Central Committee that "part of the families of collective farmers . . . in various regions of the province lack grain and potatoes and are forced to feed themselves by surrogates and begging."[41] Specific examples followed.

> The collective farmer Evdokiia Tsareva, whose husband died at the front, has three children and earned three hundred units[42] of grain but did not receive any. She has no farm animals, and she has consumed all her grain and potatoes. She and her children are ill of malnutrition. . . . On the Red Star farm the families of Ekaterina Kulkovaia, Evdokiia Ledovaia, Mariia Govorovaia, and Ekaterina Sergeevaia . . . have no food and live only by begging. . . . The tractor operator Minaev earned 493 kilograms of grain but received only 31 and is ill from malnutrition. . . . Several farmers, having no food, are selling their livestock and using the money to buy potatoes.[43]

Not only villages starved. The inspectors of the Central Committee, venturing out to examine the state of affairs in industrial enterprises of various cities, came to disturbing conclusions in a series of cases, as illustrated by one of their reports to the Central Committee.

> In the municipal industries of Mariupol in Stalin Province the number of workers ill of dystrophy has recently increased significantly. The physicians of the city concluded on 1 March [1947] that there are 3,789 cases of dystrophy in five factories of Mariupol. . . . Their examination has established that the increase of illness is related to a significant degree to the fact that the Ministry of Trade has in the course of the past five months systematically reduced the supply of grain and food products to the factories.[44]

The atmosphere of these hungry months is conveyed best of all by the letters of people condemned to the misery of the experience. Several thousand such letters were recorded by the confidential surveillance of the Ministry of State Security in two provinces of Russia in November and December 1946 (4,616 from Voronezh and 3,275 from Stalingrad). "The approaching famine is terrifying," wrote M.S. Efremova from Voronezh. "Our children are living like animals—constantly angry and hungry. From undernourishment Zhenia has begun to swell up, especially her face, and she is very weak. The children bear hunger patiently. If there is nothing to eat, which often happens, they are silent, they don't torment me with futile demands."[45] Another letter was sent from the city of Kalach, Voronezh district: "We live in frightful conditions. We have absolutely nothing, we eat only acorns, and we can scarcely drag our feet. We will die from hunger this year."[46] Letters from Stalingrad and the surrounding villages are little different: "There is no bread, and we do not know how we shall survive. No one is receiving bread. People are beginning to swell up. In our collective farm and the one next door no one has been given bread. Things are bad." "I have sold everything to save us. There is nothing more to sell. Only one thing remains: either to die or to do something decisive. Prison doesn't frighten me if I can get a piece of bread there."[47]

The thought that "we must steal in order to survive" slipped into letters, was heard in bread lines, hovered in the atmosphere. It was voiced most often in people's hearts, and what lay behind it was usually a feeling of resentment and lack of alternatives rather than real intentions. The famine did nevertheless goad people to crime. According to incomplete figures, in fall 1946 in the USSR 53,369 people were prosecuted for stealing bread, and 36,670 of them (74.3 percent) were sentenced to deprivation of freedom.[48] Among the total number of those sentenced for various categories of crime in 1946–1947, about 50 percent were women with young children who were obliged to follow their mothers into Siberian exile.[49] The wave of so-called "women's crime" of these years was a direct consequence of the famine, as was the growth of crimes committed by children and teenagers. Often the sentence—from five to eight years in a corrective labor camp—in no way corresponded to the seriousness of the crime. A person could draw such a sentence, for example, for the theft of a kilogram of flour or for digging several potatoes from a collective farm field. The minister of justice of the Russian Federation, Ivan Basavin, admitted that the judicial practice of those years was characterized by "frequent imposition of sentences on the basis of unfounded accusations."[50]

The situation in the consumers' market slowly improved. The people, as usual lacking information on the plans of the authorities, made new conjectures and circulated new rumors. In summer 1947 in Moscow it was widely rumored that there would soon be, around 15 July, another increase of ration prices. Once again, great lines formed in the stores, and people began withdrawing their money from savings accounts.[51] In the course of 1947, 1948, and even at the beginning of 1950 there were many cases of interrupted supply of bread and other vital food products. In spring 1948, for example, there were serious problems of bread supply in Novosibirsk. A number of stores in the city had no bread for several days, and lines of up to seven or eight hundred people formed. In such circumstances there were naturally outbreaks of public disorder. Observers reported that several people climbed onto the roofs of stores, jumped down onto consumers gathered in the crowd, and thus forced their way to the sales counter.[52] In other cities the militia had to be called in order to enforce order in the lines before stores. Thus the provisions crisis was not completely resolved by the end of 1947, when rationing was abolished and monetary reform was introduced.

Chapter 5

The Currency Reform of 1947: The Views from Above and Below

One of the early consequences of the war was the disruption of the financial system. Inflationary pressures, aggravated by the critical situation in the consumers' market and the growth of an economy of natural exchange, were manifested in the de facto devaluation of the ruble and threatened the program of economic reconstruction. Additional pressure was brought against the state budget by the gradual reduction of sources of revenue: the emergency wartime tax was abolished, voluntary contributions to the Red Army fund ceased, and employers' contributions to employees' savings accounts for unused vacation time were diminished.

The first effort to restore the financial position of the country was the state reconstruction and development bond issued in May 1946. The size of the issue was 20 billion rubles.[1] According to a letter of People's Commissar of Finance A.G. Zverev to the commissars of the union republics and their subdivisions, "Though it is desirable to float the loan quickly, superfluous haste is not advisable. . . . The tempo of the loan must be accompanied by a corresponding measure of organizational work and explanation."[2] Notwithstanding the warnings, however, as often happened at the grass roots when the state initiated major undertakings, the local authorities treated it as a forced loan. The psychology of administrative excess provoked its natural results. It usually began with the calling of a meeting of workers for "discussions" with party and government organs, after which "voluntary" subscriptions were encouraged in the form of a week's, a month's, and sometimes two months' wages. Of course, such methods elicited little respect for the authorities employing them or for the loan as a whole. More important, the loan was not adequate by itself to deal with the long-term challenge of restoring the financial system, though it allowed the state to acquire a part of the means to address the problem.

The logical next step to repair the state's finances was monetary reform, which was fated to have complex consequences. Typically, such economic measures were accompanied by a serious political agenda, and propagandistic aims sometimes masked economic expediency. From the beginning the monetary reform was dependent upon another reform—the end of rationing. The abolition of ration cards, which had become the very symbol of wartime, was to have been, in the opinion of Soviet leaders, a demonstration of the strength and endurance of the Soviet economy. And thus it was necessary to end rationing earlier than in the other countries that had resorted to it during the war (England, France, Italy, Austria). This action was initially planned for 1946, but the provisions crisis in autumn of that year forced its postponement. It would not be fair, however, to explain the haste with which the cards were canceled entirely by considerations of propaganda.

The forced pace of this measure is explained not only by the position of the leadership but by pressure from below to proceed with it. In the workaday mentality, the war and the ration cards were so intimately identified that the rationing system was popularly perceived as virtually the cause of the wartime supply problems. Instances of various kinds of abuse, inevitable in a rationing system, only magnified this outlook. The idea of the abolition of the cards became even more popular after the increase in ration prices of 1946. Typical were a series of opinions expressed in the summer and fall of 1947: "The most painful question is that of provisions. Everywhere people are saying: when will the rationing system be abolished, or at least when will a commercial market for bread and buckwheat groats be opened?" "All workers and office personnel are waiting for the end of bread rationing. This is a general expectation. And when there is enough bread, then prices on other food products will be lowered."[3] Many workers were expressing hope for the cancellation of rationing by the end of 1947.[4]

The view of rationing abolition as a complete panacea for provisioning problems was not, however, universal. As conversations in workers' circles indicated, many of them did not imagine that conventional commercial organizations would be able to resist the evils of speculation. Such people stood for the preservation of rationing for the foreseeable future along with an increase in the government supply of bread. "It's tough in the bread market now, not enough," said a coal miner from Cheliabinsk Province. "And if they abolish the cards, then it may get worse. The speculators will take over, and we may be left without bread."[5]

Thus there were advocates of the rationing system, just as there were enemies of it (though the latter did not condemn the practice but rather its duration). The abolition of rationing at the end of 1947 did not catch anyone by surprise. Rather the factor that caught the majority of people off guard was the simultaneous decree of the monetary reform.

A.G. Zverev, the minister of finance, recalls that this reform was prepared in circumstances of strict secrecy under the personal supervision of Stalin.[6] Conceived as an anti-inflationary measure, it in fact simply appropriated from the people their so-called superfluous cash reserves. The result, presumably, would be to punish the speculators, and the honest working people would be the winners. What in fact happened?

In reality the secret of the imminent reform was soon breached. "In places," recalled Zverev, "upon receiving the special order stamped 'Open only on receipt of special instructions,' curiosity overwhelmed devotion to duty among local authorities, and so the order was opened ahead of time."[7] Some government and party officials thus found out about the reform in advance, which allowed them to take preliminary measures of financial security with the cash that they had on hand. Even earlier the shady characters, the speculators, exchanged the bulk of their cash for gold, real estate, or other valuables. Rumors of the reform, which was decreed in the night of 14 to 15 December 1947, spread among the people and set up a veritable prereform fever.

Viacheslav Kondratiev described the scene.

> For the past several days, people have appeared on the streets before daylight. All the stores, especially shops for used goods and industrial products, are thronged by crowds. The day before yesterday, in the 'Optika' store on . . . Nikolsk Street, all the binoculars were selling like hotcakes. The excellent Zeiss binoculars—the dream of officers at the front—were now being bought by old men and women, and not one or two at a time, but by the dozen, at a hundred rubles apiece. A week ago, crowds appeared in the savings banks, anonymous people depositing, withdrawing, anticipating the reform, trying to figure out what was best to do. . . . In the evening, the restaurants were jammed with people

brawling, shouting, cursing; there were fights at the door. . . . Of course,
not only those trying to spend their money roamed the streets of Moscow. Others . . . were seized by a mixture of holiday spirit and panic. It
was interesting to watch. A few people decided to save their last couple
of hundred old rubles as souvenirs, as a new life was starting with new
money and without ration cards.[8]

The paradoxical juxtaposition of a holiday spirit and the feeling of
nervous insecurity were fed by two ingredients of the situation: on the
one hand, the abolition of rationing was associated in people's minds
with the return of peacetime; and on the other hand, nobody knew
what this new peacetime would be like, whether better or worse. This
situation was clarified somewhat on the day after the reform: the
shelves of the stores (especially in Moscow) were covered with an
almost prewar abundance. Prices of goods of mass consumption, however, were many times higher than the old ration–card prices, especially on clothes, shoes, and knitwear.[9] The prices of food products
were on the whole higher than prewar prices, and, with the exception
of the necessary minimum, out of reach of the majority of the people,
who thus bought only on special occasions.

In spite of the officially declared goals, the reform, in the opinion
of a number of specialists, hit several categories of the population
hard: the better qualified element of the workforce, persons engaged
in heavy and dangerous work or in agriculture, and those who kept
their capital and resources at home rather than in savings accounts.[10]
[Because only money in savings accounts could be exchanged against
the new currency.—H.R.] According to the calculations of the economist Aleksei Uliukaev, the accumulation of capital savings in the
country at that time was fourteen to fifteen times greater than the
annual salaries of workers and office personnel.[11]

Notwithstanding the fact that the reform reduced the volume of
the people's disposable money, it did not eliminate the gap between
supply and demand. If the necessary level of consumer goods could
be provided in the big cities—though it required a special order of
the Council of Ministers on 29 November 1947 to do so—the status of
the consumers' market elsewhere remained critical. And among the
number of items in deficit the most important was bread. As a result,
in the hinterland there was an elemental and spontaneous return to
rationing in the form of ration cards, booklets, and other documents
(*propuski*) conferring privileged access to the market.

Such a state of affairs could only alarm the people. A study prepared by Iurii Aksenov and Aleksei Uliukaev introduces documentary evidence—the letters of workers and office clerks to the Central Committee and to the newspaper *Pravda*—that gives an idea of the real conditions in much of the country after the abolition of rationing. "The lines at bread shops present a frightful picture, with officials and bouncers at the door to keep order. A worker receives two kilograms of bread for three to four days. Every day there are fist fights [*mordobitiia*]! The workers are in a terrible condition" (Semipalatinsk). "In Spassk the supply of bread is bad without exception. In order to get bread, it is necessary to stand in line from one morning to the next. I am an invalid of the war, my health doesn't allow me to fight through the crowd, and so my family and I, five people, have not seen any bread for ten days" (Riazan Province). "The lowering of prices didn't help us, and we are workers [i.e., the privileged people in a proletarian society—H.R.]. We don't buy caviar, and motorcycles and cars are of no concern to us. It would be better to lower prices on lard, shoes, and clothes" (Moscow).[12]

The end of rationing did not justify the hopes that prompted it. Life did not change instantaneously. In all of the early postwar years, this was the first occasion when stark reality collided directly with the hope for relatively painless improvements in life. Many people then believed seriously that it sufficed to take one correct decision, simple and wise, to leave behind all the fevered problems of wartime. The abolition of rationing was just such a form of that uniquely right and simple decision. The real and the ideal conflicted, and this fact formed a complex of deceived hopes. Insofar as these hopes arose precisely on the basis of one particular reform, then the common reaction was to hold that reform responsible for the disillusionment. And so the popular mind generalized from one reform to reforms more broadly conceived. Based on their negative experience of the monetary reform of fall 1947, the people developed a distrust of reform in general. For the time being, this was neither a stable nor an all-embracing fund of distrust—because the faith of the people in the justice of their leadership was not yet exhausted—but rather an impulse that changed their attitude toward the very process of change. Having previously looked forward to reform as if it would necessarily bring improvement, they now reacted with caution and apprehension. Might it not make things worse? At the same time, the illusion of prospective changes for the better persisted for at least the first of three postwar years, until it finally became clear that the authorities had no intention of reverting to the prewar order of things.

PART II

THE ILLUSION OF LIBERALIZATION

Chapter 6

The State and the Peasant: Village Antagonism to the Collective Farm

Everybody expected changes after the war. These expectations suffused the whole society, enabling people to survive and to hope that a new and better life would soon begin. Not everyone could imagine this new life in detail, a life without war, and the general picture of hopes and only partially formulated wishes clearly distinguished the different expectations and pretensions of one social group from another. Among the peasantry, hopes for the future centered on a single great question: what would happen after the war to the collective farm?

Formally organized on the basis of voluntary principles, during the war the collective farm system was finally transformed into an institution of forced, heavy, and virtually unpaid labor. In 1942, the government issued a special order increasing the obligatory minimum of individual workdays.[1] Collective farmers who failed to fulfill the minimal norm without sufficient reason were subject to legal action and to punitive corrective-labor obligations in their own collective farm for a period of six months, while 25 percent of their usual earnings were diverted to the farm. First introduced during the war, these policies continued after the end of hostilities. In addition, by an order of 31 May 1947, the government prolonged the wartime practice of the increased minimum of workdays and the legal responsibility for fulfilling the obligation.[2] The most serious problem of collective farm labor, however, was not its intensiveness but the fact that it was progressively devalued such that the level of farmers' income fell to the

purely nominal. In 1946, after the harvest and the forced appropria-
tion of grain during the procurement campaigns, the peasants in
many collective farms received no income at all. In the USSR as a
whole in 1946, 75.8 percent of the collective farms issued less than
one kilogram of grain per workday, and 7.7 percent issued no grain—
that is, income—whatever to the peasants. In the Russian Federation,
13.2 percent of collective farms were left without grain in 1946, and
in several provinces of Russia—for example, Orlov, Kursk, and
Tambov—the proportion of farms not issuing grain to the peasants
ranged from 50 to 70 percent.[3] The settling of accounts with the
peasants in grain in this first postwar year was worse than during the
wartime year of 1943, the most difficult year of the war for the agricultural economy. The peasants thus lost whatever interest they had ever
had in work on the farms, and their attitude soon showed in the
indices of their labor productivity. In 1946, 18.5 percent of the able-
bodied peasants in the USSR as a whole did not perform the obligatory minimum of workdays, and in those provinces where the pay
scale (in grain) was worse, the proportion who fell below the minimum was higher yet; for example, in Orlov, it was 31.1 percent; in
Kursk, 29.2 percent; and in Tambov, 45.8 percent.[4]

The mind-set of the peasants was manifest in their letters, which
candidly expressed hopelessness (*bezyskhodnost'*), a feeling of doom,
or sometimes simply anger. Characteristic are excerpts from
Stavropol in June 1946. "We work on the collective farm as we used to
work for the landlords in the days of serfdom. They drive us to work,
and they neither feed us nor pay us. For bait they give us a teaspoon
of gruel once a day, and sometimes—two or three times a week—fifty
grams of bread . . . to keep us breathing, so we don't kick the bucket."
"We are in a panic. The harvest has started, and everything is breaking down. This is all due to Kozlov [chairman of the collective farm—
E.Z.], who spent the winter hunting rabbits and did not service the
equipment. Now many of the men, instead of organizing the work,
are doing nothing. The women are cutting hay by hand, while the
men simply lie about." "I am crying every day. There is no bread, and
they drive us to work. The chairman of the farm simply makes fun of
me. He screams, Go to work or you'll be expelled from the farm and
won't get any bread. How can you work when you can scarcely drag
your feet?"[5]

The collective farm system was in a deep crisis, and many people,
enthralled to it by their tax obligation, would have preferred a radical
solution to the crisis: the dissolution of the whole agrarian system. An

analysis of the mood of the villages in the last year of the war and the first postwar years shows that opinion in favor of the abolition of the collective farms or their radical restructuring not only roused the hopes of its enemies but prompted illusions of possible changes even among the loyal and enthusiastic advocates of the government.

"Rumors of the liquidation of the collective farms . . . are widespread among the peasants," reported a Central Committee agent returning from an inspection tour of Kursk Province in June 1946.[6] Similar signals reached party and government organs from other regions of the country. The members of the Spark Collective Farm of Pskov District asked an itinerant government official: "Will the collective farms soon be dissolved? If there were no collective farms, we could live better and be of more use to the state."[7] Conversations reported from Penza Province alleged that "everyone is waiting for the return of the soldiers to abolish the collective farms."[8] The peasants of a number of farms of Pskov Province refused to sign the traditionally obligatory annual letter to Stalin promising to fulfill their assigned grain-quota deliveries to the state ahead of schedule.[9] They explained their refusal curiously. "This letter has a hidden motive, because Comrade Stalin asked the people to remain in the collective farms for seven more years [there is no evidence to this effect—H.R.]. The local authorities are trying to preserve the farms, and now they collect the signatures of the peasants [to support the preservation of the farms—H.R.]. If the letter is signed, then the collective farms will not be dissolved."[10] Some of these peasants actually believed rumors that the initiative in the liquidation of the collective farm system would come from the supreme authority himself, directly from Stalin. Someone said that a special commission had been formed in Moscow to do the job, while others were sure that the decree on liquidation had already been signed though not yet published.[11]

According to reports from the villages, however, the majority of peasants reacted to the supreme authority more skeptically. They did not believe that Stalin on his own initiative would repudiate the collective farms. Such a thing would be possible only upon outside intervention, as the peasants assured each other, something in the role of a "third force," which would oblige Stalin to dissolve the collective farms. This something was usually identified with the recent allies of the USSR in the coalition against Hitler—that is, the United States and Great Britain. Opinion of this kind was surprisingly uniform whether recorded in Pskov, Kursk, Voronezh, or Rostov, in the peasant homes of the western provinces or the remote Siberian villages.

The rumors proliferated quickly and grew ever more fantastic. According to the peasants in Voronezh Province, "In America, it is said, they have already decided to dissolve all the collective farms in the USSR, and that is why Molotov [foreign minister] walked out of the San Francisco [United Nations] conference [April–June 1945]."[12] The peasants of Stavropol thought that "the collective farms will be abolished in accordance with the demands of Churchill and Truman."[13] In Pskov, there were other fantasies: "At the San Francisco conference they asked Molotov to repudiate both the Bolsheviks and the collective farms. He refused to repudiate the Bolsheviks, and therefore America declared war on Russia."[14] An informer from Kursk Province reported to the authorities the content of peasant conversations: "England and America presented an ultimatum to our government: either dissolve the collective farms, or we will declare war. In San Francisco, Molotov at first refused to liquidate the collective farms but later returned and agreed. The Americans will verify by airplane reconnaissance whether or not the collective farms have in fact been dissolved."[15]

Such rumors and conversations were characterized in official documents exclusively as the work of provocateurs and hostile elements. Besides the rumors current among the people, informers recorded so-called "unhealthy" opinions among some of the collective farm administrators. Thus chairman Petrov of the True Way Farm in Pskov Province said in a conversation with one of the local government officials, "Now, when we have finally won the war, the collective farms will apparently be dissolved, as they have served their purpose."[16] It is true that far from all chairmen entertained such radical opinions. Some of them spoke more cautiously. "We must reform the collective farms, as they have become entirely impoverished," according to Chairman I.P. Ivanov of the Victor Farm in the Buriat Mongol Autonomous Republic. "We must allow the collective farm to operate independently without central government interference in its local affairs, set aside the Five-Year Plans, and define the farm's rent and tax obligations to the state, which we would certainly render. But how to do so would be our business. We would work the land better, if not as much, and we would have bread for ourselves and fill the cities with food products."[17] In these perceptions, it was necessary to liberate the peasants from the tyranny of the state and thus protect them from the arbitrariness of the authorities. This thought was common to those who believed in any kind of positive prospects for the collective farm system as well those who hoped for its transformation.

At the same time, not content to wait upon hopes, some peasants were ready to act more decisively. These peasants called on their fellow villagers not to wait for gifts from above but rather to leave the collective farms on their own initiative, as if to prompt the authorities to take the proper action. As Fedor Iastrebov, a foreman of the Lenin Farm in the region of Lake Baikal, argued, "There is no point in working on the collective farm because they won't pay you anything for it. It's better to work on your private plot, to plant your own private crops, and others, seeing your example, will do the same. And the communists will not be able to do anything with us and will dissolve the collective farm."[18] The peasant Akim Fedorov from the Shock-Worker Farm in Buriat Mongolia reasoned as follows: "Life in the collective farm has reached a dead end. We are on the verge of starvation. . . . We must leave the collective. To hell with work, let's get out of here."[19] Conversations and challenges to the authorities of this kind were regarded as anti-Soviet agitation, and the people openly behind them were hauled in for legal proceedings.

Confronted with manifestations of the anti-collective-farm disposition after the war, the authorities tried to analyze the reasons for it. Insofar as this kind of opinion was evaluated as indisputably hostile, the reasons for its dissemination were attributed above all to "the machinations of [class] enemies"; that is, the opinions were regarded as the product of an alien influence, and so the authorities began to suspect the soldiers returning to the village as the potential source of the problem. One of the reports characterized the influence of these demobilized veterans on the outlook in the villages: "A lot of comrades have been in Romania, Hungary, Austria, and the Baltic countries, and they have seen the system of private farming and individual tenure, but not all of them have the political literacy to understand the real distinction between our system and capitalism. As a consequence, they sometimes lead our peasants astray."[20]

Another channel of the penetration of sentiment against the collective farm was believed to be repatriated Soviet citizens, who, like the veterans, had spent enough time abroad or in occupied territory to experience other forms of agricultural organization. One such person, returning home from Lithuania, related to his neighbors that "all the peasants in Lithuania live well, the very poorest have three to four head of cattle and a couple of horses. There aren't any collective farms there. The Germans were well disposed and didn't touch us."[21] One woman reported that "in Lithuania there are no collective farms, the peasants are their own masters. Now as soon as we return home, they begin to torment us and reorganize the collective farms."[22] Two repatriates returning from East Prussia to a village near Smolensk shared their impressions with their neighbors: "In Germany we lived several times better than here. The peasants in Germany live well, are as well dressed as the people in town, there is no difference between village and town."[23] Similar thoughts were sometimes expressed by residents of the occupied territories during the war, chiefly those from the western provinces. The stories of a prosperous life among the German occupiers were not always believed, however, the more so as many people who had experienced the occupation had completely different memories of it. The Russian village ravaged by the war was far from fertile ground for the spread of any kind of favorable recollection of the German occupation. An absurd but characteristic rumor current among the peasants of Penza Province maintained that "the collective farm system itself was introduced on the orders of the Germans in order to ruin the economy and weaken Russia for the purpose of conquering it."[24]

Identifying displaced persons, returning veterans, and people from occupied territory as the source of anti-collective-farm sentiment, local informers deliberately avoided the chief reasons for peasant dissatisfaction with collective–farm life: the circumstances of the farms and the conditions of life on them. It is not true that they were silent about these factors. On the contrary, the informers described in detail the critical situation of farm income, the dilapidated condition of farm machinery, and the decline of work discipline. But in sum they reported these matters as if there were no connection between the facts and the growth of sentiment against the system; and the refusal of the peasants to work free of charge for the state was explained by their lack of political consciousness and the influence of hostile ideology. Unlike the peasants, who for some time after the war entertained illusions about the prospect of changes in their fate, the Central Committee's informers evidently imagined that the leadership of the country had no plans to retreat from its former principles in agricultural policy. The peasants were soon to see that the informers were right.

In the agriculturally inauspicious conditions of 1946, even before the grain procurement campaign, the government decided to raise taxes on the peasants' private plots.[25] As the peasants put it, so much for the "better life" of Soviet propaganda. "The peasants are writhing like fish pulled from water. Taxes this year are twice as high as in the past."[26] "We thought that when the war was over life would be better, and it turns out that it's worse, taxes twice as high." "With taxes like these, life is impossible," peasants were writing to their relatives.[27] This was, however, not the last tax increase of the postwar years. The tax liability of the peasants was reviewed every year, and twice, in 1948 and 1952, the agricultural tax was increased. While in 1940 the peasants paid these taxes in the amount of 2.4 million rubles, in 1952 they paid 8.7 million. The household economy of the average peasant, possessing one cow, two sheep, one pig, about one-third acre of potatoes and a bit more than one-tenth acre of other vegetables, paid 100 rubles of agricultural tax in 1940 and more than 1,100 rubles in 1952.[28] Lacking the capacity otherwise to meet their obligations to the state, the peasants cut down their orchards and killed their livestock.

The refrain "there is no living in the collective farm" was repeated in the peasants' letters and in conversations among themselves, and of course it reached the eyes and ears of the informers. The state of affairs in the village did not remain a secret from the authorities. The peasants themselves regularly informed the government organs of it in their letters of complaint. The Council of Collective–Farm Affairs (under the Council of Ministers) of the USSR received 92,795 such complaints in the years 1947–1950 alone. During the same time, officials received 3,305 petitions in personal interviews.[29] The complaints were directed chiefly at the problem of the tax burden and other obligatory deliveries. No more than half of these were examined, and only a handful received satisfaction.[30]

The policy of the state in the villages during the early postwar years persuaded the peasants that hopes for the abolition of the collective farms or even for relief of the tax burden were purely illusory. Once this fact was comprehended, the mood of the villagers changed accordingly. No longer hoping for any satisfactory changes in rural life, many peasants saw only one exit from the situation: they fled from the farms. A part of the peasants who fled became *edinolichniki*—that is, they somehow set themselves up on their own. In Cheliabinsk Province the number of such individual peasant households increased from 1,078 to 1,907 in the course of the year 1947–1948 alone, that is, by 70 percent.[31] The general trend is evidenced in the unauthorized departures of peasants from the collective farms of Novosibirsk Province.[32] One of the women at a farm meeting declared without hesitation, "Do what you want, I am getting out."[33] "You work or you don't work in the collective farm, it's all the same, a prosperous life is out of reach." The peasants came to this conclusion and left for the cities, for construction work, where it was possible to feed a family.[34] The famine of 1946–1947 was a powerful catalyst of the process. The migration of the rural population continued, however, through the succeeding years. Thus from 1949–1953 alone, the number of able-bodied peasants in collective farms (within the prewar borders of the USSR) decreased by 3.3 million people.[35]

The majority of those who remained in the collective farm could hardly make ends meet. The peasants tried to perform the required minimum of workdays in order not to fall afoul of the law, but beyond this necessary minimum they did not trouble themselves about work in the collective fields. Many did not bother about the obligatory minimum of workdays. Not even the threat of punishment could force the peasants to work without compensation. Therefore, when the circumstances of passive sabotage on the farms became clear to the authorities, they immediately took more brutal measures to coerce conformity. On 2 June 1948 the Presidium of the Supreme Soviet issued a decree "On the Resettlement in Remote Regions of Persons Maliciously Refusing to Work in the Agricultural Economy and Leading a Parasitical Form of Life Hostile to the Public Weal." The decree granted to local government the right to exile principally to Siberia practically any person, whether collective farm peasant or *edinolichnik*. Such decisions were to be made at collective farm and village meetings and might be preceded by a kind of prophylactic warning. The peasants remembered this decree as a "second dekulakization." "Now they will begin to transport us in droves, as they did in the 1930s. Whoever does not fulfill the plan goes into exile," said a peasant woman from the Better Path Farm in Novosibirsk Province.[36] "The decree is too cruel," said another from the Ninth of January 1905 Farm of the same province. "This is like the persecution of the 1930s, when they shipped off the kulaks."[37]

The reinforcement of the punitive sanctions on the part of the state provoked bewilderment and protest among some peasants: "All of this is not right, to forbid individual farming and to exile anyone who does not work on the collective farm. Why force us to live in the collective if we don't want to?" asked the peasant Lukinov from the Better Path Farm, as he proceeded with persuasive arguments. "You can't get far by the use of force, and in the collective farm people are dying of hunger, how can they not flee the farm?"[38] This was not the unanimous response to the decree on resettlement. It was not accidental that in many collective farm meetings, the discussion of the decree did not meet the expectations of the local or the higher administration. The peasants either did not vote or voted against exiling their fellows, substituting the issuance of warnings only. There were some occasions of a different kind when the peasants voted for exile as a settling of personal accounts or the making of scapegoats.

The decree put into the hands of the collective-farm administration a new stick with which to chase the peasants back into the collective. According to the foreman of one farm in the Moscow region, "The government did well to issue this decree. Going to work the next day, I was surprised how many of my people—whom I always had to nag, who were always getting out of hand—were also at work."[39] A similar situation was observed in other farms. Learning that a meeting was taking place in the farm next door on the exile of peasants who did not work conscientiously, people began to fear landing on the black list and at once went to work in the fields. The secretary of a Iaroslav Province party committee reported that "a meeting took place in the Great Wilderness (*Bolshie pustoshki*) Farm, and on the neighboring farm when the foreman came at 3:30 A.M. to issue daily orders to the peasants, no one was at home. All were at work in the hay fields."[40] Trying to avoid what was in fact prosecution and persecution at once, even adolescents and invalids went to work in the fields. In a number of farms the local administration was simply not prepared for such a comprehensive turnout of the peasants, and as a consequence many of them did not have the capacity to accommodate full participation in fieldwork.[41] Overlooking the real causes and ascribing the new attitude of the peasants to their alleged native enthusiasm, the local authorities reported to their superiors "the unprecedented growth of labor activity." Preparing to call village meetings, the chairmen of the farms sometimes obviously brandished the big stick. Not feeling confident of their own strength, they invited to the meetings local authorities and even the police of the Ministry of Internal Affairs. This tactic provoked among the peasants rumors and reports of different kinds. "There will be some kind of special meeting today. They say that fifteen people will be arrested and twenty will be expelled from the village."[42] Virtually a sign of the times was the popular observation that "if a lot of officials arrive in cars, it means that something big is afoot."[43] Such signs were not lacking. In the course of three months after the introduction of the new decree, 23,000 Soviet peasants were sent off into exile, 12,000 of them from the Russian Federation.[44] The authorities succeeded in extracting obedience from the peasants, or at least the appearance of obedience and loyalty. Far from all of them, however, surrendered the conviction that "sooner or later, the collective farms will be dissolved; no stick is big enough to keep the people in them."[45]

Chapter 7

Religion and Politics: The Revival of Religious Belief

The war years witnessed retreats from official ideology that seem strange at first sight yet are fully understandable in the circumstances. The propaganda machine, which had until recently expended enormous energy unmasking the evil past of prerevolutionary Russia, began to work in an apparently diametrically opposite direction. The Soviet regime, whose ideology was constructed in the main on the principle of opposition to the old world, to whatever existed before 1917, suddenly began to place bets on Tradition. This turnabout was manifested in the restoration of officers' epaulets, the celebration of old Russian military leaders, the establishment of new decorations evoking the glory of Russian arms, and a new presentation of historical figures, especially conspicuous in the case of Ivan the Terrible and Peter I. The appeals to patriotic feelings began to crowd out the former calls for proletarian internationalism. In his speech on the Day of Victory, 9 May 1945, Stalin addressed himself not merely to "Soviet citizens" and "comrades" but to "fellow countrymen and countrywomen."

Among these conspicuous changes of political style, one of the most remarkable was the policy of the state toward the Russian Orthodox Church.[1] During the war, the clergy used its sermons to give moral support to believers and to lift the spirits of the army. The church offered state and society great material assistance, organizing, for example, fund-raising campaigns for the Red Army and extending alms to orphans and to the families of soldiers killed in action. These activities were one reason for the liberalization of the state's policy in religious questions. The church was viewed in these circumstances as an asset in the mobilization of society against the enemy. In 1943 the government organized the Council for Russian Orthodox Affairs, which took the religious policy of the state under its advisement. In 1945–1946 the Council sanctioned the opening of 290 houses of prayer,[2] and a special order recognized the legitimacy of a hundred Orthodox monasteries liquidated in the 1930s and returned them to their previous occupants.[3] In the beginning of 1945 the Moscow Orthodox Council was organized, and its activity was widely publicized in the pages of the Soviet press, including *Pravda.*

The change of policy toward religion was prompted not only by the wish to use it as an instrument in national mobilization during the war. Another reason motivating the alleviation of policy toward the church was simply the revival of religious sentiment and activity among the people. This development, fully comprehensible in the circumstances, soon acquired massive proportions. People often found in religious faith the necessary source of moral support in the face of the loss of family, friends, and home. Faith recovered or newly discovered provided comfort if not hope. The growth of religious impulses continued into the postwar years, when a number of regions actually recorded more religious activity than during wartime. Thus 139 religious weddings took place in the Pokrov Cathedral of Kuibyshev in 1940, 403 in 1944, 867 in 1945, and 1,258 in 1946.[4] The size of congregations in church increased, and they consisted not only of women but of men as well, especially of those between the ages of 20 and 40—that is, those who had passed through the experience of combat.[5] Some documents petitioning for the reopening of churches bore up to three thousand signatures.[6]

The spark of religiosity during the war manifested not only the revival of life in the church but a conspicuous rebirth of mysticism and superstition, of faith in contemporary prophets and the traditional old Russian "holy fools." Among the people, especially in rural areas, so-called "holy letters," various forms of prophecy, the appearance of "satans," rumors of the imminent end of the world, and other such things were widespread. At times such phenomena fell upon well prepared soil. In one village of Stavropol the rumor spread that "in the next few days the Earth would collide with a comet, which occurrence would announce the end of the world." This report provoked a genuine panic. Young and old alike began to prepare feverishly to die. They bathed and dressed in clean clothes. Some lit votary candles before icons, lay down inside the front door of their homes, and crossed their arms over their chests.[7]

The significance of the church and of the great increase in the numbers of people turning to it was especially clear in these difficult years. In 1946, for example, when the drought began, the priests in a number of regions held services, at the request of the peasants, to pray for rain. In Penza Province, where a part of the crop was ruined as early as May and June, such services were held in twenty locations.[8] Moreover, on some occasions the local authorities, for example the chairmen of the district executive committees, gave official permission for the services, sometimes even speaking as one of the organizers and participants. On 16 June 1946 a priest came to the Bessonovka District committee of Penza Province to request permission to hold a service to pray for rain. On the same day a group of six hundred people marched on a kind of pilgrimage to the Sura River and then into the fields of the Gorky Collective Farm.[9] After a church service in the village of Lopatino of Chaadaev District on 12 July, four hundred people participated in a pilgrimage to the local collective farm.[10] News of prayer services for rain came in from other areas as well. The local authorities did not always take a sympathetic attitude to such things, and incidents sometimes took place. In Voronezh Province, for example, during a church ceremony the local authorities and representatives of the Ministry of Internal Affairs tried to arrest the officiating priest, which provoked resistance from the believers.[11] The party characterized this kind of action on the part of the authorities as "inappropriate," just as it did other kinds of local intervention—for example, the dispersal of religious services or other arbitrary acts in regard to religion.[12]

At the same time the Central Committee reacted with alarm to occasions of the opposite kind, when local party and government leaders entered into close cooperation with church leaders. Information reached Moscow that local government organs were using priests for the propagation of economic and political campaigns, the organization of grain deliveries, the subscription of state loans, and even Supreme Soviet election campaigns. The administration of the Proletarian Collective Farm in Stavropol, for example, asked the local priest to use his sermons to influence the attitude of the peasants toward farm work.[13] In one of the village soviets of Kursk Province the subscription of the state loan was going badly, and the authorities asked the priest for assistance. He intervened briefly, and 100 percent of the villagers subscribed.[14] As the chairman of another village soviet of Dnepropetrovsk Province confessed, "I worked with the priest. I asked him to encourage the believers to improve their labor discipline, their participation in fieldwork, and to respect the collective property. He spoke of these things in his sermon, and matters improved significantly."[15] In a number of districts the local leaders turned to the priests and religious communes with requests for assistance to the families of soldiers, invalids, and orphans.[16] The central authorities did not approve of proceedings of this kind.

The transformation of the state's religious policy was so unexpected for many local leaders and provincial communists that not all of them had time to reorient themselves properly. "Some communists are confused about the relationship of the party and religion," as the local party secretary for propaganda in Stavropol put it.[17] "How are we supposed to act?" the communists of the Machine Construction Factory in Moscow asked themselves after receiving the news of the establishment of the local congregation. "Earlier we were taught that religion is the opiate of the people, and now the government itself is accommodating the priests."[18] Sometimes the opinion of the communists was more extreme: "Communists may now without hindrance go to church, pray to God, baptize their children and marry in church."[19] The secretary of the Kursk Province party committee, Doronin, expressed himself more decisively, recognizing the real state of affairs: "In our country the church is separate from the state. Therefore our strategic goals are inviolable, though our tactics have changed. We are working with the church now for the mobilization of the people in order to deal with our principal task, the destruction of Hitler. Otherwise nothing has changed."[20]

A variety of rumors circulated among the people about the new religious policy. "You see, even Comrade Stalin admits that without the church we cannot overcome the enemy," according to one war invalid.[21] Others expressed themselves on this question more unambiguously: "As soon as we began to speak of God, things improved at the front." "The Red Army began to win from the time when the Bolsheviks turned to the church."[22] As a digest of public opinion demonstrates, the attention of the state to the problem of the church was greeted with understanding and approval. People began to speak openly of what they had previously preferred to leave unspoken. It was possible, for example, to hear judgments of a surprising kind: "Religion brings to the people a feeling of blessedness, ameliorates ugly tempers, relieves cruel torments and suffering. For this reason we must respect it and its guardians, who bring light and relief to life."[23] Letters addressed to the government or directly to Stalin contained distinctly reverent sentiments: "At prayer on the day of the sanctification of the church that opened with your blessing, we assure you, our adored Iosif Vissarionovich [Stalin], of our deep, sincere, and heartfelt gratitude and devotion to you."[24] Forced by the circumstances of wartime to appeal for the support of the church, the government was able to use this opportunity to strengthen its own influence and authority among the people, which had been shaken by the defeats of the early period of the war.

Many of the people, however, reacted to the changes in religious policy with a large dose of skepticism. "What a transformation!" said one worker in a Moscow factory. "After the struggle with rank and privilege, now we introduce officers' and generals' insignia. . . . We chased the priesthood underground, and when our allies speak up, we beat a retreat."[25] The general opinion that Stalin had struck an agreement with the church not of his own volition but under the pressure of his allies was widespread among the people. "Our policy toward the priesthood is dictated by the demands of England and America." "We did not speak of priests for twenty-eight years, and now we begin to speak of them when we've become allies of England. It's some kind of concession." "England and America have turned us back onto our old path. How else to understand the question when even the newspapers are writing of priests?"[26]

The change of religious policy provoked many questions from both communists and non-party people. People asked if it were permissible to ring church bells and when the restoration of churches and monasteries would begin. The communists were chiefly concerned about other questions. Would the new policy entail changes in the Soviet constitution and in the party programs? Did the former assessments of religion as a reactionary force, the opiate of the people, remain valid, and would the anti-religious works of Marx, Engels, Lenin, and Stalin be published again?[27] As there were no official explanations of these matters, the people contented themselves as formerly with rumors and drew their own conclusions. There was some opinion, for example, to the effect that scriptural readings would be introduced in all the schools,[28] and the students of Moscow University discussed seriously the question of organizing a divinity school there.[29] The skeptics continued to insist that the accommodating policy toward religion was a forced and transitory measure that would yield after the war to the former policy. They were right.

The return to the old attitude in religion did not take place all at once. For some time after the war the force of inertia prolonged the rapprochement between church and state. After a year or two it became obvious that the government had no intention of retreating either from basic principles of ideology in which there was no place for any kind of dissent or from its monopoly of public thought control. The authorities first proceeded to limit the sphere of clerical influence. In 1945–1946 the Council of Orthodox Affairs permitted the opening of 290 houses of prayer; in 1947–1948 it allowed only 49 new ones.[30] From 1948 through 1950, 31 Orthodox monasteries were closed.[31] At the same time anti-religious propaganda was reinforced. In 1949 the Central Committee condemned the work of the Council of Orthodox Affairs for allegedly supporting the revival of religious sentiment.[32] "It has become known to the Central Committee," according to the decree, "that during the religious holidays of Christmas and Epiphany . . . the priests have organized mass pilgrimages, christenings, and baptisms in ice-holes on the rivers, which cause serious illnesses among the believers. The rebirth of these and similar religious barbarities manifest the power of the clerics to spread religious influences among unsophisticated elements of the population."[33] The Council of Orthodox Affairs was accused of mismanaging local affairs, creating "conditions favorable for the growth of church organizations, the religious movement, and the unrestricted encouragement of barbarous religious services," and "crudely violating the instructions of the Communist Party."[34] In fact, the Council did not violate instructions. It was simply assigned the role of scapegoat. It had not adjusted quickly or fully enough to the new, postwar ideological directions. The ideological screws were rapidly tightening, and the attack on the church was only one manifestation of the massive new struggle with dissent in Soviet society.

Chapter 8

The Political Temper of the Masses, 1945–1948

The first significant political event in the life of the country after the war was the election of the Supreme Soviet in February 1946. The electoral campaign was widely covered in the Soviet press, and the newspapers exhibited the "moral and political unity" of Soviet society, the "indissoluble bond of communists and non-party people." The discussion of candidates took place in all electoral districts, a formal and rather ritualistic discussion inasmuch as the election, like the pre-war ones, left the people no alternative to the party's candidates—there was only one candidate per electoral district. In official meetings, people did what was expected of them: they spoke approvingly of the party's policies and supported the party's candidates. Such meetings proceeded by a previously programmed agenda, and the opinions and judgments expressed can scarcely be considered an adequate reflection of the real political outlook of the people. This does not mean that the persons speaking at the electoral meetings were utterly insincere. The atmosphere of the election, something like a national holiday, demonstrated that the people's faith in the authorities was real, not imaginary. Spontaneous greetings to the Communist Party, to Stalin, and to other Soviet leaders were scrawled on the back side of the election ballots. If we admit that some of these inscriptions were prompted, still the style and the spelling of others testify to their genuineness. Whether the positive nature of these expressions reflects a characteristic spectrum of opinion is another question. There were critical comments, too, and they were followed up by observers from party organizations and informers of the organs of state security.

74

In January 1946 the chief of the People's Commissariat of Internal Affairs, Sergei Kruglov, reported to the Central Committee on the so-called "anti-Soviet activities and hooliganism during the Supreme Soviet election campaign."[1] In the list of such activities he included the distribution of leaflets of anti-Soviet contents (though he did not specify their nature), the destruction of campaign posters and portraits of Soviet leaders, and disturbances in electoral districts during campaign meetings; and he gave examples: "On 20 December 1945 twenty-two anti-Soviet leaflets were strewn around the sidewalk in front of No. 18 Krivoi Lane in Moscow. The author of the leaflets, G.M. Ivannikov, an unemployed, demobilized veteran of the Red Army, was arrested. . . . An investigation is in progress." On 9 January two mutilated Supreme Soviet campaign posters were discovered at the Volga train station in Nekouzsk District of Iaroslav Province, electoral district No. 134. The guilty parties, Maksimova and Volchenkova, were arrested. In the village of Bezmintsevo of Rostov District, Iaroslav Province, a war invalid, I.F. Tulenkov, declared that "they are offering us candidates that we don't know, and we won't elect enemies of the people of the ilk of Zimin [former secretary of the Iaroslav Province party committee, arrested in 1938—E.Z.]. If we are not careful, we will elect another government that gets us into a new war." Tulenkov was arrested.[2]

Party informers observed among the population "unhealthy attitudes, manifest in harmful rumors and in the discontent of various people with the policy of the party and the Soviet government."[3] In spite of the official propaganda emphasizing the democratic nature of the elections, people correctly saw behind this mask a routine fraud and discussed it among themselves. "The government is wasting money on the election; it will elect whomever it wants."[4] "What we think is a matter of indifference; they will decide how we vote."[5] "The upcoming elections are nothing to us. If they took place as in other countries, that would be a different matter."[6] "The campaign ballot includes only one candidacy, and that is a violation of democracy, as the winner will be in any event the one they put in the ballot."[7]

A variety of rumors and conjectures about the elections circulated among the people. According to regular election procedure, government agents were supposed to verify the participation of the voters by lists drawn up in the organs of local government. It was a conventional formality, but this exercise generated fantastic stories. In Voronezh, for example, it was said that the purpose of the lists of voters was to identify unemployed people in order to send them to work on collective farms. People were known to close their apartments and leave home in order to avoid this fate.[8] Such behavior was regarded by the authorities as illegal and was subject to prosecution. In popular parlance this kind of prosecution was known as "democracy by the stick": "The elections are being carried on improperly; only one candidate is nominated, and the electoral bulletin guarantees his election. If we don't want to vote for the nominee, we can't strike the name out, as the police will investigate and send us into exile."[9] "We have no freedom of speech. If I say something today about flaws in the Soviet government, they will put me in prison tomorrow."[10]

In the course of these discussions, some very specific questions were raised. What would happen to voters if they did not like the person nominated? What measures would be taken against people who did not take part in the election?[11] Questions of this kind were also raised during the elections to the supreme soviets of the different national republics in 1947. As résumés of questions compiled by several republics and provinces show, there were several particular subjects that most interested the people. For example, what kind of electoral rights would belong to persons of tainted legal status; persons repatriated, exiled, or imprisoned; former soldiers in General Andrei Vlasov's anti-Soviet army? Why not remove from their positions of responsibility representatives who did not justify the people's confidence? When would the deputies appear before the voters in order to give an account of themselves?[12]

People often expressed doubt about the usefulness and timeliness of elections on which so much effort was being expended when thousands of citizens were on the verge of starvation. "Why not worry about taking in a good harvest and forget about the election campaign? It is of no use to anyone." "Why all of this nonsense? Better feed the people than sponsor the elections." "It's all very well to have elections, but having bread for the collective farms would be better."[13]

The subjective process of imagining the authorities as some kind of abstract force revealed an element of alienation that took the form of progressively apolitical attitudes. "If you need to vote, then vote . . . but we're fed up with all of it, let them vote without us." "I don't plan to vote and will not. I have not seen anything good from this government. The communists have nominated themselves; let them elect themselves."[14] Such attitudes were not always spoken in public, but they were present in the spectrum of public opinion, and they influenced at least the views of families and friends, if not their behavior.

In spite of the notoriously abstract nature of the perception of the government by the masses, they nevertheless made a clear distinction between its national and its local branches. The local branch consisted of the directors of enterprises, the chairmen of collective farms, the leaders of local soviets and party organs, and it was these people who were the objects of most of the public criticism. The people blamed most of their misfortunes on the proximate powers (*nachalstvo*). The local power structure was similarly exposed to constant criticism by the central authorities. So the focus of criticism by the people and by the supreme power in this case coincided, which sometimes gave rise to the illusion of a coincidence of interests. This illusion nourished the viability of the whole system and belief in the infallibility of the supreme power personified by Stalin. It was no accident that unpopular decisions of the government—for example, the increase in ration prices or the postponement of the abolition of rationing—were either attributed by the public to Stalin's ignorance of the matter ("Stalin knows nothing about it") or justified as an unavoidable evil ("if Comrade Stalin made the decision, it means there was no alternative"). According to one characteristic example, "Life is tough at present. Everybody is stuffing himself, filling his own belly, sitting around and deceiving Stalin."[15]

Conceptions of some kind of vague "dark forces" that "deceived Stalin" not only pointed to the persistence of the image of an enemy in the public mind but demonstrated the subjective perception of the unity of people and *vozhd'*—the leader. The exclusion of the name of Stalin from the permitted parameters of criticism secured not only him but the very regime that his name inspired. For millions Stalin was the last hope, the most reliable foundation. Without Stalin, life would fall apart. And the more complicated the internal situation of the country became, the greater was the popular faith in the role of the *vozhd'*. Alarm about the health of the leader, who in 1949 was seventy years old, was a constant topic of questions at lectures, interviews, meetings.

A respectful attitude toward Stalin was not only a matter of personal conviction and personal choice. It was cultivated by the entire Soviet ideological machine and carefully controlled by the responsible organs of state. Punishment was imposed not only for opinions and actions directed one way or another against the *vozhd'* but for deeds entirely unrelated. Many people suffered from mere oversights of his cult. An editor making an ordinary typographical error, or a schoolchild using Stalin's portrait for a prank, could be accused of

counterrevolutionary activity. During a party meeting at a textile factory in Ivanovo (Moscow Province) a speaker made a slip of the
tongue. He said that "Comrade Stalin was the organizer of German
fascism and Japanese militarism," omitting the word "defeat" (of the
Germans and Japanese). The result was hardly catastrophic. For the
"anti-party expression addressed to the leader of our party, Comrade
I.V. Stalin," the unfortunate speaker received only a reprimand from
the party.[16] The occasion itself was indicative, however, of the atmosphere of the time, when not only real criticism but an uncharacteristic
gaffe was perceived by the government as a factor threatening its
stability. To express an honest opinion openly, if it contradicted the
official line, was risky—in a number of cases, not only for one's career
but for one's life itself. Nevertheless, such opinions, few though they
were, existed, and both official and voluntary informers reported
them to the responsible authorities.

In the event of critical opinions, the dilemma of *us* versus *them* was
resolved in a typical fashion. "What good can we expect when the government and the party are robbing each other? That is why our life is so
difficult."[17] "Life will be good when we no longer have these officials
who have ravaged all of Russia."[18] "The only people who live well are
those who work in the stores and the bosses in the government."[19] Some
thought the Soviet government guilty of all the misfortunes of Russia:
"There will be no good times so long as the Soviet government lasts."[20]
The problem was perceived somewhat differently in the villages: "Without these damned collective farms, our life would have been a lot better.
Only the communists live well under the Soviet government."[21] "It
seems to me that where there are no Soviets and no collective farms,
people live in abundance. There is more of everything, and it is all
cheaper. Where there are Soviets and collective farms, everything is
ruined, everything is expensive."[22] In these people's opinions, the government is no longer impersonal; it consists of tangible people, who in
this case are not confined to local administration. The subjects of criticism here are the government, the officials, Soviet power as a system, all
levels of it, and communists in general.

The attitude of the population toward the communists as responsible officials was an important factor in the development of the political opinion of the masses after the war. Although in the villages
during the war and immediately afterward the most common rumors
had to do with the dissolution of the collective farms, they were usually accompanied by similar reports of the abolition of the Communist Party, and not only among the rural population.[23] The masses

often conceived of the liquidation of the collective farm system and the liquidation of the party as related measures, which should logically take place at the same time. In order to understand such an attitude toward the party, we must consider the party's situation in the early postwar years.

Before the war the party counted a membership of somewhat more than 4 million; toward the end of the war, more than 6 million.[24] These statistics suggest that the party had passed through the war without serious losses and significantly increased its numbers. In fact the figures obscure quite a different picture. From the beginning of the war the reception of new party members acquired an unprecedented tempo, as nearly 9 million new members entered it before the end of 1945.[25] While the party began the war with a membership of 4 million, it lost during the course of the war 7 million members. Combat losses amounted to more than the total party membership of 1945.

The forced pace of growth in the Communist Party during the war was driven above all by Stalin's plan of national mobilization, which called for the concentration of all efforts on the problem of Soviet survival. The slogan "Communists, forward!" was not mere wartime propaganda but everyday practice. The principles of dedication to the party assisted military commanders and facilitated the solution to military problems. Unlike the purely military or disciplinary codes of conduct, the party's principles were voluntary and spontaneous, and cases of entry into the party from egotistical or careerist motives were unusual at the front. In the rear, or after the war, of course, it was another matter. One caveat must be entered here: even after the war, there were people who entered the party with the most selfless convictions, not seeking advantage or privilege. At the same time, belonging to the party clearly opened access to privilege. It was considerably easier for a party member to climb the ladder of career promotion. Positions of leadership were reserved largely for communists. Party leaders benefited from special systems of food supply and of social security—medical care, vacation facilities, access to apartments and dachas, and so on. All of these advantages were beyond the reach of the majority of ordinary communists, and in this respect their circumstances differed little from those of their ordinary fellow citizens. For those who could wrap themselves in the mantle of the power structure, however, membership in the party not only conferred social privileges but a variety of opportunities to exploit and abuse the system as well. Thus cases of entering the party out of self-serving motives either before the war or after it were by no means rare. The presence in the party of an element of corruption diminished its authority and the authority of the government that it served. In the eyes of the public the corruption of one tarnished the image of the other as well. The upper levels of government tried to combat corruption in the party. Before the war this effort took the form of periodic violent purges, and after 1939, when such purges were discontinued, of exclusion from the party.

As the statistical tabulation of reasons for exclusion from the party from 1945 to 1953 shows, the bulk of communists were deprived of party cards for dereliction of duty, corruption, embezzlement, moral dissipation, drunkenness, and disorderly conduct. During the period from July 1945 to July 1947, expulsion from the party for these causes accounted for 37.8 percent of the number of party cards canceled.[26] The next most common reason was the presence of communists in occupied territory during the war—29.2 percent of expulsions. About 9.3 percent were expelled for breaking party or labor discipline; 4.7 percent for failing in economic or political campaigns, breaking the law, deception, or "conduct unworthy of a communist." It seems noteworthy that only a minority of those expelled were accused of political shortcomings. Only 0.5 percent were accused of treason; and 1.6 percent were accused of anti-Soviet agitation, relations with foreigners, or hiding their social origins.

In May 1946 the Central Committee decreed an examination of party decisions and proceedings at the various republican, provincial, and local levels with special reference to cases of malfeasance and abuses of public trust. According to incomplete data, from 1 July 1945 through 1 May 1946 a total of 4,080 party workers at ninety different regional levels of responsibility were summoned to account for their unsatisfactory discharge of duties. Among these were 1,256 persons suspected of infractions of party responsibilities; 1,156 employees of district Soviet executive committees; 728 officials of law-enforcement agencies (Ministry of State Security, Ministry of Internal Affairs, courts, and procurators' offices); and 940 officials of economic administrative offices.[27] Of the 4,080 regional officials reprimanded for infractions of party discipline, 1,158 were relieved of their duties and 978 were expelled from the party. The most common reasons for expulsion were: (1) violation of Soviet law and distortion of party and government instructions, 71.2 percent; (2) drunkenness and dissipation, 14.5 percent; (3) stealing from the supply system and illegally harvesting on the collective farms, 9.2 percent; (4) deception of the government, 5.1 percent.

It is interesting to follow the relationship between the administrative position of these people and the nature of the infractions or abuses for which they were punished. Party officials and officials of the central Soviet government were punished more frequently than local leaders for "violation of Soviet laws and distortion of the instructions of the party and the government": such cases comprised 31.1 percent and 29.8 percent respectively of the total number of punishments handed out. According to a report prepared for the Central Committee, "Many local officials behave arbitrarily in regard to the peasants, follow crude administrative practice in carrying on agricultural campaigns, intimidate collective farmers, fine them, search their homes, etc. In various collective farms . . . local leaders have permitted beatings of peasants, and such outrages in a number of instances have not been stopped by party organs or the local procuracy."[28]

Most of those summoned for stealing from the supply system or illegal harvesting on the collective farms were officials of local soviet executive committees (35.4 percent of those punished) or officials of economic administrative units (29 percent)—that is, persons whose positions gave them greater opportunities for such abuses. The same circumstances explain the high proportion of economic administrators and local soviet executive committee officials who were punished for deception of the state (36.8 percent and 29.2 percent respectively). Those accused of drunkenness and moral dissipation, if we judge by the statistics, were most commonly officials of the Ministry of State Security, the Ministry of Internal Affairs, the courts, and the procuracies. These officials constituted 36.7 percent of those punished for infractions of party discipline.

Obviously such figures are approximate. The real facts were not always passed along unvarnished from local officials to higher ones. Sometimes the local authorities sought scapegoats of a type demanded by a particular party campaign. Thus instructions from the Central Committee to the effect that crude administrative abuses of the peasants were inadmissible were often treated by the local authorities as idle moralizing in view of the fact that other instructions of the Central Committee obliged them to fulfill the excessive quotas for grain procurements, for the agricultural tax, and for the delivery of other collective farm obligations. In the event of the nonfulfillment of obligations to the state, the secretary of the local party committee was subjected to punishment almost as a matter of course, whereas reports of his administrative abuses for the sake of fulfillment of instructions did not always reach the responsible authorities. Even if such reports reached them, the authorities did not always hasten to mete out punishment. Thus the arbitrariness of local officials became a common occurrence.

The facts about officials' abuse of their positions, their crude manner of address to the people, their aspiration to live on a grand scale while others could scarcely make ends meet—all of this provoked the discontent of those living around them. In order to prevent popular dissatisfaction with the behavior of various local officials from growing into dissatisfaction with the government in general, the higher organs of power from time to time fined their local counterparts for behavior that offended the people. This was one means of relieving social tension and neutralizing social discontent that the regime utilized actively in order to preempt social disturbances.

Besides discontent with various representatives of the government, there was in addition considerable criticism of certain decisions of the supreme power. Social discontent in this period centered on basic decisions of the government as well as on abuses of its officials. If we judge by the questions most often raised at lectures and interviews at industrial enterprises, on collective farms, and in government institutions, there were a lot of doubts about the wisdom of supplying other countries with food, something really difficult to understand in view of the food supply crisis at home. This particular concern reached massive proportions in 1946–1947, the period of the greatest problems in the domestic food market. In words recorded in the cities of Sverdlovsk Province: "What on earth is our government doing? It sends grain abroad, and it keeps us on a starvation diet. It is feeding all other states with our grain, and we ourselves starve." "These agreements of the Soviet government to supply Bulgaria, Yugoslavia, and other countries with grain are not right. We must first feed ourselves before we supply foreign countries." "We are angry about these supply agreements. We feed the bourgeois while we ourselves starve."[29] Such opinions were recorded also in other cities.[30] For similar reasons questions were raised about the Soviet refusal to participate in the Marshall Plan.[31]

Information, however scanty, on life in the West only fed such reflections. People could not understand why a country suffering more than others from the war should extend aid to countries admittedly also damaged by the war but not so seriously. The contrast between the standard of living in Russia and in the West, especially the contrast with defeated Germany, simply deepened public pessimism. These musings, in the absence of any credible explanation, often grew emotional and sometimes provoked a feeling of flagrant injustice. Here was the origin of the unsatisfactory results of the war and resentment against English and American allies who, not without the assistance of Soviet propaganda, became the chief malefactors in poisoning the international climate and thereby helped to aggravate difficulties in the Soviet domestic market. At times doubts arose whether the war was carried to a victorious conclusion, and sometimes one could hear fanciful suggestions: "We did not do well, having taken Berlin, not to destroy our allies, too. We should have pushed them into the English Channel. America would not now be rattling its weapons."[32] Such a simple solution to complex problems was fully in the spirit of the times, as was the attribution of Russian problems to the intrigues of "hostile encirclement." The regime's persistent application of propaganda eventually yielded results, directing popular discontent into the channels that it needed.

The old myth of hostile encirclement was reinforced by rumors of the inevitability of a new war. The people interpreted the most various decisions as preparation for war, whether the increase of ration prices ("before a war they always raise prices") or the abolition of the rationing system ("so the people will fight better"). This same point of view also explained the foreign policy initiatives of the Soviet government. Central Committee Secretary A.A. Kuznetsov reported to Stalin that the convocation of communist parties in Poland in September 1947 was reported to be occasioned by the imminent threat of a new world war.[33] "The governments of England and America have always spoken against the spread of communism. Will the alliance of the communist parties then not lead to a new war?" "The Americans and the English understand very well that this meeting of parties is called on the initiative of the Soviet Central Committee. Can this not complicate relations between the USSR and America and hasten a third world war?"[34]

It was the experience of the recent war that prompted the people's sensitivity to a new one. The threat of war would long be perceived in the people's view as the explanation of their economic problems, and the saying "just don't let there be war" would serve as the ultimate justification of the deprivations of the postwar period, for which there would otherwise have been no explanation. Once the world entered the Cold War, the explanation of all problems was facilitated by reference to military factors. In 1946, for example, the Novosibirsk Province party committee reported to the Central Committee that "in a number of collective farms after Churchill's speech in Fulton [Missouri] people long expected English and American military moves against the USSR at any time."[35] When prices were raised on food products sold on ration cards, people interpreted it as evidence of the preparation of a new war, though they sometimes conjectured that the war might have already begun. Such rumors were current not only in remote regions but in Moscow as well. "I heard," said a worker of one of the Moscow factories in 1946, "that the war is already going on in China and Greece, where America and England have intervened. Any day now they will attack the Soviet Union."[36] During the Korean War panic attacks were recorded among the people of the Soviet Far East. People imagined that the proximity of the war would certainly bring it across the Soviet frontier. As a result the stores were emptied of such goods as matches, salt, soap, kerosene, and the like. The people were putting in long-term "war reserves."[37]

Rumors of the prospect of a new war were not confined to the unsophisticated masses. A part of the intelligentsia was also inclined to explain the domestic political events of 1946–1948 by military factors. In particular the ideological change of direction proceeding under the rubric of the struggle against Western influence was understood as the regrouping of forces prior to the beginning of a new confrontation of the world powers.[38]

War introduced its own system of values in Soviet society. Zdeněk Mlynař, one of the leaders of the "Prague Spring," studied at Moscow University in the 1940s and early 1950s and recalls one characteristic particular of Russian thinking about war. "The most fundamental conviction was that the Soviet Union had at the price of enormous sacrifices decided the fate of mankind during the war, and it was thus entitled to the special respect of all nations. These people regarded any criticism as an insult to the memory of the dead. In this respect they were at one with the government, however critical they were of it in other questions."[39]

The aura of heroism surrounding the war did not immediately appear, as the euphoria of victory in the war's aftermath quickly gave way to recognition of the magnitude of the losses. The war remained in the minds of the people as the greatest of disasters. Under the influence of experience the people soon ceased to believe in the fantasy of a better life after the war. People's material ambitions necessarily grew ever less demanding, and the dreams of wartime, that there would be abundance and a happy life afterward, floated back to earth and deflated. The collection of blessings comprising for most people the upper limit of their dreams began to diminish such that a stable income allowing them to feed themselves and their families, or assured living space, even a room in a communal apartment, soon seemed a gift of genuine good fortune. The unconscious transformation of such an outlook on happiness had been described by Sigmund Freud.

> Under the pressure of . . . suffering, men are accustomed to moderate their claims to happiness—just as the pleasure principle itself, indeed, under the influence of the external world, changed into the more modest reality principle—, if a man thinks himself happy merely to have escaped unhappiness or to have survived his suffering, and if in general the task of avoiding suffering pushed that of obtaining pleasure into the background.[40]

The perception of happiness as the absence of unhappiness took form among people experiencing the disasters of wartime, especially the attitude toward life and its problems. Here is the origin of the incantation "but for the war," and the willingness to forgive the government for all of its unpopular policies if only it fulfilled the people's wish to avoid a new war.

This attitude of the people was consciously utilized by the government and its propaganda. The recent allies were transformed into enemies whose aggressive intentions obstructed social programs and thus weighed heavily on a people still suffering from the recent war. At the same time this explanation of the government cannot be considered exclusively as a propagandist trick or an example of the clever manipulation of public opinion. The psychology of hostile encirclement was part of the Soviet mentality, a characteristic feature of the thinking not only of the people, but of the leader as well. The circumstances of the Cold War, which changed the international climate and ruined people's hopes for peaceful cooperation among the wartime allies, worked actively to reinforce this psychology. The arms race was not fiction but reality. It had to be taken into account by modifying plans for postwar reconstruction. We must not forget the consequences of the psychic shock that Stalin experienced at the time of the German attack on the USSR. He could not afford to be unprepared again in the event of a new military conflict, even if we admit that the possibility of such a conflict existed only in his imagination. This factor explains why the Soviet leadership gave such priority to defense industry in its postwar plans. The Soviet economy was to a significant degree militarized even after the war. According to the data of Nikolai Simonov, who studied the military-industrial complex of the USSR, in 1950 the expenditures of the Soviet military (including all police forces) accounted for 14.2 percent of the national income. If we add the budget for the ministries of aviation, defense, shipbuilding, and development of atomic weapons, then military expenditures absorbed up to a quarter of the national income.[41] After the war many military industries were shifted to peaceful civilian production. In the course of 1946–1950 the tempo of development of military-industrial production fell not only relative to the period of the war but by comparison with the prewar year 1940 as well.[42] This turn toward consumer production was insufficient, however, to satisfy even the modest needs of the population. The increase of the budget for the development of a new defense complex in 1953–1955 only made matters worse.[43]

The myth of hostile encirclement was supplemented by the myth of a fifth column inside the country, and suspicion turned on internal enemies. The illusion of simultaneous resistance to internal and external enemies served to unify people and government, and this illusion, in spite of the accumulation of attitudes critical of the government, preempted the growth and focus of criticism such as to avoid bringing it into open conflict with the government.

The prerequisite of survival in conditions of such rigid social control was an apolitical attitude or a ritualistic political activity. The government sought the participation of the population in different political campaigns, elections, discussion of party and government decisions (after they had been made), and the persecution of dissenters. All of these measures had to have the stamp of popular approval. In fact, political questions seriously interested only a small part of the population, while the remainder was concerned with simpler and more essential problems: where to get bread, how to clothe the children, where to find the money to pay taxes, and so on. The list of questions asked by audiences during discussions of routine party and government policies shows that many had nothing to do with the announced subject but turned again and again to the ordinary economic needs of life. A good example is from the summary reports of the questions most often asked during the elections to the supreme soviets of the national republics in January 1947. Fourteen questions were related to the elections; thirty-four questions dealt with the problem of difficulties in the food supply and the situation in the consumers' market in general; and eighteen questions concerned the work of community services and the urban economy.[44]

Another peculiarity of the openly expressed political interests of the masses was their increased attention to questions of foreign policy by comparison with internal problems. Usually two-thirds of the questions in the résumés prepared for the central authorities concerned matters of international affairs, the situation in different countries, and foreign-policy initiatives of the Soviet leadership; and only one-third of the questions dealt with the internal situation of the country. This might give the impression that Soviet citizens had little to worry about other than developments in Greece or China or discussing the aggressive plans of the capitalist world and sympathizing with the national liberation movements. In fact, matters were a good deal more complicated. People's interest in problems of international life was largely explained by their need to be reassured that there would be no new war. Here was the reason for the special thrust of the questions: they were aimed at establishing the reality of the aggressive intentions of other countries, the capacity of Soviet diplomacy to preserve the interests of peace, and the stability of the Soviet bloc (which was viewed as a guarantor of peace).

Another reason for the heightened interest in questions of foreign policy was the impossibility of openly discussing internal problems. There was always a circle of forbidden subjects that were dangerous to bring up. The famine in the country, for example, could not be mentioned, though the euphemism "provisioning problems" could be. The supreme authority could not be criticized (such criticism was regarded as anti-Soviet agitation). Even the question of a "living wage" in the USSR was considered a provocation. The same prohibition applied to questions of a comparative nature: where, for example, was the standard of living higher, in Russia or in the United States?

So what could people ask about? About matters of local significance: for example, when the deficit of bread supply in the cities would be eliminated, when public transport and the public bath would be restored, and when the rationing system would be abolished. Questions of internal politics were admitted, but they had to be neutral in nature.

It was as if relations between people and government were regulated by a secret treaty, though it was from time to time broken, as evidenced by the appearance of questions considered hostile or maliciously provocative.

Chapter 9

"Something Must Be Done":
The Intelligentsia and the
Intellectual Mavericks

The political outlook of the public in the early postwar years reflected a broad spectrum of feelings, emotions, and expectations. Some people accepted the situation as it was. Others could not and criticized everything from particular personalities to the system as a whole. The former and the latter were alike in one respect: they lacked constructive ideas to turn their hopes and expectations into a program of concrete deeds. The function of generating ideas in this society traditionally devolved upon the supreme power, which, as it seemed to many, should propose a program to reform and reorganize the country. Not everyone, however, shared the outlook of the modest little man whose role was to await orders from above. There were people ready to take the initiative to share with the government their ideas, reflections, and plans. Immediately after the war, the intelligentsia lived with the illusion of liberalization, occasionally finding hopeful signs of its coming. Only in the course of several years did it become apparent that Stalin had no intention of changing his political course.

In 1946 a commission charged with preparing a draft of a new Soviet constitution finished its work. The draft in general fell well within the bounds of prewar political doctrine, yet it contained at the same time a number of progressive features, especially in respect to personal rights and liberties, and democratic principles in public life. Though recognizing state property as the predominant form of property in the USSR, the constitutional project nevertheless admitted a modest expanse of private economy, peasant commerce and handi-crafts "limited to the individual's own labor and excluding hired labor."[1] When the draft was distributed to the national republics and the government commissariats for comment, many responses sug-gested the necessity of decentralizing the economy and granting sub-stantial economic autonomy to the economic commissariats and the provinces. Some suggested the liquidation of the special military courts and tribunals.[2] Although the editorial commission rejected such proposals as undesirable—on grounds of superfluous detail—the mere suggestion of them was symptomatic of public opinion.

Similar ideas surfaced in the discussion of the new draft Program of the Communist Party in 1947. These proposals concentrated on broadening internal party democracy, relieving the party of the func-tions of economic administration, and rotating personnel in positions of responsibility. In view of the fact that neither the constitutional project nor the project for the new party program was published and that the discussion of them was conducted in a rather carefully re-stricted circle of officials, the mere appearance in such select circles of ideas rather liberal for the time suggests the new outlook of ele-ments of the Soviet managerial class.

Admittedly, the officials advancing these views were new people who had risen to their posts before the war, during the war, or in the first year or two after it. The conditions of wartime demanded a special type of personnel, people of high professional qualities capa-ble of bold initiatives. Their knowledge, experience, and willingness to take risks made them capable of independent thought. Although the official documents of the time do not exemplify such characteris-tics, private correspondence and conversations do.

What were the thoughts of these people positioned closer to the government than their fellow countrymen, what did they share among themselves? What worried them especially in the first year after the war?

On 28 December 1946, the technology of the Ministry of State Security recorded a conversation between two generals, Vasilii Gordov and Filipp Rybalchenko, in the apartment of one of them. This was no ordinary dialogue; it was occasion for a death sentence. Such was the price of candor in confidence.

> *Rybalchenko:* What a life, might as well lie down and die! Pray there's no more harvest failure.
> *Gordov:* What kind of harvest failure? The harvest can't fail if it's not planted.

Rybalchenko: The winter crop failed, of course. Stalin travels by train, doesn't he look out the window? People are dissatisfied with their life, they say so openly, in the trains, everywhere.

Gordov: Ah! Everything depends on bribery and bootlicking. . . .

Rybalchenko: Yes, on bribery. You see what's going on, incredible hunger, everybody is discontent. And as everybody is saying, the newspapers are pure eyewash. The most essential goods are lacking. We've literally become beggars. I'm surprised, doesn't Stalin see how the people are living?

Gordov: He sees it, he knows it all.

Rybalchenko: Or is he so confused that he doesn't know how to get his head straight.

Gordov: What are you saying, Filipp? What's to be done. . . ?

Rybalchenko: . . . We must begin by writing him, bombarding the boss [*khoziain*].

Gordov: Write what? It's not allowed. . . .

Rybalchenko: . . . It seems to me that this situation cannot continue for long, there must be some kind of order. . . . This policy will lead to some kind of . . . . On the collective farms they are consuming the last drop of grain, leaving nothing for the next sowing.

Gordov: How has Russia gotten itself into this predicament?

Rybalchenko: Because we have adopted a policy that makes nobody want to work. We have to admit straight out that all the collective farmers hate Stalin and wish for his death.

Gordov: Is it true?

Rybalchenko: They think that when Stalin is gone, the collective farms will go, too.

Gordov: But the people say nothing, they are afraid.

Rybalchenko: They have no hope. They are completely isolated.

Gordov: There's no way we can realize the slogan "Proletarians of all countries, unite!" . . . It has all come to nothing.

Rybalchenko: Right, nothing has turned out right.

Gordov: But it would have if things had been done at the proper pace. We should have had a real democracy.

Rybalchenko: Exactly, a real, pure democracy in order to pursue our goals *gradually*. Now everything is ruined, all mixed up, land, livestock, people. . . .[3]

The trial was not held until August 1950. Accused of treason to the Fatherland and anti-Soviet activity, Generals Vasilii Gordov and Filipp Rybalchenko were sentenced to be shot. They did not plead guilty.

Recognition of the critical situation into which the country had fallen, the demand for action to change the situation, doubts about the competence of the government, including Stalin himself, to take the necessary measures—all of these factors led to a mentality of alarm that tested the endurance of former convictions, faith in their reliability. This is how the historian A.Ia. Gurevich recalls his perceptions of those years.

> After the victory, we began to sober up. Fascism was overthrown, but our minds would not accommodate the things going on in the country. The colossal gap between words and deeds, between the real nature of the system and its official packaging, gradually began to occur to me. Therefore when I hear from people who were adults in those years that only the revelations of Stalin's crimes at the Twentieth Party Congress [February 1956] opened their eyes, I shrug my shoulders. Either these people are lying to themselves and to others or they had chosen the position of the ostrich. It is understandable in the circumstances but does not flatter their memory, their intelligence, or the quality of their judgment. Some elements of society might have preserved their illusions, but those who did not want to be blind could not have avoided seeing long before 1956 that our society was not progressing. In those years it seemed obvious that we had taken a wrong turn.[4]

As for the opinion of the authorities on possible reforms, there is no reason to suppose, on the basis of documents currently available, that there were in Stalin's immediate entourage any serious disagreements on the principal issues of political strategy. At that time a tough struggle for power was proceeding in the upper echelons of government, but the substance of it was personal rivalry rather than political opinion. Therefore any radical or even liberal ideas not only met with no understanding but were actively opposed. And such ideas existed. The most constructive new ideas appearing in the first postwar years had to do with questions of reformulating economic policy. The Central Committee received more than one letter of interesting, sometimes innovative thoughts on economic reform.

Among these is one document of 1946, a manuscript by S.D. Aleksander entitled "Postwar Economic Policy." The author was a bookkeeper in one of the factories of Moscow Province and did not belong to the party. In essence, he proposed (1) to transform the state enterprises into joint-stock companies owned by employees and managed by a board elected by them; (2) to decentralize the supply of raw materials; (3) to abolish the system of mandatory procurements of agricultural products and to grant state and collective farms the right to sell their produce freely in the market; (4) to institute a system of currency backed by gold; and (5) to liquidate state control of internal trade and transfer its functions to trade cooperatives and joint-stock companies.[5]

There were others who shared Aleksander's thoughts. As one of the reports presented in the Institute of Marxism-Leninism put it in February 1946, "Our journals and research institutes continue to receive manuscripts on the postwar development of the Soviet economy. They propose to introduce competition among our enterprises, to found joint-stock companies, to abolish the system of state procurements immediately, to develop private trade governed by free prices, etc."[6] These ideas may be viewed as the foundation of a new economic model constructed on the principles of the market and limited dissolution of the government economy, suggestions extremely bold and progressive for that time. Of course, they were not destined to be implemented. They were either stamped "harmful" or simply consigned to the archives.

The same fate was in store for all new ideas and proposals, whatever sphere of life they concerned, if these ideas infringed upon the chief postulates of Stalinist doctrine, state property, centralized control, and intolerance of private interests. In October 1948 the chairman of the Council of Collective Farms, A.A. Andreev, received an anonymous letter from a "group of leaders of collective farms of Kirov Province." The letter analyzed the miserable situation of the Russian village and concluded with a proposal of six measures to bring the rural economy out of the crisis.

> (1) To diminish grain procurements, the milling tax, and the payment in kind for the work of the Machine-Tractor Stations in the northern regions of the country; (2) to raise the standard of living of collective farmers, leaving them enough grain to avoid famine; (3) to sell less grain abroad, to feed the Russian people sufficiently, to show more concern for the patient and long-suffering people; (4) to diminish the tax burden on the people by cutting back the costly administrative apparatus of the country, which will also add billions to the resources of the state, and strengthen the lower levels of government and collective farm organs by the addition of qualified personnel, at the same time removing the superfluous plenipotentiaries of oversight and surveillance; (5) to summon more workers to the village in order to strengthen the collective farms; (6) to strengthen democracy in the country in deeds rather than in words alone, and periodically to take account of the people's condition in order to know their needs.[7]

These suggestions do not look so radical as the ideas about reforming the economic model itself, and they represent a sober accounting of past practice, especially if we consider, for example, the episode at the end of the 1920s when 25,000 workers were sent out to do the ugly job of collectivization. Still the postwar proposals were represented as sufficiently seditious. It was no accident that policy in the villages was founded on precisely opposite principles, as subsequent experience was to show. The possibility of introducing progressive ideas depended upon the degree of their conflict with the prevailing economic and ideological doctrines. There was perhaps a slight chance for those that proceeded by small, incremental steps. The freedom of maneuver here was very limited, but that does not mean that it was entirely absent.

The war opened the door to the rules of common sense, which was stimulated by the need for practical decisions. Its impact in the biological sciences is a good example. As is well known, after the defeat of the advocates of Academician N.I. Vavilov and the affirmation of the opinions of Academician T.D. Lysenko, the development of genetic research in the country was brought virtually to a standstill. The situation began to change only toward the end of the war. As the archival research of historian V.D. Esakov[8] shows, it was precisely at that time that the position of Lysenko grew somewhat less secure. "It was not only a matter of his brother going over to the occupiers and remaining after the war in the West," writes Esakov, "nor that S.I. Vavilov, the brother of N.I. Vavilov, rose to the leadership of the Soviet Academy of Sciences. More significant was the consolidation of international cooperation as a regular part of the military and political collaboration of the great powers in the ranks of the coalition against Hitler."[9] Exploiting these conditions, one of the followers of Vavilov, Academician A.R. Zhebrak, tried immediately after the war to restore the discredited theses—and lost positions—of sound genetics. It seems likely that his efforts were met with understanding by the leaders of the party, because Zhebrak was appointed Director of the Scientific Division of the Propaganda Administration. As for Lysenko, his mere visit to the Presidium of the Academy of Sciences as new elections approached was considered questionable. An influential opposition to him was forming inside the Academy. For this reason the Director of the entire Propaganda Administration, G.F. Aleksandrov, was forced to ask V.M. Molotov and G.M. Malenkov to instruct the members of the Presidium of the Academy to give Lysenko the majority of votes necessary to elect him.[10]

Lysenko was reelected, but his power in the biological sciences had lost its plenary scope. The Presidium of the Academy asked the government in 1946 to organize a new Institute of Genetics and Cytology alongside the Lysenko Institute, and N.P. Dubinin, a partisan of Vavilov, was elected as a corresponding member of the Academy.[11] The general attitude of the geneticists began to shift, and opinions critical of the work of Lysenko began to surface in the Central Committee and in the specialized journals. The chief of the science division of the Central Committee, S.G. Suvorov, reporting on opinion in the scientific community, described what many biologists thought.

> They are in fact deprived of the chance to discuss important questions of biology and to defend theoretical positions in science against which Lysenko writes. A monopoly of one opinion has been established in biology. The academics observe that this state of affairs has effectively established the appearance of official approval of the theoretical views of Comrade Lysenko in biology. . . . I suppose that the discussion of disputed biological questions in the specialized press would be useful for the development of science.[12]

The mobilization of intellectual forces in the postwar period was observed not only in scientific circles. The idea of a dialogue, of a broad discussion of essential problems, broadly public as well as scientifically specialized, took hold in many good minds. That sector of intellectuals not yet losing faith in the capacity of the government to realize long-awaited reforms, and at the same time not belonging to the number of those indebted to the regime, was ready to be mobilized, but only on its own agenda. The relations between this element of the intelligentsia and the government were not based on Vera Dunham's principle of the "Big Deal."[13] The essential feature of this relationship consisted in something else described by the poet and veteran David Samoilov.

> We considered poetry a civic affair. Civic duty in our conviction consisted in serving political missions in whose usefulness we believed. . . . But we considered that in taking a civic mission on ourselves we were entitled to the honesty of the government. . . . We needed an explanation of its ideas and the wisdom of its decisions. We decidedly did not want to be witless executors of whatever it was pleased to do. We were ready to become mediators between government and people: the eternal dream of Russian idealists.[14]

David Samoilov and his like-thinking colleagues defined their position as open-minded Marxism, and they saw their relations with the government as open-minded dialogue. "I want to write for clever secretaries of provincial party committees," as the poet Boris Slutskii said in a circle of friends.[15] Readiness to serve, but not to cringe, was a characteristic feature of the postwar generation of intellectuals and one of the reasons for their subsequent disappointment and disillusionment. "The generation as a whole did not correctly assess the prospect of the struggle for the rights of man within the bounds of the Stalinist state," as David Samoilov wrote. "Raised in an environment of a willful government, we overestimated the power of the individual, of the intellectual level and the good will of the people in power. We imagined able provincial party secretaries and honest leaders of government agencies ready to listen to the voice of social criticism."[16] They recognized their mistake, however, somewhat later. Immediately after the war, many of them were the prisoners of their illusions.

"As I recall, at the end of the war and immediately after it, in 1946," wrote Konstantin Simonov, "to a rather large circle of intelligentsia it seemed . . . that something should move us to the side of liberalization . . . of indulgence, of greater simplicity and ease of socializing with the intelligentsia even of those countries together with which we fought against the common enemy. . . . There was in general an atmosphere of ideological optimism."[17]

Many thought so at the time, even the most cautious. In November 1945 the senior editor of the journal *Oktiabr'* (October), F.I. Panferov, sent to the Central Committee a note outlining his views on the future principles of editorial work and literary policy in general.

Comrade Stalin more than once said to us in interviews, "Literature is a delicate affair," "writers are not to be administered," "deal with writers cautiously," "understand that the writer sometimes sees farther than we politicians." Here is the working style of the journal *Oktiabr'*. . . . In fact, we make mistakes, of course, but they do not come from malicious conceptions. . . . Who wanted the fascists to attack our country and advance to Stalingrad? The explanation of some people that it was planned, that it was simply to wear out the enemy, is naive. And if a writer were to write of the Fatherland War and dismiss the retreat of the Red Army, beginning only with the victorious counterattack, he cannot exhibit all of the heroism of our country. We do not need a saccharine, comforting literature. We are a nation of great and beautiful truths and are accustomed to looking everything straight in the eye. . . . We must plan in the journal *Oktiabr'* a forum on "The Writer and Criticism" in order to discuss all the acute questions of literature, giving writers and critics the chance to express themselves in full voice, not to whip writers and critics might and main if they make a mistake. We must assist the

creative work of the writer and poet and not thrust our judgments upon
them. We must grant the writer and poet great independence and let
them answer before the party and the people for their work."[18]

The writers reflected on their problems, trying to resolve the eternal question of the truth of life and the truth of art, thoughts that
would find an outlet in the literary discussion of 1948. At the same
time the film directors sought new trends in cultural life after the
war. The well-known Soviet director I.P. Pyriev described their outlook at a meeting of the Central Committee in April 1946.

> In the 1920s and 1930s we shot many scenes of Soviet people. We
> understood the substance of these people, their internal world . . . and
> now, shooting scenes or looking at scenes of these comrades, it seems
> that our people of the years 1945–1946 are mentally older in many
> respects than the people of the 1930s. It turns out . . . that we some-
> where lost the spirit of the new Soviet man, and we all find ourselves in
> the 1930s.[19]

The thought on the mental maturity of the man who had been
through the experience of the war deserves special attention, as it
contains the key to the puzzle of many postwar problems. The appetite for reform that seized the country after the war nourished an
entirely natural impulse: the society, outgrowing its old traditions,
demanded new forms of the organization of its life. Here was the
aspiration to emancipation of thought, spirit, and deed. Though ever
so timid at this point, who knows how it might have developed if
these first impulses had not been extinguished?

There were some genuine breakthroughs—for example, in the
theory of socialism, the holy of holies of the world of ideology. In
1947, E.N. Burdzhalov gave a course of lectures at the Higher Party
School devoted to the problems of eastern European countries, the
so-called people's democracies.

> Marxism is not a dogma but a guide to action. It is easy to study the
> texts, much more difficult to take account of contemporary life. . . . The
> general lawfulness of historical development discovered by Lenin and
> Stalin is fully confirmed by life itself. But the specific situation during
> and after the Second World War was much more complex and peculiar
> than could have been foreseen. . . . In several countries the question of

socialism was already posed as the order of the day, but posed how? Not exactly as it was posed in our country. . . . The paths of transition to socialism were for several countries quite different from our path: the dictatorship of the proletariat is not unavoidable.[20]

A trifle later this last thesis would be evaluated as "subversion of Leninism,"[21] not to speak of Burdzhalov's positive references to the experiences of Tito and Kardelj in Yugoslavia, which were denounced by vigilant auditors of the class. The ideological sphere remained as formerly quite conservative, reacting morbidly to even the most timid attacks on its principal postulates.

The dialogue of the intelligentsia with the government never materialized. The government did not come forth immediately after the war with a program that might have served to confirm the expectations of the people after their victory. In spite of that, people continued to hope for the best. Expectant anticipation became the dominant element in the atmosphere of the postwar years. The prospect for reform at this stage consisted more of anticipation and an accumulation of relatively uninsistent demands than of ideas ready for implementation. These ideas circulated in postwar society, but they lacked massive support. As for the critical opinions of the masses, they usually reflected discontent with particular practical features of life and did not amount to a systematic program.

What the masses and the intellectual mavericks shared was dependence on the policy of the authorities. They looked to the supreme power, and above all to Stalin himself, to initiate the expected reforms. Stalin had no plans to retreat, however—at least on the principal issues—from his prewar political doctrine. If any changes in the previous political course were permitted by the government, they had to fall well within the parameters of the traditional political, ideological, and economic system. Relying on the trust of the people and the priority of restoring civilian authority, the government postponed decisions that would have laid the foundations for the future modernization of the country. Instead of a policy of renovation of society, the government offered the people the idea of temporary hardships and an assessment of the situation justified now by the complexity of the reconstruction of the country after colossal destruction, now by the intrigues of hostile encirclement. This course of policy succeeded. The people, notwithstanding the expression of sharp criticism, were compelled to consent, to wait patiently, to accept the real difficulties of the postwar situation. Thus a coincidence of interests developed: the government's unwillingness to engage in bold reforms and the people's willingness to temporize. And so a social consensus was reached. But it could not be long-lasting, because the very conception of temporary difficulties presupposed their eventual end. Sooner or later a critical moment would arrive when the idea of the temporary no longer seemed plausible. In fact, this moment occurred in the winter of 1947–1948.

1–3. On 9 May 1945 Soviet radio broadcast news of the capitulation of Germany. Thereafter 9 May, known as Victory Day, would be a major national holiday. At that time it seemed that the worst was over. The photos are of Red Square and the streets of Moscow as the news of the end of the war was announced.

4. The first demobilized veterans began to return home in June 1945. They were to be known as the Generation of Victors.

5. As the roar of the victory salutes died away, the scope of the destruction and the magnitude of the losses became clear.

6. People returned to places of residence from which they had been driven by the war.

7.

8.

7–8. Rationing was abolished in the Soviet Union in 1947. More goods appeared in the stores. The majority of people could not, however, afford many of the products. Only the fortunate could buy meat, sweets, and sausages. The photos show the chief food stores in Moscow after the abolition of rationing.

9. The most essential products were much in demand, for example, *valenki* (felt boots) for children.

10. There were annual price cuts on retail items between 1947 and 1954—a policy that enjoyed great popularity among the people. The photo shows GUM, the largest department store in the country, on the day of such a price cut. The banner reads: "The price of bath soap will be lowered on 1 April 1954."

11. The life of people gradually returned to normal. In the photo: An urban family at dinner (early 1950s).

12. The first TVs appeared in Russian homes in 1949. Thereafter an evening of TV became a favorite form of relaxation, attracting not only members of the family but neighbors as well. The majority of families in those years lived in communal apartments, several families sharing a common kitchen.

13. The problem of housing remained acute throughout the postwar years. Moving into a new apartment was a festive occasion.

14. If TV long remained an inaccessible luxury, no one was denied the old favorite treat of ice cream. It was always popular, even in winter.

15.

16.

17.

15–17. In Soviet times all citizens without exception were expected to participate in political life. After work, people attended so-called Marxist-Leninist study groups, where they studied the latest decisions of the party as well as the works of Marx, Lenin, and Stalin (no. 15). Prior to elections propagandists advised the electorate how to vote, although there was only one candidate to vote for (no. 16). During the war and in the postwar years state loans were commonly floated among the people. Such loans were subscribed at the workplace (no. 17).

18. The popularity of Stalin reached its height in the postwar years. He was known as the "father of the country," the "leader and teacher," the "best friend of children," etc. In the photo: Participants in a physical culture parade in Moscow (1946). The banner reads: "To the best friend of the sportsman, the Great Leader of the people, Comrade Stalin, a hearty greeting!"

19.

20.

19–20. Stalin died on 5 March 1953. Millions of citizens felt his death as a personal loss. In order to pay their last respects to him, people stood for hours in line in the Hall of Columns of the House of Soviets, where his body lay in state. In the photo: People at the entrance and inside the Hall of Columns.

21. The death of Stalin opened a new chapter in the life of the country. It initiated the period known to contemporaries as the *thaw*. One of the first signs of change was the opening of the Kremlin for public visits in 1954. In the photo: One of the first excursions through the Kremlin.

22. It was not only life inside the country that became more open. The Soviet Union opened up to the world outside as well. A real international holiday was the World Festival of Youth and Students in Moscow in July 1957. The authorities were still afraid of the influence of the West on Soviet youth. In order to keep contacts to a minimum, it was decided to transport the foreign guests on tall trucks. But these barriers did not work. In the photo: Muscovites greet the foreign guests.

23. The experience of the war reawakened in the people a religious sensitivity. After the war, notwithstanding a new persecution of the church, religious practice persisted. In the photo: Believers before an icon of one of the Moscow cathedrals (1957).

24.

24–25. By 1957 the war was simply history for children who had grown up afterward.

25.

26. The generation of 1957. In thirty years they would live in a new Russia.

PART III

REPRESSION

Chapter 10

"The Situation Doesn't Change":
The Crisis of Postwar Expectations

The war was in no hurry to retreat into the past. Although the victory salutes were long since silent and the Soviet Information Bureau no longer brought news of the course of combat, reminders of the war were everywhere. There were belated burials, ration cards, villages without men, cities in ruin, military garments in place of civilian dress—all this a year and more after the end of the war. The majority of people who lived through this period clearly think of the war and the postwar years without any distinction. And the basis of this lack of distinction was emotional, the extraordinary stress of life, the initial wish to win the victory at all costs and then to return to normal peacetime life. The great aim uniting millions of people and the principle of victory at any price as the means of achieving that aim created a special spirit in postwar society, formed a kind of spiritual bond among contemporaries.

At the same time the very principle of sacrifice became something like a psychological instrument of motivation, strong enough on the one hand to bring millions to the commitment to victory but limited by the fact that it could not be exploited indefinitely. In order to activate this principle, it was necessary to have, at a minimum, an extreme situation and a limited period of time for its application. Otherwise, as fatigue accumulated, the sensation of extreme stress and extraordinary commitment receded.

The extreme conditions of the first postwar years were occasioned principally by the task of rapid restoration of the country. The aspiration of people to enter as quickly as possible into a normal life in this case coincided with the program of the government, which proposed a very urgent tempo of reconstruction. Thus even at the level of the everyday outlook there was no open expression of protest, notwithstanding many critical remarks. In spite of their complaints, the people regarded the material deprivations of the time as temporarily unavoidable ("temporary problems"), as the legacy of the war.

The situation began to change in 1947 or 1948. Public consciousness began gradually to focus on the boundary between wartime and peacetime, a focus that by itself constituted a demand for reforms, an alteration of the previous outlook. The principle of sacrifice gradually lost its role of justification. And a new attitude—"we can no longer tolerate this situation"—began to form around one simple fact: "the war is over, we have shouldered the burdens of the war, and now we know without a doubt: it is time for peaceful construction."[1]

The confidence of people that the period of peaceful construction had *already begun* testified to their exhaustion with the idea of stress and sacrifice. This attitude marked the psychological frontier of the end of the war, prompted by both real and symbolic factors. By 1948 the industrial production of the prewar period was fundamentally restored. About the same time the demobilization of the army was completed. A short time earlier, in December 1947, the rationing system, that quintessential symbol of wartime, was abolished. Against the background of these quite promising developments, which contemporaries perceived as evidence of the end of the period of transition, the life of the majority of the people, having remained essentially like the life of wartime, formed a striking contrast.

The memory of the great famine of 1946–1947 was still vivid in 1948. The famine conditions had not been overcome, as the bread supply problems of various regions of the country demonstrated. The problem of housing remained acute, especially in the areas occupied during the war and thus subjected to more war damage. Two years after the war, for example, more than 800 families in Velikie Luki lived in dugouts, and in Novgorod 9,000 of the population of 29,000 were sheltered in temporary barracks, basements, or dugouts.[2] The problem of living space was addressed extremely slowly. By way of illustration we may consider the figures of 1956, eleven years after the war. A special survey undertaken in 85 cities, 13 workers' settlements, and 144 rural areas subjected to occupation or combat during the war (Briansk, Velikie Luki, Kalinin, Kaluga, Novgorod, Orlov, Pskov, etc.) established that 1,844 families continued to live in dugouts or makeshift structures, 1,440 of them in rural areas, 1,512 lived in the ruins of buildings, 3,130 families in crude and dark basements, and 32,555 families in other places unfit for human habitation (barns, bathhouses, kitchens, attics, railroad cars, etc.).[3]

In 1947 the Central Committee undertook a review of the coal mines of Kemerovo, Stalino, Karaganda, Tula, Rostov, and Cheliabinsk provinces. It found that working conditions in the Kuzbass and the Donbass [Kuznetsk and Don River Basins] remained much like those of wartime. The signs of the war were evident in the composition of mining personnel as well. The experienced miners composed between 20 and 25 percent of the whole number. The others had gone to work during or after the war.[4] In spite of special decrees of 1940 and 1941 punishing workers for absenteeism and tardiness, the number of infractions increased. In 1947, 29,000 miners left the mines in Kemerovo Province.[5]

The housing situation was extremely difficult for the miners of the Kuzbass. In the Stalin Mine, for example, more than 350 workers continued to live in dugouts two years after the war. In the Kirov Mine ten to twelve families lived in dugouts of 40 square meters (that is, there was 1 square meter per occupant).[6]

The iron industries struggled with similar conditions. In eleven months of 1947, while they hired 163,000 new workers, 155,000 workers quit, 30 percent of them without authorization.[7] Labor turnover, abandonment of work, grew from isolated examples into a massive tendency. Not all of the so-called deserters left the workplace because of bad labor and living conditions. Among them were many evacuees from wartime combat zones who now wanted to return home. Laws attempting to limit this natural right could only provoke discontent. "During the war they kept us on a leash, we had no right to leave a job," as one of them said. "Now it's time to give us freedom to work wherever we want."[8]

Abandonment of the workplace turned into a singular form of protest on the part of people who refused to accept the material norms of wartime as they entered the promise of peacetime. To make matters worse, administrative personnel often continued to resort to the forceful and summary practices of wartime. As the minister of the coal industry for the western regions of the country, A.F. Zasadko, informed Central Committee Secretary A.A. Kuznetsov, "A close acquaintance with the problem of living conditions of workers and engineers shows perfectly clearly that it is not considered by the economic, party, and trade-union organizations a high-priority question."[9] He further explained that "during the war years the leaders [of these organizations] grew accustomed to dealing with such contingencies as prisoners of war, repatriates, internees, victims of enemy encirclement, convicts, and recruits, and notwithstanding the great changes in the composition of the work force now that such special contingencies are past, they continue to deal with the workers as they dealt with people under military escort."[10]

A serious irritant to workers was the wartime law forbidding them to change jobs without authorization. A law of 26 July 1940 began to limit this freedom in certain industries, stipulating prison sentences of two to four months for violations, and a law of 26 December 1941 extended this provision to a whole series of industries, including all enterprises in Moscow and Leningrad, and increased punishments to five to eight years. By an order of the Council of Ministers of 7 March 1947, the application of the law of 26 December 1941 was suspended. Nevertheless, in 1948, 24,600 persons were sentenced for leaving work without permission under the law of 1941, and the number of persons sentenced under the law of 1940 grew from 215,700 in 1947 to 250,000 in 1948.[11] Martial law was prolonged until May 1948 in railroad and water transport, where special legal organs had jurisdiction. The maintenance of these features of the wartime regime was not always justified in conditions of the transition to peace, and it became one of the chief grievances of the people. By a decree of 31 May 1948 the Presidium of the Supreme Soviet abrogated the law of 26 December 1941, but legislation stipulating legal liability for leaving a job without authorization, for absenteeism, and for tardiness continued in force until 1956.[12]

In the villages conventional Soviet measures were maintained, both economic and noneconomic. The peasants lived without passports.[13] In 1948, the agricultural tax was raised. At the same time the government began a campaign to expel from the collective farms those who, in the opinion of the authorities, did not participate sufficiently in collective labor. The price that the government paid for the procurements that the farms were compelled to surrender did not even equal the cost of their production. In order to diminish the burden of taxation, the peasants cut down their orchards, gave up their own livestock, and curtailed the size of their private garden plots. These measures, of course, further undermined the already miserable standard of living of rural families. The income of the collective farms often did not suffice to pay the individuals' workdays. In 1950, 22.4 percent of the collective farms distributed no income for peasant workdays, and more than 20 percent gave out less than half a kilogram of grain per workday.[14] The peasants had more grounds for discontent with the government than any other group of the population. The villages, unlike the cities, had little respect for the higher authorities, including Stalin. The memory of collectivization, the exile of the kulaks, and postwar grievances were alive and well in the villages.

Also uncertain at that time was the political loyalty of the veterans, who, in spite of the prevalence of pro-Stalin sentiment, had good reason to be dissatisfied with their circumstances. At the end of the period of reconstruction the former soldiers had the right to demand from the government a certain compensation for the victory in the satisfaction of their hopes and wishes for a life worthy of victors. Eight million demobilized soldiers were an influential social force whose potential politicization might represent an eventual threat to the regime.

A special problem was the prisoners of war, many of whom returned home without finding the reception on which they rightly counted. Suspicion became the lot of all who had found themselves in occupied territory, were deported to Germany, or were taken prisoner. Communists who had been in occupied territory for whatever reason, for example, had practically no chance after the war to hold on to their membership in the party. In the first two years after the war 60,000 communists were expelled from the party on this ground.[15] Thus their social status was incomparably lower than that of their fellow citizens who escaped this sad fate.

The suspicious attitude of the authorities to anyone who crossed the borders of the USSR was aggravated in the case of people who for any period of time whatever were beyond the reach of the Soviet ideological machine. This misfortune applied not only to Soviet citizens falling into captivity or coming under occupation but those shipped out of the country as *Ostarbeiter*, forced laborers in Germany. The majority of them were repatriated after the war. At the beginning of 1946, 5.2 million Soviet citizens had returned from Germany and other countries, 1.8 million prisoners of war and 3.4 million civilians.[16] In spite of the assurance of the authorities that "most Soviet people finding themselves in German slavery remained loyal to the Soviet Fatherland,"[17] the attitude toward repatriates, especially on the part of the local authorities, was distinctly negative and consistently suspicious. As one local official described his method of receiving repatriates, "We are not allowing them to conduct counterrevolution, we are going to mobilize them and send them off to float timber down the rivers [i.e., in Siberia]."[18]

Despite the government's assurance of a benign attitude toward repatriates, a drive to isolate them undoubtedly took place. The chief reason for distrusting people returning from abroad was evidently the fear of the government that Soviet citizens who had experienced the West might become a source of uncensored, uncontrolled information on life beyond Soviet borders. And yet it was impossible to deprive Soviet people entirely of access to that kind of information. It would have been necessary to isolate not only the repatriates but the whole of the demobilized army.

Cases of collaboration during the war took place, of course, but in accusing all prisoners of war or residents of occupied territory of potential collaboration, the authorities clearly over-reacted. After the war all of these people bore the invisible stigma of inferior citizens. In questionnaires obligatory for taking a job or entering an institution of higher education, a special question was posed about POW status or residence in occupied territory. A person answering the question affirmatively had practically no chance to study in higher education or develop a decent professional career. There were exceptions, of course, but they were few enough to prove the rule.

Among the various groups of citizens substantially disadvantaged— partly or wholly disfranchised—were those peoples deported during the war from the North Caucasus, the Volga, Crimea, Ukraine, and other regions of the USSR. More than a million Volga Germans, 575,000 people from the North Caucasus (Chechens, Ingush, Karachais, Balkars), 91,000 Kalmyks, 183,000 Crimean Tatars, 94,000 Meskhetian Turks, Kurds, and Khemshils had been deported to exile.[19] Suspected, like other people regarded by the government as "ill-disposed," of collaborating with the enemy, these people were forced to begin a new life in a completely different, unfamiliar climatic and cultural environment. The difficulties of economic reorganization were aggravated by psychological problems, the absence of any hope. As a result of the high death rate and accompanying low birth rate among the resettled peoples, several of them were threatened with extinction. Thus, according to the figures of 1946, among the Kalmyks living at the time in Novosibirsk Province, the death rate exceeded the birth rate by three times (for purposes of comparison, the contemporary figures for Russians in the same area were exactly reversed, the birth rate exceeding the death rate by three times).[20]

Hopes of possible rehabilitation and restoration of political autonomy rose among the deported peoples after the war. The authorities, without intending to, sometimes inadvertently activated these hopes of returning home. For example, the decision to abolish the

Chechen-Ingush Autonomous Republic and to reorganize the Crimean Autonomous Republic was interpreted by the exiled peoples not included in these plans—the Karachais, Kalmyks, and others—as oblique evidence of the government's intention to reestablish their autonomy.[21] They soon had to part with this illusion, however, as the government took no such steps either immediately after the war or later. This situation soon contributed to the accumulation of great bitterness: "The evil that the Soviet government has done to us, that we bear the notorious name of 'specially resettled people,' we will not forget in the seventh generation."[22] Thus postwar policy set off conflicts that would require years and even decades to resolve.

On the lowest rungs of the social ladder stood those in the camps and colonies of the GULAG. Estimates of this population range from one or two million to tens of millions of people; but even the most modest total, calculated on the basis of documents of the Ministry of Internal Affairs, finds 1.7 million prisoners in 1947, 54 percent of whom were condemned for so-called counter-revolutionary activity.[23]

The repatriates, the exiled, the prisoners (above all, political prisoners), independently of particular motives, could all easily be grouped in the category of people aggrieved by the regime, unhappy with their situation and driven by dissatisfaction to change their fate. Given the instability and the humiliation of their social status, a favorable opportunity—any sufficiently serious crisis—could provide this force the necessary volatility and capacity for active opposition.

Thus, at all levels of social life in 1947–1948 it is possible to uncover various strata and social categories having claims of one kind or another on the developing order of the authorities. Conceptions of the monolithic unity of the society and its absolute dedication to the leader, true in general at the moment of victory in 1945, turned ever more surely as time passed into an illusion. The chasm between government and people was too great to hope for the harmony of their interests while maintaining the status quo. In the galloping alienation of the higher and the lower orders the single link uniting them, combining this political conglomerate into an apparent whole, was Stalin himself. But he evidently overestimated the strength of his position and his capacity to focus in himself the will and the aspirations of this society. Not all of his fellow citizens hastened to demonstrate their loyalty. Stalin knew it, but he did not know how many of them there were and how dangerous, even to himself personally, this incipient opposition was becoming. It did not come to open protest, but the ferment of minds was real, as the résumés of the attitudes of different social groups confirmed.

Events beyond the border challenged the preservation of social calm as well. As the Cold War began, Stalin lost the position of first statesman of the world, a position that he felt he enjoyed at the time of victory. He retained primacy only in Eastern Europe, where the peoples, or rather the governments, had already begun to structure their life after the pattern and image of the Soviet elder brother. These countries were concerned essentially to unify their internal regimes according to the Soviet example as defined by the first meeting of the Communist Information Bureau in 1947. Not all of the Eastern European leaders, however, conformed to such a subordinate position and such strong pressure from the Soviet Union. Milovan Djilas recalls:

> No one anywhere wrote about it, but I remember from confidential conversations that in the countries of Eastern Europe—in Poland, Romania, Hungary—there was a tendency toward independent development. I will give an example. In 1946 I was at the Czechoslovak party congress in Prague. [Kliment] Gottwald [leader of the Czechoslovak party] said that the cultural levels of Czechoslovakia and the Soviet Union were different. He emphasized that Czechoslovakia was an industrially developed country and that socialism there would develop otherwise than in the Soviet Union. . . . Gottwald spoke against collectivization in Czechoslovakia. His views did not in essence differ from ours [Yugoslav]. But Gottwald did not have sufficient character for a struggle with Stalin. Tito, on the other hand, was strong enough.[24]

The culmination of the disagreements between the USSR and the countries of Eastern Europe occurred at the Soviet-Yugoslav meeting in Moscow in February 1948, after which the break between Stalin and Tito ensued. This was a great defeat for Stalin.

Such a confluence of events could not fail to be reflected in the internal life of the country. Admitting opposition in the international arena, Stalin could not now admit even the embryo of it around himself at home.

Chapter 11

The Birth of the Anti-Stalinist Youth Movement

The year 1948 is often compared with the purge years of the 1930s—two waves of repression that rolled over society, leaving in their wake painful memories. The comparison is prompted not only by the tragic similarity of these events. It is also simpler and deeper. The latter year is both the continuation and an admission of the inadequacy of the former. The elements of continuity are plain enough: the same methods, the same grand dragnet, the same hopelessness for those falling into the net, the uncertainty and fear of those not yet sharing the fate of the enemies of the people.

Yet in spite of the massive nature of the purges of the 1930s and the relentless work of the machine of intimidation thereafter, 1937 did not avert 1948. It is sometimes suggested that the terror of 1948–1952 was an artificial phenomenon, that there were in the Soviet Union after the war no forces of opposition sufficiently serious to threaten the government. In fact there were not. Did Stalin then strike out at phantoms? Hardly. The campaign of 1948 was intended chiefly to intimidate, but the very fact that the authorities used such severe preventive measures suggests that the struggle was directed against a real rather than a phantom phenomenon.

The first shoots of political dissent sprouted where the regime least expected it, among the youth, whom, it would seem, the dark secrets of life scarcely touched. As Alexander Solzhenitsyn observed, "Along those very strips of asphalt over which the Black Marias scurried at night this tribe of youth marched in the daytime with banners and flowers, singing their irrepressible songs."[1]

In kindergarten, they had sung "Thanks to Comrade Stalin for our happy childhood." Later in school, in the factory, and in higher education all of their training and experience worked to reinforce the feeling of gratitude to Stalin and the party that they had mastered in earliest childhood. The fact that some few of them rather than singing irrepressible songs suddenly turned up in the Black Marias may seem nonsense, a misunderstanding, an absolute exception to the general rule. The absence, however, of a massive scale of opposition does not mean that protest itself was not present. In any event, in the persecutions of 1948–1952 the so-called youth groups were by no means insignificant.

The behavior of the younger generation began to alarm the authorities almost as soon as the war ended. By today's standards there was nothing criminal in the thoughts or conduct of the youth of the time. Nevertheless, something about them put the government elders on guard. In 1946, 163 graduates of the schools of Cheliabinsk were given a questionnaire to determine their interests, their future plans, their sentiments while in school.[2] The results were remarkably conventional. Half the respondents spent their leisure time reading, a third were active in sports, and only a small number were interested in music or painting. Their favorite authors were Gorkii and Tolstoi, then, in order of preference, Pushkin, Lermontov, Sholokhov, Maiakovskii, Fadeev, Ostrovskii. No one named Zoshchenko, Akhmatova, Esenin, or other authors disgraced by the Soviet government, not to speak of foreign authors. Neither was there anything unexpected about their favorite fictional heroes: Pavel Korchagin, Andrei Bolkonskii, Tatiana Larina, Pavel Vlasov, Natasha Rostova [for identification, see note below—H.R.]. Several students, it is true, preferred heroes who, from the viewpoint of Soviet pedagogy, were not exemplary choices—Platon Karataev, Ostap Bender, Nekhliudov, Pechorin.[3]

What bothered the teachers was something else: the untutored interests of the students. Chief among these were what was then termed "personal interests," the most conspicuous of which were love and friendship (the same findings occurred among a group of university students). It was feared that such interests might divert the youth from the ideals of socialism into a world "of philistine illusions."[4] Yet the more this world was forbidden, the more predictably attractive it grew, unlike the dull routine of school life where everyone was above all a member of the collective. No more than their peers elsewhere did this young generation accept personal values by paper-doll patterning, not to speak of paradigms imposed on them. They made their own self-images.

In the girls' secondary school in Cheliabinsk the students of the upper classes formed an unofficial circle called the "Italian Republic." Here they talked about what was not conventionally discussed in school—the basic personal problems that invariably bother fifteen- and sixteen-year-old girls. Asked what attracted her to the circle, one student responded: "It was the fact that we didn't discuss politics, which didn't appeal to us. We rarely read the newspapers. . . . We enjoy playing at being a republic. This was so much fun that we didn't want to leave school."[5] This was a mere game, but in the language of adults it was "an attempt to found an organization."

Not unexpectedly, the Komsomol (Communist Youth League) looked upon the rise of this kind of organization with great disfavor. After the war there was a decline in the growth of the Komsomol in educational institutions. In Cheliabinsk in 1940, for example, 65 percent of students in higher education belonged to the Komsomol; in 1946, 42 percent. On the one hand, the contraction of the Komsomol was explained by limited enrollments during the war and older student bodies afterward. But there was another cause: in a number of educational institutions the older students refused to enroll in the Komsomol on the grounds that it was "boring and uninteresting."[6]

The cohort of youth in the army, the most highly disciplined element of the age group, displayed a similar retreat from good Komsomol standards. After demobilization, two-thirds of army personnel (statistics of 1946) were of Komsomol age (typically, ages 14–27). As a letter of the Chief Political Directorate (security police) informed Central Committee Secretary A.A. Zhdanov, the number of violations of discipline admitted by Komsomol members had increased, as had the number of Komsomol members condemned by military tribunals.[7]

All of these facts suggest that the younger generation, to whom the role of support of the regime was entrusted—the first generation educated from beginning to end under the aegis of the Stalinist system—was becoming ever more difficult to manage. This does not mean that they were oppositional. Questionnaires show that one of the major goals in life for the majority of the youth was still to serve the Fatherland, to work honestly for the well-being of the country.[8] In the system of values imbibed by the younger generation since childhood, Stalin, Party, and Country still composed a single indivisible triad. The experience of the war had intervened, however, and notwithstanding all the subsequent ideological efforts, it had assigned top priority to the sentiment of patriotism. When the virus of doubt was born in the minds of the young, it was this feeling of patriotism as the highest value that, if it did not nudge them into the ranks of the opposition, preempted in any case the development of pure cynicism.

The end of the war marked symbolically a change of generations. In the seventeen-year-olds of 1945, we confront a unique generation, unique in the potential to pursue its plans, a generation distinct from its predecessors, not knowing the fear of 1937, and in this respect free of the collective responsibility for the past. Yet neither would it share the disappointing shortfall of the hopes of the next generation. This generation took its pedigree from the high moral purity of the war years. Though it had not gone to the front, it was related to the veterans as the next link in the chain of generations. Only four years separated the seventeen-year-olds from the veterans of 1945; but between them lay the war, and the war aged the prewar generation overnight. Having gone to the front, these boys returned home wiser, having seen and learned a lot. The critical capacity of the generation of victors remained for a whole series of reasons entirely unrealized, but it fed the thoughts and the deeds of the postwar generation. By comparison with its predecessors, the new generation had experienced fewer disappointments and harbored more illusions and more hopes. And in the eyes of these youths, those who could and wanted to think, the Stalinist system did not have a halo of sanctity or the unchallenged presumption of exclusive reasonableness. The generation whose childhood was spent in the tough years of the war had, by comparison with its contemporaries growing up in peacetime, some kind of special reserve of inner independence. It also had the need to express this independence outwardly.

These youths began modestly enough with a kind of extracurricular study in secondary school and in higher education. The conventional textbooks did not satisfy them, and so they read the appropriate monographs on their own. The recommended literature did not suit them, and so they turned to other writers and poets, not forbidden ones but those belonging in official Soviet literary studies to the second rank. Such were the innocent origins of the youth movement. Political motives were utterly absent at this stage. The youth simply gathered in circles of friends for independent study of literature, philosophy, and history. The effort to avoid the clichés of school and university and the concomitant approved values and judgments grew out of the appetite to think for oneself. The natural process of learning advanced from questions of literature and philosophy to problems of contemporary politics. In the beginning it all developed in legal fashion. Only after the first prohibitions were imposed did a system of conspiracy begin to form.

In Cheliabinsk Pedagogical Institute the students organized their own literary almanac, *Student*. The idea alarmed the school administration, and the almanac was forbidden. Several students (O.L. Plebeiskii, F.L. Sorokin, A.I. Levitskii, B.Ia. Bruk) then founded an underground almanac called *Snow Wine*.[9] The aesthetic principles of the almanac were the traditions of Russian Symbolism. The students issued two collections of poetry, which were passed from hand to hand at the institute, and prepared a third before the security organs took an interest in their work. An investigation followed, and their poetic efforts were evaluated by characteristic criteria. *Snow Wine* was classified as "an illegal, anti-Soviet society" which carried on "counterrevolutionary activity" masked by Symbolist devices.[10] The Supreme Court of the Russian Federation sentenced the students to different periods of imprisonment under the notorious article 58 of the Civil Code of the Russian Federation, which covered cases of counterrevolutionary crimes, anti-Soviet agitation, the founding of anti-Soviet organizations, terrorism, and treason.[11]

Two different trends gradually developed in the youth movement. The first continued the tradition of self-education in the spirit of catacomb culture. One participant in the self-educational circles who later became a famous sculptor, Ernst Neizvestnyi, described the experience.

> We did not pose any political questions, we did not in any event have political conceptions. I was not even in the Komsomol, although one of my friends was a member of the party. We all intended, however, to educate ourselves well, and the reading of, say, Trotsky, or Saint Augustine, or Orwell, or Berdiaev was punishable. Therefore we needed a conspiracy. . . . Before *samizdat* ["self-published" underground opposition materials of the Democratic Movement of the 1960s ff.—H.R.] we procured and copied privately the whole circle of the Vekhovtsi [liberal political writers of the *Landmarks* school, 1909—H.R.]. . . . Besides this, we heard reports on theosophy, on genetics, on subjects forbidden in the USSR. If the authorities had asked us whether we studied politics, we would have had to answer honestly, No.[12]

Other circles, especially during 1948 and 1949, acquired a political direction and began to accentuate a political outlook. Thanks to Anatolii Zhigulin's autobiographical story, "Chernye kamni" (Black

Stones), we know the history of the Communist Party of Youth, a group founded in Voronezh in 1947. Similar circles of older students were active in Moscow at the end of the 1940s and the beginning of the 1950s: the Army of the Revolution and the Union of Struggle for the Cause of the Revolution. Such circles also formed in Leningrad, Cheliabinsk, Sverdlovsk, and other cities.

What did these groups, classified in the briefs prepared against them as anti-Soviet and even as terrorist, really represent? Let us begin with the "terrorists." As a rule these were older students in high schools or technical schools—that is, students between the ages of 16 and 20. Sometimes, it is true, they were younger. In Cheliabinsk, for example, the police arrested a group of students in the seventh class (14 years old) who duplicated materials by handwriting (block capitals—printing was merely a conspiratorial fantasy here) and posted on residential doors sheets summoning the people to overthrow the government.[13]

The circles usually numbered from three to seven people, rarely more. An exception was the Voronezh Communist Party of Youth, which counted more than fifty members.[14] The very names of the groups indicate clearly that they were based on a Marxist, communist platform. The independent study of the works of Marx, Engels, Lenin, the theory of socialism on the one hand and the observations of real life on the other became the chief stimulant of doubt, the operative motive of their activity. Anatolii Zhigulin describes the characteristic outlook.

> Yes, we were kids of seventeen, eighteen years of age, and those were terrible years, 1946 and 1947. People swelled up from hunger and died not only in the hamlets and the villages but in cities, like Voronezh, destroyed by the war. They moved in throngs, mothers and infants both swollen from hunger. They begged for mercy, as they used to in old Russia, for Christ's sake. But we had nothing to give them. We were ourselves hungry. The dead were pretty quickly hauled off, and so tolerably decent appearances were maintained. . . . Yes, we experienced that terrible hunger. The disgusting thing was to read in the newspapers of the happy life of Soviet people. That is what made us heartsick. That is why we wanted to see everyone fed, clothed, wanted to see no more lies, wanted the accounts in the newspapers to coincide with life itself.[15]

Propaganda and reality were incompatible, and the youth began to search for the reason why. Then arose the idea, We have been deceived! The Stalinist regime was not at all what it claimed to be. The development of this idea took various forms; but one particular aim, the struggle against the regime, the "monster," was everywhere the same, just as were the general positive principles—loyalty to socialism, democracy, and communist ideals.

In the platform of the Moscow Union of Struggle for the Cause of the Revolution, the situation in the country was described as having nothing in common with the ideas of communism. Stalin's dictatorship was identified with Bonapartism, his internal policy was described as tyranny and his foreign policy as another form of imperialism. "Socialist property of the people does not exist in the USSR. Rather there is state capitalism in which the government pursues a policy of collective exploitation."[16]

The program of the Voronezh Communist Party of Youth had a distinctly anti-Stalinist tendency. It condemned the practice of deifying the leader[17] (the conception of the "cult of personality" appeared much later). The Cheliabinsk group adopted a document called "Manifesto of Ideas of Communist Youth," which spoke of the degeneration of the Soviet Communist Party into a bourgeois kind of party and of the degeneration of the Soviet government into a bureaucratic, undemocratic system incapable of leading the country.[18]

The ultimate aims of the youth groups were posed in various forms. The aim of the Communist Party of Youth was to "build a communist society throughout the world."[19] The Cheliabinsk group was dedicated to the "struggle against the existing Soviet order." They did not, however, envisage resorting to force or terror as a means of reaching their goals. On the contrary, as a rule, the participants in the movement condemned the use of terror in principle as immoral as well as ineffective. Their chief instrument of influence was to be explanation and persuasion. They dreamed of a time when by virtue of the development of the movement and the growth of insight on the part of the public, a majority of the people would be behind them. "We did not set ourselves the goal of the violent overthrow of the Stalinist system," said a member of the Union for the Struggle for the Cause of the Revolution, Svetlana Pechuro, "but considered it our primary task to persuade as many people as possible that they were cruelly deceived by a well-organized counterrevolution."[20]

A charge of treason was at that time the most terrible of accusations. Therefore the idea of Stalin's "betrayal of the interests of the revolution" and the related idea of "reestablishing justice" were not only constructive principles encouraging the rise of these motley and scanty groups; they illustrate as well what is all too characteristic of them, that is, their primary motivation by sentiment rather than by reason. Could it have been otherwise among seventeen-year-olds? In these first breakthroughs to justice and liberation from an environment of lies there is so much of youthful romanticism. Conspiratorial meetings, pseudonyms, secret tests of newly recruited members of the organizations could all very well be seen as an extension of the school playground—but for the fact that the punishments meted out were all too real, were monstrously disproportionate to the deeds.

The fates of the members of the Moscow Union of Struggle for the Cause of the Revolution were illustrative: three were sentenced to execution; ten, to twenty-five years in the camps; three, to ten years in the camps. Of the members of the Marxist Workers' Party of Leningrad, three were executed; seven were given twenty-five years in the camps; two, ten years; and three people, one year for failure to report the organization. Similar sentences were handed out to participants in other groups.

The youth groups were a short-lived phenomenon, lasting, as a rule, about one year. Then followed arrests, interrogations, trials, executions, the camps. Thus the prototype of a social force that in the future might have spearheaded the process of democratic renewal of the country was destroyed. It had no chance to survive, but it has every right not to be forgotten.

Chapter 12

The Struggle with Dissent

The general mood changed in 1947–1948. A shift of opinion could be seen in the outlook of the authorities as well. As early as the beginning of 1947 motifs reminiscent of the Great Terror of the 1930s could be discerned in their public speeches.[1] They quoted Central Committee documents of 1935 and 1936 having to do with the murder of Sergei Kirov, and they summoned the people to vigilance against the "intrigues of enemies."[2] They referred to Stalin's speech at the February-March 1937 Central Committee plenum, which was the real precipitant of the Great Terror. "Comrade Stalin said that the bourgeois states . . . constantly send among each other masses of spies. There are thus no grounds for supposing that they send fewer among us. On the contrary, the bourgeois states send us two to three times more than to any bourgeois state." This was the spirit in which Central Committee Secretary A.A. Kuznetsov spoke in September 1947.[3] It seemed that a wave of witch hunts for spies and wreckers was about to roll over the country again. The mechanism of the Ministry of State Security was always ready. And still the experience of the 1940s did not duplicate that of the 1930s. The political repression of the postwar years did not resort, for example, to show trials. After all, the circumstances of the two periods were different.

In the trials of the late 1920s and the 1930s Stalin struggled with real opposition to his bid for absolute power—from partisans of Trotsky and of Bukharin, from various kinds of "deviationists"—and he won. His strongest rivals were physically destroyed, and their supporters either ended their lives in the camps or returned hopelessly old and ill. After the war there were no oppositionists of this kind. Moreover, the Stalinist regime had reached its mature form by the end of the 1930s, and thus it possessed a vastly more powerful arsenal

117

of resources for dealing with enemies than it had during its evolution. This power had not lost its punitive function, but the forms, nature, and scale of terror had changed. In the postwar period the terror itself had grown more adequate to its social role.

The Russian psychologist L.N. Voitolovskii described the influence of terror in the traditional Russian political system.

> To gain a victory over an opponent, the tsarist government sought above all to *paralyze effective collective action* in social groups hostile to it. The main role of terror and repression was to stifle opposition. For the aim of any terror against a social class is by no means vengeance or the destruction of the individual. *The goal of terror is rather to spoil the collective perception of the enemy,* to sow in his ranks the numbing of social consciousness, to remove from his political arsenal the capacity to respond well to factors of public life.[4]

To "deaden collective perception" is nothing more than to paralyze the capacity to think freely and to analyze a social situation critically—or to engage in dissent in general. A dictatorial regime is capable of dealing with opposition not only in its active form but at the level of thinking, attitudes, and feelings as well, that is, at the formative stage of opposition, when it is scarcely aware of being an opposition. The method of open political terror is used as formerly, though partly out of inertia, and basically to form a necessary atmosphere of intimidation, to charge it with fear and suspicion.

Meantime ideological campaigns assume a fundamental role, and the attack on dissent acquires at that point a simultaneously prophylactic function. Although they borrowed from the show trials, these campaigns were marked by a different choice of methods. These features of the process began to be worked out as early as the 1930s, but the basic stage of their evolution took place after the war.

However strange it may seem, it was not only the development of progressive reforms that proceeded by trial and error; the process of political repression relied to a great degree on the same sort of intuitive probing. The two processes differed chiefly in that the developmental stage of the repressive process was much shorter, a fact easily explained by the persistence of the tradition of surveillance in the political history of Russia. The tradition notwithstanding, however, the process was approached through experiments that enabled the authorities to assess the society's readiness and the mechanism's ideological effectiveness—from the selection of the objective to the projection of the results onto groups initially beyond its reach.

At the end of the 1940s and the beginning of the 1950s experimentation in the struggle with dissent assumed two forms. One was the so-called "court of honor," and the other was the no less odious "creative discussion." Both of these campaigns centered on one pivotal idea. They began at the time when the Soviet government identified its enemy No. 1. This enemy was "kowtowing before the West." This was the government's reaction to the attitude of that part of the intelligentsia seeking more access to international contacts and a liberalization of the internal regime.

The first mention of kowtowing before the West appeared in August 1946 in the Central Committee order "On the journals *Zvezda* and *Leningrad*," which signaled the incipient ideological campaign to suppress the liberal leanings of the intelligentsia. The large-scale attack on the influence of the West, however, began only in the summer of 1947 after the appearance of the confidential Central Committee letter "On the Affair of Professors Kliueva and Roskin."[5] The letter affirmed "the presence among a certain part of the Soviet intelligentsia of obeisances and servility before foreign and reactionary bourgeois Western culture unworthy of our people."[6]

> Scientific work in Russia has always suffered from this cringing before foreign culture. Lack of faith in the vitality of Russian science has led to lack of respect for Russian scientific discoveries, as a consequence of which the most important discoveries of Russian science have been ascribed to foreign scientists or have been dishonestly appropriated by them. The great discoveries of Lomonosov in chemistry were attributed to Lavoisier, the invention of radio by the great Russian scientist Popov was attributed to the Italian Marconi, and the invention of the electric lamp by the Russian scientist Iablochkov was assigned to foreigners.[7]

In order to avoid such errors in future, the Central Committee moved to reinforce educational measures of the Soviet intelligentsia. The result was the order to organize the courts of honor (28 March 1947).[8]

These novel institutions had been endowed with broad and plenary powers "to examine acts of an antipatriotic, antistate, and anti-Soviet nature committed by leaders, executives, and scientific personnel of the ministries and central organs of administration of the USSR when these acts do not fall within the jurisdiction of the civil code."[9] From April to October 1947, courts of honor were summoned to eighty-two ministerial and other central administrative branches of government.[10]

The first one sat in the Ministry of Public Health on the case of

Professors Nina Kliueva and Georgii Roskin. It lasted three days, 5 to 7 June 1947, and pronounced a sentence of public reprimand (*obshchestvennyi vygovor*) on the accused.[11] This kind of procedure was to be repeated in all the ministries and administrative units of the state and the party, including those of the Central Committee. According to the scenario handed down from above, all scientists and all the personnel of the ministries and administrative units should hold meetings to discuss the confidential letter of the Central Committee on the Kliueva-Roskin affair, after which they were to search their own institutions and bring before courts of honor those guilty of "worshiping foreign culture."

Meetings for the discussion of the Central Committee's letter were duly held in all the appropriate offices, and the required number of examples of kowtowing before the West were uncovered. Judging by the accounts of the meetings in the scientific establishment, especially in the institutes and divisions of the Academy of Sciences, the facts identified as criminal consisted chiefly of the use by Soviet scientists of foreign sources of information and the publication of their own works in foreign languages. One example from the Technical Division of the Academy of Sciences may serve as typical.

> In 1946 . . . V.V. Sokolovskii published a book, *The Theory of Plasticity*, which contains twenty-two pages of English text. The author's preface appears in both Russian and English. There is a summary of each chapter in English. It is symptomatic that the author Sokolovskii sent his book to the English scientist Folke Odqvist, and the latter, responding to this courtesy, sent to Sokolovskii his brochure in English. The text of this brochure and the accompanying letter contain, of course, not a word of Russian.[12]

Such accusations might well appear merely amusing if the officials in charge of the campaign had not taken their duties more than seriously. They scrutinized closely scientific journals and counted the number of pages published in foreign languages as well as the number of references to native and foreign authors. The Central Committee, and especially Secretary A.A. Kuznetsov, was offended by a group of physiologists, headed by Academician L.A. Orbeli, who gave their presentations in English at the World Congress of Physiology in London.[13] Among the evidence of worshiping foreign culture was the use by Soviet scientists of the research of foreign colleagues and the exchange of raw materials and laboratory instruments for experiments.

Not all Soviet scientists, however, agreed with this policy position.

As several of them said at a meeting of the All-Russian Union of the Cooperative Society of Invalids, "We may not consider utilization of the scientific and technical achievements of other states as servility before foreign culture."[14] Physicist V.L. Ginzburg explained at a party meeting at the P.N. Lebedev Institute of Physics that Soviet scientists often simply did not have at their disposal the instruments necessary for experiments and hence were dependent on foreign technology. "The stronger, more developed, and more powerful our science becomes, the less we will need imported technology," said Ginzburg. "We must at present take account of the science of other countries and consider it with respect. When you are strong, then you may look first of all to yourself, think of your own work and not that of others."[15]

Many scientists supported the need to devote more attention to the achievements and inventions of Russian science, but at the same time it was necessary, in the opinion of Academician S.I. Vavilov, to reach an understanding among scientists, production experts, and the leaders of industry, in order to relate theoretical work to application. "We all know," he said, "that in the majority of cases Soviet work is implemented only after it becomes well known or after we recognize that similar work is done somewhere abroad. Only then do we begin to introduce it and make the transition to new technology on a crash basis."[16] Obviously the scientists tried insofar as possible to avoid searching for antipatriotic and antistate elements in their own ranks. They tried instead to direct the attention of the authorities to the real problems and needs of Soviet science. In some scientific institutes, however, they did not dare to resist the government campaign, and it was not unusual for discussions of the Central Committee's letter to turn into a settling of personal accounts.

The participants in party meetings reacted in different ways to the court of honor judging Kliueva and Roskin and expressed different opinions about the sentence. The discussion in the scientific institutes took the basic form of unemotional and ritualized approval. In several ministries the nature of the discussion was reminiscent of the reaction of people in the streets. When the party meeting in the Ministry of Trade heard the decision of the court of honor, there were demands for heavier punishment: "What an outrage! They must get twenty years. Let them work it off. How could they have deceived Stalin?"[17] The opinion that Kliueva and Roskin got off lightly was heard at other party meetings as well.[18]

Immediately after the discussion of the Central Committee's letter, several ministries and scientific institutes proceeded to elect courts of honor. But by no means all. None was elected in the Ministry of Aviation Industry because the minister, V.M. Khrunichev, thought that none of its business fell within the jurisdiction of such an institution.[19] The leadership of other ministries took a similar position: Geology, Armaments, Communications, Electrical Industry, and Northern Sea Transport. Others adopted a wait-and-see attitude. The Ministry of Fishing Industry for Eastern Regions organized a court of honor, but it did not undertake any work, as its chairman, Deputy Minister B.A. Starikov, explained, "We are awaiting the accumulation of the experience of other ministries."[20] This kind of conduct on the part of the central organs of state could not fail to alert the authorities, who initiated a campaign of indoctrination of the intelligentsia. Central Committee Secretary Kuznetsov recognized the situation plainly.

> It seems to me that we are running into resistance to the instructions [confidential letter] of the Central Committee. Whether we want to recognize it or not, it is a fact. We are encountering resistance from the local party leaders as well as from the economic administrators. The fact that the comrades do not want to elect courts of honor indicates that they are resisting this new form of propaganda among the intelligentsia.[21]

The ministers of aviation and of the electrical industry were summoned to the Central Committee for explanations. In the course of October–November 1947 the Central Committee instituted a series of investigations into the implementation of its confidential letter and the work of the courts of honor. It was only after this booster that the business began to move forward. "The ministries overcame their passive attitude . . . and proceeded from discussions to practical implementation," according to one investigator's report. "The courts of honor have abandoned their passivity."[22] By this time the affair was four months old. The initial failure of the measure, however, did not pass without consequences. This was the first time since the war that the authorities had confronted disobedience, and what made it especially significant was that it occurred in the very social category that was regarded as unstintingly reliable. The campaign against dissent in the intelligentsia and the civil service, relying on the intrinsic support of the latter, did not elicit the desired response. The courts of honor were clearly unpopular. To a large extent this fact decided their subsequent fate. On 7 July 1948, an order of the Council of Ministers and the Central Committee prolonged their mandate by a year; however, upon the expiration of this period they were not reconstituted. Stalin had evidently lost interest in this form of indoctrination, but it was the courts of honor together with the other ideological campaigns of the 1940s that prepared the transition from preventive measures of struggle with dissent to political repression.

Another contribution to the atmosphere of ideological rigor was the campaign of so-called "creative discussions." The first was devoted to philosophy. Its target was the textbook of G.F. Aleksandrov, *History of West European Philosophy*. The author was chief of the Soviet Propaganda Administration. Though the book had received the Stalin Prize early in 1946, Stalin later made seriously critical comments on it. It is hard to say whether the book fell into his hands by accident or by design, but in the coming ideological campaigns Stalin's observations were a necessary element of discussion. It was on the basis of his remarks that the discussions of Aleksandrov's book took place in January 1947. Soviet philosophers, however, innocent of experience of such campaigns, evidently failed to discern the political role that the authorities assigned them. The Central Committee was dissatisfied with their proceedings and ordered further discussions. It then placed no less a figure than A.A. Zhdanov in charge of the campaign and distributed a mandatory agenda of discussion.

At this point Aleksandrov was accused of "objectivism," that is, he had derived the evolution of Marxism from its philosophical predecessors, including—and this was the criminal element in his work—the work of bourgeois philosophers. Of course, whatever tribute he paid to Western European philosophy was assessed in the spirit of the time as kowtowing before the West. There is no need to review the content of the discussions,[23] as it was hardly significant. The essence of the proceeding revealed a premeditated model of attack on dissent in pursuit of ideological monism. Garbed in the trappings of democratic criticism and self-criticism, the discussion in fact conformed entirely to the promptings of the Central Committee. In the words of Yurii Furmanov, "the force of argument yielded to the argument of force."[24]

In place of the accepted authorities of classical philosophy stood a new authority. Philosophical thought itself was defined by the Central Committee, which presumed hereafter to serve as the high court of social science. The role of scholars degenerated into that of commentators and popularizers of decisions taken by the Central Committee in its role of ultimate academic arbiter. Whoever erred was expected to make public recantation. The letter that Professor Aleksandrov himself wrote to Stalin and Zhdanov in July 1947 may serve as a general example.

> I am fully aware that without the Central Committee's correction of my work in theoretical questions I would be of little use to the party as a professional philosopher. The [recent] philosophical discussion, and especially the profound and powerful speech of Comrade Zhdanov, has charged the philosophical workers with enormous Bolshevik inspiration, has called forth in all of us a sincerely ardent ambition to put an end to the traditionally accepted methodology in scientific work.[25]

At this professional level the design of Zhdanov and Stalin was completely successful. The philosophers drew the appropriate conclusions. It remained then to devise a means of transmitting the newly adopted outlook down the steps of the professional hierarchy, to indicate the proper political lessons. This assignment proved quite complicated not only because it was difficult to apply soaring abstractions to the mundane features of Soviet society—the problem of production, for example—but also because of the absence of professional personnel to do the job. The campaign against dissent was weak at its most critical link: the lack of competent and informed ideologists to carry the message to the people.

This fact soon confronted the Central Committee's agents sent to assess the impact of political propaganda at the grass roots. As their notes indicate, a large part of the party's propagandists, both the rank and file and the leaders of party committees, had not the most elementary idea of the decisions taken at the center, did not know what was going on either in the country or in the world at large. Their interviews with local party personnel reveal the problem.

First interview:

> Q: What political literature do you read?
> A: Comrade Stalin's first volume.
> Q: What in particular have you read in it?
> A: I forget, I can't remember, I can't say.
> Q: What else do you read?
> A: I read Comrade Aleksandrov on bourgeois theories.
> Q: What kind of fiction do you read?
> A: I read *Ivan the Terrible*, a book by one of our writers. I don't like the book. It speaks well of the people, but among the bourgeoisie and the capitalists there isn't one good person. That is all that I have read this year.[26]

Second interview:

> Q: Have you read the report of Comrade Zhdanov on the journals *Zvezda* and *Leningrad*?

A: No, I haven't read it.

Q: Which of the recent decisions of the Central Committee guide you in your work?

A: I cannot now name any.

Q: What English political parties do you know?

A: I don't remember.

Q: Who is the head of the government in Yugoslavia?

A: I don't remember. Tito is in the government either in Yugoslavia or in Bulgaria.[27]

At the rank-and-file level, matters were worse yet.

Q: Name the highest organ of government in the USSR.

A: The working class, the Central Committee? The RKK [sic?—H.R.]? The All-Union Communist Party?

Q: What is Comrade Stalin's position in government?

A: He has many offices, I can't say.

Q: Who is the head of the Soviet government?

A: I don't know.

Q: What is Comrade Molotov's position in government?

A: He travels abroad.

Q: What is currently going on in Greece?

A: A gang is making war on the working class.[28]

These notes hardly need any comment. They were likely analyzed with some care by the Central Committee, as it was taking measures to correct the situation. First it undertook to strengthen party schools and courses. In 1947 there were around 60,000 Soviet political schools enrolling 800,000 people. During the year the number of such schools grew to 122,000 and the number of students in them to more than 1.5 million. During the same time the number of circles studying party history doubled from 45,500 to 88,000, while the number of persons attending these circles increased from 846,000 to 1.2 million.[29]

Along with the measures devoted to strengthening the ideological front through the preparation of cadres, the policy of surveillance was extended to different spheres of science and culture. In August 1948 the meeting of the All-Union Lenin Academy of Agricultural Sciences completed a long-term discussion among biologists; in the summer of 1950 there was a discussion of the problems of linguistics; at the end of 1951, a discussion of the problems of the political economy of socialism. All of these discussions, like the one in philosophy, proceeded by a prearranged agenda delivered from above. To attribute all initiative in these colloquies to the authorities, however, is unwarranted. The reality was more complicated. The authorities were able to utilize genuine impulses in the cultural life of the nation. In fact, the intelligentsia felt the need for a broad discussion of questions born of wartime and of material life in the postwar period. Public opinion sought a forum for the discussion of the most painful problems of life, and the professional colloquies convoked by the government were a suitable means of satisfying the demand. It was no accident that talk of professional problems usually led to talk of far broader issues than those originally envisaged. Konstantin Simonov observed one of these strange professional gatherings. When he summed up a discussion of problems of literary criticism in 1948, he found that the conversation soon turned to the literary process more generally and to public life in general.[30] The change of emphasis in these meetings was often unwelcome to the organizers.

In order to avoid the introduction of undesirable subjects, it was necessary to turn for cover to a powerful arbiter of discussion. This was a tried and true device. In the 1930s Stalin routed his opponents by wielding the authority of the Leninist course, the authenticity of which was beyond appeal. Lysenko and his colleagues used a similar ploy, citing the authority of the famous Russian biologist I.V. Michurin. The reference to Michurin, however, as suitable as it was to demonstrate patriotism in the face of the threat of kowtowing before the West, could not silence the arguments of critics. Rather what was necessary was an authority whose opinion was not subject to discussion, an infallible authority. Such a position belonged to only one man, Stalin. The logic of the function of absolute power preordained the subsequent course of developments. Stalin had no alternative to becoming the great philosopher, the sovereign economist, the grand linguist, and so on. Insofar as the struggle with dissent presupposed a highest authority, that authority must pronounce the decisive word, and the pronouncement of that word served to resolve the discussion. The intervention of Stalin ordained the victory of Lysenko over the geneticists and sketched the boundaries of discussion about issues in economics and linguistics.

This is not to say that until this time Stalin stood aside from discussions. Rather he was present as an observer and followed the course of events closely. In the linguistics debate, the article of the Georgian philologist A.S. Chikobava, attacking the theories of N.Ia. Marr,[31] was written directly on Stalin's orders, and it initiated the discussion. The disposition of scholarly opinion at the time is clearly conveyed in the letter of the philologist L.F. Denisova to the editors of *Pravda*, the paper that published Chikobava's article.

There is an unprecedented ferment in the minds of linguists. Some, chiefly old enemies of Marr, say, "Well, thank God, Marr has finally found a genuine critic." Others declare directly that they now "make a 180-degree turn," although recently these comrades were ardent Marrists. . . . Others yet refrain from expressing an opinion, afraid of putting their foot in their mouth, fearing that Chikobava is supported by comrades of superior authority. . . . If the editors of *Pravda* would in some fashion dispel these fears and persuade the comrades that the discussion may proceed in an open fashion and that there are no potentially unpleasant consequences behind it, then this article would serve to stimulate a genuine discussion.[32]

As attention turned to the controversy over linguistics in 1950, many scholars took a more cautious approach in expressing an opinion. The years of ideological terror had left their impression. In any event the threat of "unpleasantnesses" could not be regarded as groundless. The whole course of the linguistic controversy illustrates that people had already learned to await the opinion from above and to adjust their own opinion accordingly. This opinion from above appeared in summer 1950 when Stalin published three articles in *Pravda*. In their wake came a chain reaction of people dissociating themselves from the views of Marr. *Pravda* began to receive not letters but express telegrams. "Please insert in my article immediately corrections of the following content: in any class society, language reflects not the class structure but the national culture. The remainder of the article may be left as it is." "I beg you not to publish my article on the linguistic question and to return it." "After the articles of Comrade Stalin I reject the fundamental propositions of my article and beg you not to publish it." "I beg you to withhold my article 'For the Complete Defeat of the Idealists and the Metaphysicians in Linguistics.'. . . I consider this article erroneous and harmful." "After the brilliant article of Comrade Stalin it is no longer necessary to publish my article." "Do not publish my article on the linguistic question. I will send another in a few days."[33]

In the case of the linguistic debates we can gauge how effectively the dynamism of social demagogy worked, especially if Stalin stood at the head of it. Faith in the word of the leader transformed people into prisoners of phrases. A student of the philological faculty of Moscow State University addressed himself to Stalin in this style.

Iosif Vissarionovich! Your pronouncement on questions of Soviet linguistics has been for me the most significant event of the past five years in academic life. . . . It forces us to think creatively and not to live by the dogmatic hair-splitting of classical Marxist citations. . . . Whatever you undertake in the affairs of our country is an inspiration. . . . I wish you good health and good health and good health. May your achievements always be with us.[34]

This letter is reminiscent of another written by a student of the philological faculty of Leningrad State University: "Dear Iosif Vissarionovich! You have taught us to love the truth more than life. We have grown up in a society constructed and developed under your leadership. We have been raised according to your books and articles. We have learned to believe you, Iosif Vissarionovich, more than ourselves. Every word of yours we honor as sacred."[35]

But these words were a mere preface. This Leningrad student obviously found several points in Stalin's article on linguistics difficult to understand. Her confusion can be sensed between the lines of the letter. Nevertheless, as she wrote, "I want not simply to believe you, I want to be convinced . . . of the truth of your every word."[36] The word itself of the *vozhd'* did not admit of doubt, but blind faith in its truthfulness, as evidenced by this letter, was at some level of subconsciousness not sufficient. In addition to faith, she needed conviction based on knowledge, and this was to turn from emotion to reason. This student's letter is a solitary example of such a shift, and we have no evidence that it took place on anything like a massive scale.

The story of these discussion campaigns illustrates not only the power of the ruling regime to control the minds of the citizens, not only the power of social demagogy but its weaknesses as well, one of which was the capacity to reduce any decision to absurdity. Thus miners were obliged to participate in the discussion of genetics, and collective farmers had to study Stalin's articles on linguistics. In Fedor Abramov's novel *Puti-pereputia* (The Paths of Confusion), there is an episode in which the hero, collective farm chairman Lukashin, happens upon such a discussion.

Everyone was busy studying [Stalin's] works [on linguistics]. They appeared in *Pravda* exactly at harvest time. . . . And so the harvesters were summoned to a meeting. . . . The room was full to the brim, nowhere to sit. . . . Fokin was reading from a paper, but he was growing excited. . . . The last words Lukashin caught with difficulty. They were drowned in a wave of applause. . . . He wanted to rush to the party office, to read it with his own eyes. And so he read. He looked out the window. It was raining. He looked at the portrait of Stalin in his generalissimo's uniform and began to read again. Here was the program of the party and the people for the next few years, and he must somehow grasp it.

Lukashin was somewhat comforted when he spoke with his colleague Podrezov. Podrezov did not mince words. Lukashin asked what practical conclusions were to be drawn by collective farm chairmen from Comrade Stalin's works on linguistics. Podrezov answered directly, "To work hard."[37]

Beyond the organization of comprehensive public discussions, the campaigns of the 1940s and 1950s ran into other substantial difficulties. Like any administrative decisions based on control and pressure from above, they demanded great expenditures. The burden on the central apparatus increased. The Central Committee determined what books Soviet people might read, what films they might see, what recordings they might hear.

The massive network of libraries and bookstores was purged of books that lacked, by the standards of censorship, "academic and literary value" and were "littered with names and citations of enemies of the people."[38] Special lists of such forbidden literature were confirmed by the Central Committee along with black lists of theatrical productions that were to be removed from the repertoire. On 28 August 1951, the Council of Ministers vested control over all artistic production in the organs of censorship. A bit later lists of forbidden sound recordings were published.[39]

In July 1952 the Presidium of the Council of Ministers prepared a draft to extend the authority of local organs of censorship and to increase their staffing.[40] Suggestions were heard to transfer the duties of censorship to the Ministry of State Security.[41] Though this proposal was not accepted, it indicates clearly enough the direction in which the internal policy of the leadership was evolving in the last years of Stalin's life. In addition to introducing ideological campaigns and reinforcing control over public opinion, the regime ever more frequently resorted to nakedly repressive practices.

Chapter 13

The Wave of Repression, 1949–1953

The psychological impact of terror, designed as it was to paralyze the collective capacity of resistance, was nevertheless used selectively, however large its scale. The selective approach was employed to instill in the masses an attitude of righteous indignation against dissenters and faith in the justice of the measures taken against them. The formula "we don't imprison the innocent," an omnipresent element of the atmosphere of the time, shows that the motifs of the campaign fell on well-prepared ground. The impatience of the citizenry, raised to an emotional pitch by the deficits of postwar life, required release. The force of aggressive emotions was not hard to raise in these conditions, and an explanation of the causes of the disorders of life was essentially diverted onto the question, Who is guilty? This kind of reaction is endemic to the behavior of crowds, which are easily drawn to search for simple reasons for the extremity of their condition. Stalin exploited this familiar stereotype of mass behavior when he began to divide society into friends and enemies.

The repressions of the postwar years touched in one degree or another all strata of the population. If we judge by the numbers convicted on political grounds, the peak period was 1945 and 1946. The Commissariat of Internal Affairs convicted 123,200 persons in 1946 and 123,300 in 1947.[1] The victims of this wave were chiefly returning POWs, repatriates, former soldiers of the Vlasov army, Ukrainian national separatists (mostly Banderists), and other elements of the population classified by the authorities as "socially dangerous persons."[2] These were all people with a military background of one kind or another, and they were not directly involved in the processes that began to develop in Soviet society after the war. In the succeeding years the figures on persons convicted by the Ministry of Internal Affairs and the Ministry of State Security diminished progressively:[3]

1947	78, 800
1948	73, 300
1949	75, 100
1950	60, 600
1951	54, 800
1952	28, 800
1953	8, 400

These figures reflect only those convicted of counterrevolutionary activity, treason, and other crimes against the state. Statistics on other forms of crime—murder, burglary, armed robbery, larceny, absenteeism and tardiness at work, leaving a job without permission, and so on—were tabulated under the conventional civil code. The rubric of larceny and theft included not only real crimes but stealing of food during the famine years, when people out of desperation—and often through the fault of the state, which did not always pay them for working—took grain or potatoes, which they had themselves raised, from the collective farm fields. The sources do not allow a reliable calculation of the numbers falling victim to prosecution under the civil code. The general numbers of the convicts must take into account not only those sentenced to deprivation of freedom but peasants sent into exile, deported peoples, and other categories of resettled persons.

If we compare the scale of political repressions of the prewar and postwar years, it is obvious that the postwar phenomenon did not reach the magnitude of the Great Terror of 1937–1938. In the year 1937 alone 790,700 persons were sentenced for political crimes, while the comparable number for the whole period from 1945–1953 is 626,300.[4] The distinguishing feature of the postwar repressions is that they were confined to the level of the elite, both central and local. Repression of this social stratum sought to discipline the party and state apparatus, making examples of individuals as a lesson for their peers. It also unleashed the rival ambitions of political clans and thereby served as an instrument for revolving and renewing personnel. The majority of people were not touched by these processes, but the atmosphere that they created influenced the relationship of government and people everywhere.

The "Leningrad affair" of 1949–1952 occupies a special place in the postwar political processes. It afflicted an elite circle in one of the most significant party organizations in the country. At the upper level, the Leningrad affair was a product of clan rivalries, the outcome of a struggle for power between two blocs in the leadership of the country—those of Zhdanov and Kuznetsov on the one hand and of Malenkov and Beria on the other. Zhdanov and Kuznetsov had at different times served as first secretaries of the Leningrad party. Until approximately the middle of 1948, the leading positions in the Soviet government were occupied by persons from the Leningrad organization, including Zhdanov, Kuznetsov, and N.A. Voznesenskii, the chairman of Gosplan (State Planning Agency) and a member of the Politburo. In August 1948 Zhdanov died, and his death provided an opportunity for the Malenkov-Beria bloc.

The formal reasons for instituting the Leningrad case, whose victims were comparatively few, were two violations of the law. First was the organization in January 1949 of a nationwide wholesale market without the required permission of the Council of Ministers. Second was the falsification of the results of elections to the city party organization. The chairman of the electoral commission reported the voting as unanimous, although in fact there were votes against several candidates.[5]

For these reasons the Politburo on 15 February 1949 lodged charges not only against the first secretary of the city and provincial party committees, P.S. Popkov, but against Central Committee Secretary A.A. Kuznetsov, who had long ago ceased to work in Leningrad, and the chairman of the Council of Ministers of the Russian Federation (RSFSR), M.I. Rodionov, who also had a history in the Leningrad party. The essence of the accusation was that these leaders had manifested an "unhealthy, un-Bolshevik deviation, apparent in demagogic intrigues in the Leningrad organization . . . and in the effort to build a barrier between the Central Committee and the Leningrad party."[6] As it developed, the Leningrad affair proceeded at two levels, the central and the regional. The link between the two was an alleged clique formed between the Leningrad leaders and their protectors in Moscow.

P.S. Popkov and Ia.F. Kapustin, the first and second secretaries of the Leningrad city and provincial party committees, were relieved of their posts in February 1949. At the end of March and the beginning of April a massive purge of the Leningrad party apparatus began. From 1949 through 1952 over 2,000 Leningrad officials were removed from office, including 1,500 party, soviet, trade-union, and Komsomol (Communist Youth League) personnel.[7] Both the leadership and almost the whole administrative structure of the city were decimated.

G.M. Malenkov was in charge of collecting compromising material against the accused: Kuznetsov, Voznesenskii, Rodionov, and others. As the whole affair was conducted secretly, a special prison known as the "party prison," administered by the Central Committee rather than by the Ministry of State Security, was established. The investigation was conducted simultaneously by the party and by the Ministry of State Security. The big trial was held on 29 and 30 September 1950 in Leningrad. It was allegedly an open affair, but the audience consisted almost exclusively of the officials of the security organs, and there was no mention of an open trial in the press. The accused were charged with "constituting a hostile group, which since 1938 carried on sabotage and wrecking" with the aim of "turning the Leningrad organization into a support base for carrying on a struggle with the party and its Central Committee."[8] All of the accused, nine persons, confessed their guilt. Six of them (Voznesenskii, Kuznetsov, Popkov, Kapustin, Rodionov, and Lazutin) were sentenced to be shot, and the remainder were sentenced to different periods in the GULAG. The executions took place on 1 October 1950. In the wake of the big trial, there were several secret mini-trials in which more leaders of the Leningrad party were executed. Others yet, including family members of the condemned, were sentenced to various terms in prison or the camps. The victims included hundreds of communists in Moscow, Gorkii, Murmansk, Riazan, Simferopol, Sevastopol, Novgorod, Pskov, Tallin, and other cities.

The Leningrad affair was the most conspicuous and, by reference to its consequences, tragic in the chain of postwar political persecutions. Still, it was only a part of the purges afflicting the party elite of the time. Not all of the cases against party leaders developed according to this scenario. By way of contrast, we may consider the "Moscow affair" in which the first secretary, G.M. Popov, was removed from office. According to the Politburo decision of 12 December 1949, "On Shortcomings in the Work of Comrade G.M. Popov," he was simply relieved of his duties and transferred to other work. Several Moscow provincial party secretaries underwent this same merciful fate, and the Moscow party apparatus as a whole was spared the devastating purge that Leningrad experienced.

Lighter purges of the local, chiefly republican, elite accompanied that of the central apparatus. Among the more conspicuous were those that took place in Estonia and Georgia. The first secretary of the Estonian party, N.G. Karotamm, and the chairman of the Estonian Council of Ministers, A.T. Veimer, were relieved of their posts. Other Estonian officials were subsequently arrested and convicted: the deputy chairman of the Presidium of the Supreme Soviet, Nigol Andresen; the president of the Academy of Sciences and minister of foreign affairs, Hans Kruus; the chairman of the Union of Soviet Writers, Johanes Semper, and others. The principal charge against the Estonian leaders was "local nationalism": they did not carry on the requisite struggle against "bourgeois nationalism," and they manifested "political negligence" in the promotion of personnel and allowed the development of anti-Russian attitudes in the republic.[9]

On 7 March 1950 the Politburo issued an order "On the Shortcomings and Mistakes in Party Work in Estonia,"[10] which set in motion a purge of the state and party structures there. Karotamm and Veimer were twice summoned to the Central Committee in Moscow, in February 1950 and in December 1951, where a special commission investigated their cases. Both of them, while admitting a series of mistakes, nevertheless rejected the accusation of bourgeois nationalism. Karotamm confessed only to acts of "deviation toward local nationalism."[11] The commission concluded that the former leaders of Estonia "have not disclosed all of their mistakes." It considered, however, that Karotamm and Veimer deserved nothing more than "a severe reprimand for anti-party conduct."[12] Unlike the Leningrad party organization, the Estonian apparatus was not subjected to a thorough purge. Rather, the purge was directed chiefly against the state apparatus. The party personnel were to a significant degree imported from other regions of the USSR, and they represented in fact the sole social support for the policy of Sovietization. Therefore, the Estonian affair left the local republican party largely untouched.

The Mingrelian affair of 1951–1952 in the Georgian party developed by the same principle—hit the headquarters first. This case was precipitated by the receipt of multifaceted evidence of corruption and abuses implicating several prominent persons. The affair took its name from the fact that the majority of the accused had Mingrelian names (Mingrelia was a historic province of Georgia). Having arisen as a case under the civil code—the facts of corruption in the Georgian leadership were undeniable—it quickly acquired political overtones. All persons tainted by corruption, at the head of whom was the former second secretary of the Georgian Central Committee, M.I. Baramiia, were accused of forming a nationalist group that aspired "to seize the most important party and state posts in Georgia."[13] Several months later the Baramiia group was convicted of attempting to liquidate Soviet power in Georgia and to divide the republic into "separate party principalities."[14] A total of thirty-seven party and government officials were arrested in the Mingrelian affair, and several thousand were exiled from the republic.[15]

The purges instituted at the beginning of the 1950s among the leaders of Estonia and Georgia illustrate the difference between personnel policies applied at the center and in the regions. The essential feature of this policy was the struggle against manifestations of so-called bourgeois nationalism, one of the consequences of the birth of imperial ideology persistently cultivated by Stalin after the war. The nationalists were useful to the regime in conditions of permanent struggle with run-of-the-mill enemies of the people. They were assigned the role formerly taken by the Trotskyites, the representatives of the non-Bolshevik parties, and various kinds of party deviationists and wreckers. At the same time, the purges of the Estonian or Mingrelian type were consistently confined to the regional and republican level. For the fabrication of a nationalist threat on an all-Union scale, a development comparable to the drama of the show trials of the 1930s, a conspiracy of a wide-ranging ethnic perspective had to be found.

For this purpose Stalin's selection fell by no means accidentally on Soviet Jewry. The Jews were not only distributed throughout the territory of the Soviet Union, but many of them belonged to the elite of Soviet science and culture or occupied responsible positions in the government. In addition, Soviet Jews had their own public organization, the Jewish Antifascist Committee,[16] to which in case of need the role of nationalist center could be attributed. The organizers of the campaign took into account the anti-Semitism widespread in various strata of Russian society. The story of the anti-Semitic campaign of the end of the 1940s and the beginning of the 1950s has been related in detail in the academic literature,[17] and so we can content ourselves with an account of its salient features, those crucial to understanding the public atmosphere of the time.

The first displays of anti-Semitism as a matter of state policy were observed immediately after the war. Its targets were the Soviet Information Bureau and its director, the Deputy Minister of Foreign Affairs, S.A. Lozovskii. In September 1945 and July 1946 the Propaganda Administration instituted two investigations of the work of his office, which was subjected to serious criticism for "negligence in personnel work." This negligence consisted of an "inadmissible concentration of

Jews."[18] Lozovskii and a number of his colleagues were relieved of their duties for "manifestations of nationalism." These were the first steps in a campaign that gathered full force in the course of 1948–1949, when the attack on so-called "cosmopolitanism" was inaugurated throughout the country.

The new campaign came to the assistance of the campaign of fawning before the West, which in fact had failed to meet expectations. The old campaign was evasively abstract; the new one was convincingly concrete. Cosmopolitanism emerged as the highest form of kowtowing, as a cultural betrayal of the interests of the society. In addition, unlike the campaign against kowtowing, which lacked a clearly identifiable target—anyone could be accused of servility to foreign culture—the circle of rootless cosmopolitans, as they were then called, was clearly enough delineated. No one had to declaim it officially, as everyone understood instinctively who these people were.

The turning point in the campaign was the year 1948, the time of the foundation of the state of Israel. It was then that the murder of S.M. Mikhoels, chairman of the Jewish Antifascist Committee, took place. At the same time arrests began among members of the Committee. In order to render plausible the charge of a Zionist conspiracy, the Ministry of State Security simultaneously fabricated several modest conspiracies, which were supposed to demonstrate a whole network of Zionist organizations in state institutions, industry, the sciences, and so forth. In 1949 a purge of personnel began in all state institutions, scientific organizations, and editorial staffs: the Jews were expelled. Even the Ministry of State Security was purged of Jews.

In the spring of 1952 an investigation of the Jewish Antifascist Committee was completed, and the trial of members of the Committee proceeded from May through July. All of the accused, with a single exception, were sentenced to be shot. This affair led to the purge from 1948–1952 of 110 persons.[19]

This series of anti-Semitic purges did not, however, bring the persecution of Jews to an end. Its final stage was the "doctors' plot" designed by its instigators to uncover a conspiracy of Kremlin doctors against the leaders of the party and the country. The doctors' plot was the only one of the series of postwar purges to be given wide publicity. The communiqué on the arrest of a group of doctors—called "murderers in surgeons' gowns," "medical wreckers"—was published in *Pravda* on 13 January 1953. Not all of the arrested doctors were Jews, but the communiqué emphasized that "the majority of participants in the terrorist group . . . belonged to an international Jewish organization called 'Joint.' "[20] The "medical wreckers" were accused of the murders of the first secretary of the Moscow party committee, A.S. Shcherbakov, in 1945, and of Central Committee Secretary Zhdanov in 1948, and it was alleged that they had plotted other terrorist acts against prominent people of the government.

The seeds of falsehood fell on favorable ground, and the campaign against rootless cosmopolitans bore its grim fruit. Of course, not everyone believed the nonsense about medical murders, but the public reaction to the doctors' plot was quite positive. A citizen Nazarov wrote to *Pravda* from Novocherkassk: "Hearing the news on the radio, I curse the vile murderers of Comrades Zhdanov and Shcherbakov. The vermin must be hanged."[21] Soldiers, housewives, schoolchildren, and pensioners demanded the death penalty for the doctors. Many of these people did not consider themselves anti-Semitic. As a worker in the Dynamo Factory in Moscow wrote, "I am a simple worker and not an anti-Semite, but I say straight out, it has long been necessary to chase the Jews out of the medical institutes, pharmacies, hospitals, rest homes, sanatoria. These places are controlled by Jews, they are Jewish businesses. . . . In a word, it's time to clean these people out."[22]

The newspapers received indignant anonymous letters. "All of us residents of the apartment house were terribly irate when we read the report of TASS in *Pravda*. . . . Is it not time to settle the national question, in particular the Jewish question, from the perspective of building communism? Do they obstruct the building of communism? Yes! From this perspective it is necessary to settle the Jewish question. Exile them from the big cities, where there are so many of the swine."[23] Some of those condemning the doctors were Jews who addressed the "honest Jews of the world" with the appeal to "disown the shameful murderers," "American hirelings."[24]

The public reaction to the doctors' plot is recalled by one of its victims, the well-known Soviet pathologist, Ia.L. Rapoport.

> The unlikeliest rumors spread among the public, including "reliable" reports that in many maternity wards newborn infants were being killed or that some sick person died immediately after the visit of a doctor, who was then, naturally, arrested and shot. Visits to clinics declined sharply, and the pharmacies were suddenly forsaken. At the institute where I worked, a young woman came and demanded an analysis of an empty vial of penicillin. Her child had pneumonia, and immediately after he was given the penicillin, according to the mother, he grew worse. Allergic reactions to antibiotics are common enough, but she attributed this reaction to the work of poison allegedly contained in the

penicillin, declaring that she would not give him any more medicine. When I told her that she would thus condemn him to death, she replied, "Let him die from illness but not from poison that I give him with my own hands."[25]

In an atmosphere charged with such massive hysteria, a society is easily managed. It is capable of overcoming or destroying whatever stands in its way, barriers real or imaginary. It is not capable, however, of constructive activity. Thus it is no longer a genuinely coherent society. It is a crowd or a mob. More subtle methods are necessary to activate public reason. In this case, an atmosphere of mass psychosis turned into mass aggressiveness. As a result there was a great confusion of ideological fiat and spontaneous social terror. The threat of public reprisals was in the air. Manipulating the general mood, the authorities managed their campaign with the blessing of public approval. The public, psychologically prepared for a campaign of intimidation, was surprisingly easily persuaded of the intrigues of rootless cosmopolitans and medical wreckers. Unconcerned with the substance of the issues, it was ready to condemn those identified as wreckers in philosophy, biology, economics, or in whatever was asked of it. But could such a situation long continue?

The responsibility for total social control inevitably strengthened the influence of the Ministry of State Security and the Ministry of Internal Affairs. The leadership of the country thus found itself in a complex situation. It was approaching a critical limit of the abuse of power beyond which it dared not go. If recent political trends continued, the security organs would be in a position to threaten the Central Committee and the Council of Ministers themselves. At this point the instinct of self-preservation and the law of diminishing returns began to assert themselves.

Chapter 14

The Evolution of Public Opinion: "Whose Fault Is It?"

Political intimidation in a highly charged atmosphere always has a psychological limit. "A society seized by panic," according to L.N. Voitolovskii, "loses its sensitivity to the discord of public life [as the Stalin regime intended it to do—E.Z.], while the society itself begins to generate oppressive and alarming emotions that lead to a numbing feebleness, apathy, and defeatism."[1] This kind of outcome was directly contrary to the principles of a functioning socialist society, which depended on the support of a highly developed public discourse. If this society required an organic mechanism of terror to safeguard its security, then it needed other instruments to stimulate its cultural and economic life. The terror diverted people's attention from the real reasons for their misfortune, sending them on a false search for enemies. This search, however, only led from negative results to endless pretexts and excuses for them, while what was needed was a policy to engender positive, forward-looking, and inspiring attitudes that would elicit support for the government. The crucial feature of such policies is that their results are not calculated exclusively by material output but by the popularity of the government legislating them. Such policies, whatever their particular content, are always essentially populist.

Lowering prices naturally comes at the head of the list of populist policies. Therefore Stalin in 1947 did precisely that, a politically unimpeachable success. From 1947 through 1954, retail prices were reduced seven times. This tactic brought enormous strategic gain. The advocates of the regime invariably argued on such occasions that it demonstrated Stalin's constant concern for the well-being of the people. The calculations of economists showing that these price reductions were insubstantial[2] were simply ignored. The most important element of this question was not economic, ideological, or rational; rather it was emotional, and it is defended today on emotional grounds alone. So how did the people react to the price reductions?

The majority reacted positively, which was natural, but there were a few expressions of criticism. As one Leningrader put it after the price decrease of 1949, "Why such a lot of fuss over a modest reduction of prices? This price reduction amounts merely to propaganda."[3]

The priority of political aims notwithstanding, decisions on prices, like any other such measure, had economic consequences. Lower prices naturally led to increased demand, especially in the particular products most affected by the reduction—in this case, foodstuffs and manufactured goods. In the forty largest cities of the country after the price reduction of March 1949, the average daily sale of meat increased by 13 percent, and of butter and salt, by nearly 30 percent, while in various categories of industrial goods the increase of sales was more dramatic. From February to March the sale of gramophones grew by 4.5 times, and bicycle sales doubled.[4]

The growth of demand gave rise to doubts: would the supply of products at the new prices be sufficient?[5] Inasmuch as the price reductions scarcely touched the items of primary consumption, questions naturally arose. "Why is the reduction on bread, flour, and cooking oil so small?" "Why is there no reduction on sugar, soap, and kerosene?"[6] Apart from the issue whether such questions were well founded, their mere expression is interesting for another reason. They illustrate how a policy calculated to maintain the image of a regime devoted to popular well-being began to work to the government's disadvantage. The people gradually grew accustomed to such blessings, even came to expect them, and their demands for more soon outpaced the supply of largesse. As the price reductions were handed down from on high and were unrelated to labor productivity, the people were indifferent to the source of good fortune. In fact, the source, the government treasury, reacted to this policy painfully, because it did not at all resemble a horn of plenty. Accepting the voluntary practice of regular price reductions, the government found itself in a trap: the threat of growing inflation. The logic of things required that this costly price policy be rejected, but to do so would damage the prestige of the government. And so the practice continued through inertia; and the same inertia fed the people's annual expectations of further reductions.

The price reductions did not provide labor incentives, and stimulants of labor productivity were extremely limited in the economic policies of the postwar period. Of course, the legacy of the war took its toll: severe financial limitations and scanty resources limited the prospects of progress, including raising the pay scale. Thus labor productivity and the general pathos of reconstruction depended for inspiration on non-material sources, in fact on psychological and ideological factors. The functional principle of these factors derived from the influence of "the grand goal." During the war, that goal was victory. When the goal was achieved, it left a great vacuum to fill, and the authorities evidently found nothing better to fill it than "the building of communism." In the words of the projected party program of 1947, "The Communist Party sets the goal of building a communist society in the USSR in the course of the next twenty to thirty years."[7]

The advantage of the grand goal of victory consisted not only in its enormous appeal but in its concretely credible nature. Every city liberated, every village recovered brought the nation closer to the goal, turned the ideal into the real. In contrast, it was hard to confer a credible concreteness on the idea of the building of communism. The government tried to inculcate into the public consciousness a singular symbol of the future, the "grand construction projects of communism," the hydroelectric dams on the Don, the Volga, the Dnepr, the Volga-Don and Turkmen canals. For their sake, steel was poured, new devices and machines were employed. The start-up of each new grand project, the scheduling of the "great plan for the transformation of nature" [the diversion of the great Siberian rivers from the north, where they spill uselessly into the Arctic, to the south, where they would water the deserts of Central Asia—H.R.], and even the skyscrapers of Moscow were supposed to be perceived as landmarks, as one more practical step along the path to communism. The fact that these communist structures were built in large part by the hands of convicts hardly bothered the ideologues of the country. Many contemporaries did not know it, and those who knew were obliged to look upon the construction sites as places of reeducation in the spirit of communism.

The appearance of the grand communist projects caught the theoreticians unaware. They had suddenly to revise academic courses and curricula and to plan new subjects of research. The Institute of Economics of the Academy of Sciences sponsored a theoretical conference in June 1950 on "The Gradual Transition from Socialism to

Communism." It was agreed to concentrate on the elements of communism already present rather than to project the characteristics of the future communist society. The conference concluded that the Soviet Union possessed all the necessary and sufficient conditions for the building of communism in the nearest future.[8] There was much discussion of the forms of transition and of the mode of distribution of goods—for example, when and in what order the gratuitous distribution of food products and services would take place.[9]

Neither this conference nor other gatherings like it even approximately realized a tangible conception of the construction of communism or a conception of the promising development of a Soviet economic and political system. There was a lot of talk to the effect that Soviet society should strengthen its economic base, its system of social relations, its cultural life, etc., but the question how precisely this strengthening and development might be realized remained open. After the appearance of Stalin's brochure "Economic Problems of Socialism in the USSR" (1951), all comment on the subject began to mimic his contribution, and genuine discussion of the problem ceased.

Much more interesting things were going on at this time among the practitioners of socialism than among its theorists. A dramatic shift took place in the mood of the workers, a change of focus from material demands to pretensions concerning production and even politics. These pretensions generally took the form of dissatisfaction with the organization of production. The workers felt that they were reduced to a strictly subordinate role of carrying out orders. There was a lot of criticism of the conduct of workers' meetings. "At the meetings it is impossible to discuss matters in a businesslike fashion. Administrative pressure often preempts a genuine discussion."[10] Resolutions at such meetings were usually passed in a perfunctory fashion, more or less as follows: "not content with what we have achieved, we must raise the productivity of labor and labor discipline," "our results are good, but we are not content with our success," etc.[11] The workers were dissatisfied with the meetings, which they considered practically useless, because no one listened to their opinions. "The whole problem is that they don't listen to us. A lot of chatter and little business. I go to the meetings, but the waste of time makes me angry." "I have at times been active . . . , but I now feel that my efforts to improve work have been wasted, and willy-nilly I have given it all up, I have stopped going to the meetings. They don't listen to us."[12]

Workers speaking critically of the factory administration were sometimes subjected to harassment. They said that it was useless to bring up the shortcomings of factories in city or regional organizations, that the economic administrators would always find defenders. According to a widespread opinion, "There is only one hope, to write to the Central Committee or to Comrade Shkiriatov [chairman of the Party Control Commission]. They will help."[13]

This passive reaction was nevertheless not universal. The early 1950s witnessed the development of a new kind of initiative in which workers sought to establish the independence of their position on the production line and to assert their role in the collective management of the factory. A movement to safeguard the maintenance of plant and equipment arose among them, and they began to imitate the old Russian handicraft masters who affixed their personal mark to their products. These new initiatives did not last long, however. They were condemned as inexpedient, as if they impinged on the responsibility of the factory management.[14]

A proposal to develop new forms of factory administration and communications networks encountered more resistance yet. In January 1950 G.M. Malenkov's secretariat received a letter from the head of the financial planning department of one of the divisions of the Ministry of Communications in Latvia, I.M. Stulnikov. The author developed in detail his ideas on electing a collective leadership in industrial management.

> Experience shows that in our time, when the political consciousness and the professional qualities of the greater part of the Soviet people have reached an unprecedented level of maturity, the principle of one-man management established in economic administrations, organizations, and enterprises has ceased to justify itself. In a number of instances it has even brought undeniable harm to the interests of the state. It is well known that there are not a few economic administrators whose love of their duties has seriously turned their heads. Others wrap themselves in their exclusive authority and do not take account of anyone's opinion or advice. It is time to engage in a fundamental reconstruction of the economic administration, to base it on completely different, more democratic principles.[15]

The author envisaged a system administered by elected committees, a hierarchy of economic soviets from bottom to top, from individual enterprises to the ministerial level.[16] In fact, he proposed to retain but modify the principle of one-man management by requiring that the decisions of the head of an administrative unit be approved by an elected committee also attached to the office.[17]

Stulnikov's ideas did not meet with approval in the Central Committee, and not only on account of the debatable nature of his particular proposals. The question was one of principle. The logic of the economic administration, founded on the principle of rigidly fixed responsibility and an elaborately structured hierarchy, was fundamentally incompatible with the idea of decentralization in any form whatever. Stulnikov's proposals are interesting not only from the view point of their possible application to actual administrative practice but above all as evidence of the development of practical economic thought, seeking, within the bounds of the permissible, ways and means of reforming the economic mechanism, the conservatism of which impeded the optimal functioning of the economy. Only a handful of people at the time made suggestions of this kind. The bulk of the public remained as indifferent as usual to such questions.

It is interesting in this respect to analyze people's reactions when asked about their attitudes to the difficulties and shortcomings of the time. At the beginning of the 1950s, the journalist Anatolii Zlobin described them. "Talking with various people, I repeated a single question: 'What interferes with your work, the work of your factory?' To my surprise, a lot of people answered more or less, 'Why, nothing, what might interfere?' "[18] This response was no mere coincidence. It was the reaction to an unexpected question. It reflected the distinctive outlook of the society, which habitually sought to explain its difficulties by reference to personal factors. Not the usual "Who is guilty?" But rather, "What interferes?" When the conventional question—"Who is guilty?"—was posed, a tangible person could be envisaged. The answer to the question who was guilty was simple and simple-minded, and hence it was a customary question. But behind the surprising question—"What interferes?"—was an abstract social phenomenon. To answer this question required an analysis of the content of public life in general, a search for its sore spots, the nexus of problems of development and prospects of their solution. It inevitably raised the question "what to do?" It was a question that required thought, a problem that could not be resolved merely by replacing personnel, bad leaders by good ones. Here was an idea out of the usual context of discourse, and this fact explains the inadequate reaction of the everyday mentality to the enigmatic nature of the question.

A distinguishing feature of the Soviet system from the 1930s to the 1950s is that it was allegedly always open to criticism. The phrase "criticism and self-criticism" was among the most hackneyed elements of propaganda. And it was not merely a propagandistic trick. The constant search for particular flaws, alternating with more transient campaigns against enemies of the people, not only directed public emotions into prepared channels but increased both the dynamism and the stability of the system itself. The regime used the manipulation of the public mood as a mechanism for overcoming crisis situations. The system did not allow highly charged mass emotions to form a scheme of specific claims that might damage the foundations of the governing body. It is not surprising, therefore, that a lack of constructive ideas is one of the characteristic features of the group grievances of this period. The ability of the regime to maintain control of the emotional disposition of the society secured the government, protected it from unpredictable impulses from below. In this respect the state managed the public mentality quite successfully. It did not, however, always provide a positive program that elicited good practical performance.

This point is easily seen, for example, in the development of intraparty politics. The Nineteenth Party Congress of 1952 introduced a series of changes in the party rules, the document that governed the conduct of every communist. The chief purpose of these changes was to strengthen control of party organs over rank-and-file members. If formerly the communist "had the right," now he "had the obligation" to communicate all shortcomings in the work of anyone, and failure to do so constituted a "crime before the party."[19] A regular crusade against shortcomings began in the party. Organized in such strict conditions, however, it turned in fact into a process of the displacement of guilt onto the shoulders of the humble and the defenseless. The local party workers, afraid of being found guilty of insufficient vigilance or of criminal inactivity, tried to reinsure themselves, and the regional parties whipped up a veritable orgy of investigations of personnel. Even *Pravda* expressed alarm at massive proceedings of excessive zeal.[20]

But that was the limit. At that point the mechanism of control threatened to turn from an instrument of political stabilization into an instrument of destabilization. If there was anything that inhibited the further escalation of the situation, it was the resistance from below, where in addition to the laws of the system, the laws of humanity, in spite of everything, continued to work as well.

The historian Iu.P. Sharapov recalls how in the fall of 1949, when he was a graduate student at Moscow State University, his father was repeatedly arrested.

> They called me to the party committee and then to the faculty party meeting. They threatened to expel me from the party. But when they

said so aloud, my old prewar schoolmate, also a graduate student and a veteran of the war, stood up in one of the back rows, went to the speaker's podium, and said a word in my defense. And when the Krasnopresnensk party met on my case, two more people defended me, the secretary of the faculty party bureau, Pavel Volobuev, and a member of the provincial party committee, the director of the provincial railroads, General Karpov. And so they left me in the party.[21]

The occasion described by Iu.P. Sharapov occurred in the party bureau of the history faculty at Moscow State University when the party secretary there was P.V. Volobuev (now a member of the Academy of Sciences). This event was not unique, although Volubuev was not always supported by a majority of the faculty. Nevertheless, the special significance of party membership in personnel decisions even in those circumstances of acute vigilance could help people, capable and worthy people whose biography was tainted by association with persons under suspicion or in the camps. As Volubuev recalls, "I simply spoke out against going to extremes. For example, the extremes in the campaign against cosmopolitanism. Now, where the hullabaloo over cosmopolitanism was concerned, it continued, including in my own reports to the party. But not a single person in the faculty was fired, although blacklists of a sort existed."[22] When I asked Pavel Vasilievich why he took a position that might have brought him very unpleasant consequences, he said, "You must understand, I was no hero. I was sufficiently severe and demanding. And I acted in accord with the laws of common sense. It is simply that we must leave a place in life for personal moral choice, however difficult the situation."[23]

The features of this atmosphere were not all uniform. One person, risking his career or his head, spoke out for a close friend or for someone utterly unknown to him; another person publicly repudiated relatives, teachers, and mentors. The range of choice was not great, but the capacity for moral resistance persisted—and all the more because of the war, which left a legacy of the brotherhood of the front and of reciprocal rescue. It helped people to live—and to survive. The former soldiers were the first to emerge from these new trenches, as did, in their own way, for example, Valentin Ovechkin and Alexander Tvardovskii. It was through the efforts of these two that the novel *Raionnye budni* (District Routine—everyday life in the provinces) appeared. It was the first harbinger of spring in that new genre of postwar literature destined to become the disturber of public peace.

The publication of *Raionnye budni* began in *Novyi mir* in the fall of 1952. It was then republished in *Pravda*. The public response was enormous. "Readers had not seen such writing," recalls Nikolai Atarov. "It was about the restoration of Leninist norms of democracy, the style of leadership, a proper relationship between peasant and plowland, between the collective farm and the state. The issues of *Pravda* were passed from hand to hand."[24]

Using the story of a single region, Ovechkin in fact dealt with the problems of the rural economy nationwide, raising questions of national significance. The work was received as a comment on the conduct of the party, and the honest dialogue in it was perceived "not as literature but as a letter to the Central Committee."[25] The questions that Ovechkin raised—on administrative practice, on material incentives, on the conflicts of duty and conscience—were obviously not new. What was new was his unequivocal treatment of them. Ovechkin opened a vent for more candid public expression. As one of his colleagues recognized, "Reading Ovechkin, writers realized that they could no longer write in the old way."[26]

Ovechkin cited those problems that lay on the surface and directed public attention to them. While writers broke lances over his novel, and several party workers summoned the author to account for his "libeling" of party leaders, another kind of literature, a good deal bolder, was quietly conceived in the background. Vladimir Dudintsev began early in the 1950s to plot his novel *Ne edinym khlebom* (Not by Bread Alone). "Stalin was still alive," he recalled later. "I wrote, and I worried about the GULAG. I was afraid, but I worked out a cipher for secret notes. I was qualitatively free."[27]

Thus the grimmest of all the postwar years ended, if not with hope, then with the anticipation of some new ray of light. Nothing in everyday life spoke of the looming changes, but they were in a sense already pre-programmed. Stalin was alive but ill and increasingly decrepit. He was not so able as formerly to control the conduct of his entourage, and rival cliques had already begun to scramble for the legacy of his authority. The economic decisions made after the war had driven the country into a blind alley of superprograms. The grand construction projects were a heavy burden on the state budget. Economic policy followed its same old course of heavy industrialization and in fact slowed the process of scientific and technical development. The social programs so important to assist a people emerging from a war were kept to a minimum. The practice of price reductions had evoked great public approval, but the standard of living had scarcely improved.

The village was on the verge of ruin. "If we look for the most tragic time for the Soviet village—in terms of hopelessness and outrage of every human sentiment," as Ales Adamovich wrote, "it falls, in my opinion, somewhere in the years from 1946 through 1953."[28] The constantly expanding zone of forced labor, divided between the collective farm on the one hand and the GULAG on the other, was a potential source of social tension. The situation of the authorities began to resemble that of people sitting on a volcano inside of which the energy of an enormously destructive force gathered and accumulated.

The political repression of 1948–1952 did not destroy the potential forces of destabilization. It simply rendered them more massive, although the negative reaction remained for the time being latent. The repressions saved the regime for a while from the pressures of criticism from below, but they could not prevent the slide of the country down the slope of crisis. Worse yet, the repressions complicated the process of overcoming the elements of crisis, as they destroyed or deformed the constructive social forces born of the war, those that might have taken charge of social renewal. The mood of the masses was dominated by the syndrome of expectancy. The only way of overcoming the crisis that was nearly certain to occur in these circumstances was the path of reform from above. And the only barrier standing in the way was the figure of the *vozhd'*/leader. In this sense, Stalin was doomed, although in fact the situation resolved itself in the most natural fashion. Stalin died on 5 March 1953.

PART IV

THE THAW

Chapter 15

Without Stalin: The New Public Atmosphere

Two hundred people gathered around the Mausoleum. It was cold. Everyone thought that the sarcophagus with Stalin's body would be carried out through the main entrance. Nobody noticed the wooden screens to the left of the Mausoleum, electric lights burning over them.

Late in the evening a covered military truck approached the Mausoleum from the right. Someone shouted: "They are moving him!" The soldiers carried a glass coffin through a side door of the Mausoleum and loaded it onto the truck. And then we saw behind the screens soldiers digging a grave. There were no cameras or TV reporters around the Mausoleum at that time.[1]

These are the journalist Viktor Strelkov's memories of the second burial of Stalin [when he was expelled from the Mausoleum, 1961—H.R.], not at all like the one that took place in 1953. *Pravda* announced Stalin's death on 6 March. Ilia Ehrenburg recalls his feelings that day: "I began to wonder: what will become of us now? But I could not think. I felt what many of my compatriots likely felt at the time: I was numb."[2]

And then there was Trubnaia Square in Moscow [where a procession gathered to walk to the Hall of Columns in order to view the body—H.R.]. Poet Yevgenii Yevtushenko was there.

The breathing of tens of thousands of people huddled together formed such a thick white cloud above the crowd that the naked limbs of the swaying trees were reflected in it. It was an eerie, fantastic spectacle. People gathering in the rear of this crowd put ever more pressure on it. The crowd turned into a terrible maelstrom. Suddenly I felt that I was slowly, involuntarily moving. The crowd was a veritable organism. I lifted my feet, and the crowd carried me along. I was for a long time afraid to put my feet down. The crush of people grew ever tighter and tighter. I was saved only by my height. Short people suffocated and died. We were confined on one side by the walls of buildings and on the other side by a row of military trucks.[3]

Ilia Ehrenburg describes the scene at the Hall of Columns.

I stood with the writers in a circle of honorary pallbearers. Stalin lay embalmed in solemn attire without any signs of what the doctors had described [stroke—H.R.], covered with flowers and stars. People filed past, many of them cried, women lifted their children, mournful music mixed with sobbing. People were weeping on the street as well. Shouts rang out, and people burst into the Hall of Columns. They told of the tragedy on Trubnaia Square. Additional detachments of police were brought from Leningrad. I don't think there ever was such a funeral.

I was not sorry for the god who had died from cerebral hemorrhage at seventy-three years of age as if he were not a god but a conventional mortal, but I was afraid. What would happen now? I feared the worst.[4]

Many people felt such sentiments when Stalin died. "It was a shattering event," recalled A.D. Sakharov. "Everyone understood that something must soon change, but no one knew in what direction. We feared the worst (although what could be worse?). But a lot of people who had no illusions about Stalin feared a general breakdown, civil conflict, a new wave of massive political repression, even civil war."[5]

The principal element of the atmosphere of those days was not hope of changes for the better but fears of the worst. It took people a long time to emerge from the shock of Stalin's death. This situation was more favorable for the leadership than the demand for urgent reforms that is usual during crises of power. In this case, the crisis of power on the surface was the function of Stalin's death, and both the impossibility of remedying it and the unimaginable consequences of it gave birth to an altogether natural thought: leave everything as it is. The people would approve any initiatives of the post-Stalin leadership so long as they did not make matters worse, but on the condition that the new leaders must act in the spirit of Stalin's successors. That is, they would continue at least the outward appearance of his political course. In reality, this course meant that they would consciously proceed along the same hopelessly unpromising paths. It was not accidental, then, that the leading positions came to be occupied by a group of people (Malenkov, Beria, Khrushchev) committed in the long run to reforms but in the short term to reassurance and iner-tia—to not rocking the ship of state. Both because of a certain confu-sion in their ranks and because of the sentiments of the bulk of the population, they proceeded cautiously.

During the several months following Stalin's death, the Central Committee, the editorial boards of newspapers, and the local organs of power received thousands of letters and telegrams expressing the sincerest condolences and the indispensable demand to perpetuate the memory of the departed leader. One of the more frequent vari-ants of this demand was the building of a pantheon, for the sake of which the grieving citizens proposed to expand Red Square at the expense of the Kremlin walls, the GUM department store, and several other architectural monuments.[6] Among other popular ideas were the proposal to establish an Order of Stalin, to open Stalin museums in various Soviet cities, and to write books and make films about him.[7] There were some altogether original ideas: to construct a "fountain of tears," to establish and confer on Stalin a decoration entitled "Hero of Political Labor," or to move International Women's Day, traditionally 8 March, to some date further removed from the day of Stalin's death.[8] It is obvious that in these circumstances any talk of Stalin's crimes was not merely untimely but dangerous, at least for the supreme authorities.

Stalin's death alone introduced substantial adjustments in the rela-tionship of people and government. As the chief link between them had disappeared, so did the harmony of their interests, and thus there was a progressive alienation of the two (which reached its apogee in the time of L.I. Brezhnev). The simplest way out of the situation would have been the acquisition of a new leader. The return to such a super-human authoritarian system seemed, however, hardly possible. The earthly god had ceased to exist as an ordinary mortal, but this fact did not for a long time sink into the minds of many people.

The journalist Iu.S. Apenchenko, then a student at Moscow Uni-versity, recalls that after the tragedy on Trubnaia Square, he went to the university infirmary. "It was obligatory to have one's temperature taken before seeing the doctor. An elderly nurse approached with a thermometer and asked, 'Why are you so disheveled?' I said that I was at the Hall of Columns, that there was a great crush of people. 'And why did you go there? Have you not seen dead people?' This was the first person for whom Stalin was simply a dead person."[9]

It was as if Stalin's death had conferred on him human dimen-sions. It was an irony of fate: Stalin as human seemed superfluous. On the day after the funeral, *New York Times* correspondent Harrison Salisbury was walking around central Moscow. "Half a dozen workmen were busy at the Hall of Columns, some on the little balcony at the second floor, some on the sidewalk below. They were taking down Stalin's great portrait. One workman said, 'Careful there.' Another replied, 'Never mind. We'll not be needing this one again.' "[10]

The masses' perception of Stalin as a human being changed their attitude to his successors, who also became mere mortals. The authorities were deprived of their divine aura, but not completely: although they began to be judged as fallible humans, they were still expected to dole out gifts as formerly. This new outlook was not at first appreciated there on high, where they relied more on the accumulated credit of trust and failed to consider that such credit must actually be earned. The authorities' sober analysis of the situation was also impeded by disagreements among themselves. The struggle for power took precedence over immediate economic and political decisions.

In the first period after Stalin's death (March to June 1953), the most active of the new leaders was L.P. Beria. Appointed chief of the combined administrations of internal affairs and state security, he proposed a series of measures designed to reform these offices: to transfer the camps and labor colonies from the Ministry of Internal Affairs to the Ministry of Justice (with the exception of camps for political prisoners); to limit the use of forced labor in the economy; to terminate the expensive and unprofitable grand construction projects of communism (hydroelectric dams, etc.); to reexamine the fraudulent political affairs (purges) of recent years; and to abolish the use of torture in criminal investigations.[11] His colleagues also tended to agree with his proposal to reconsider the bases of Soviet nationalities policy in the non-Russian regions, where the practice of Russification had encountered increasingly strong resistance (in the Baltic republics and the western regions of Ukraine and Belorussia). After Beria's removal from the political arena, these proposals, extremely promising in their fundamentals, remained unrealized. The reason for his fall, however, must be sought not in his reformist ideas (in this respect he had no serious opponents). Rather it was something else that put his rivals on guard: his very activeness, his bold and independent initiatives, which were understood as his aspiration to seize exclusive power. That is what decided the fate of the marshal of the Lubianka [security policy headquarters—H.R.] in June of 1953.

After the arrest of Beria, initiative passed into the hands of G.M. Malenkov, and the leadership on the whole began to undertake some significant practical steps to formulate a new political and economic course. At a session of the Supreme Soviet in August 1953 Malenkov presented the fundamentals of his economic program. The heart of it was the idea of reorienting the economy from the priority of heavy industry to the priority of consumer goods. He proposed a sharp change of investment policy, turning special attention to the development of the rural economy and converting even heavy industrial enterprises to at least partial production of goods in popular demand. Thus the course of social spending was chosen, and it soon bore fruit in terms of goods, money, and living space.

Another key feature of the new economic program was the different approach to the production problem, a great part of which was aimed at bringing the agricultural economy out of protracted crisis. Several measures designed to raise the level of village life were given high priority: decreasing the agricultural tax, writing off tax arrears, increasing the size of the farmers' private garden plots, raising the price of compulsory procurement deliveries, and expanding the scale of the collective farm market.[12] The introduction of this complex of measures had an impact both political and economic. According to a letter of the village teacher M. Nikolaeva to N.S. Khrushchev, the newspaper reporting these new policies "was read until it fell apart, and the simple poor peasants said 'here is something for us.' "[13]

The measures undertaken in the so-called "struggle with bureaucratism," which had by the end of 1953 developed into a serious campaign, met with an entirely different reception. In one of the early post-Stalin gatherings of party workers and economic administrators, a meeting organized as usual for the traditional purpose of handing out demanding assignments, Malenkov made an unusual presentation. Fedor Burlatskii was present and recalls his impressions.

> The fundamental thrust of his speech was the struggle against bureaucratism "until its total destruction." Over and over he used such scathing phrases as "the degeneration of the organs of the state apparatus," "the escape of several organs of state from party control," "the complete neglect of the needs of the people," "bribery and dissipation of the moral temper of a communist," etc. And the persons present to hear this diatribe represented precisely the target of the thunderous attack. Bewilderment was mixed with dismay, dismay with fear, and fear with indignation. The end of the speech was followed by a deathly silence, which was interrupted by the lively, and I thought, jolly voice of Khrushchev, 'That is, of course, exactly right, Georgii Maksimilianovich, but the apparatus is our own support." And only then did long and lively applause break out.[14]

The fear of those present in the hall is fully understandable. Such expressions as those that Malenkov used could be perfectly plausibly understood as the signal to begin a new great purge. No one knew the real political position of the new leadership and its immediate intentions. This situation was characteristic of the years 1953–1955, when the ambivalence of the political line prompted a variety of prognoses, both entirely optimistic and far from reassuring. The leadership, lacking the confidence to define its position, accentuated this ambivalence. In the first months after Stalin's death not only were there no guarantees, above all of a political and legal nature, against a return to the past, but on a number of occasions there were distinct hints of a Stalinist revival.

In June 1954, for example, N.S. Khrushchev said at a Central Committee meeting that "the hope of several people for a change of the party's orientation, for a rejection of the policy of Stalin, is unjustified."[15] The likely reason for such a declaration might have been the authorities' fear of losing control over the situation, as the public reaction to the early post-Stalinist decisions gave grounds for such fears. The hopes for warming up the political climate were stimulated by the suppression of the purges fabricated during Stalin's last years and by rumors of the beginning of political rehabilitations. The politically sensitive part of the society could not resist hoping that there was real substance behind the change of both the tone and the content of the press, where the formerly militant attacks on such persons as cosmopolitans, enemies of the people, foreign spies, etc., had gradually disappeared. In fact, the terms themselves soon ceased to be used. This adjustment was perceived as a modest reassurance that an element of cautious self-expression was now safe. The same process had a more conspicuous impact in literature, and publications began to appear that were utterly unlike those so familiar just a year earlier.

The last issues of *Novyi mir* for 1953 published Vera Panova's novel, *Vremena goda* (Seasons of the Year) and the article of Vladimir Pomerantsev "On Truthfulness in Literature." In 1954, the journal opened its pages to the critical articles of Fedor Abramov, Mikhail Lifshits, Mark Shcheglov, and others.[16] This was the beginning of that *Novyi mir* tradition that defined so much of the cultural life of the 1950s and 1960s. Its inspiration was the great ethical tradition of Russian literature, and especially the moral quests of the Russian intelligentsia, the search for truth and the meaning of life. The conscious or subconscious sense of the falsehood in which more than one generation of Soviet people had lived prompted the primary demand, the demand for the truth. This demand had not yet turned onto the past, as that prospect was still closed, but aspired to understand the present, not waiting for explanations from above but seeking on its own a new vision, one without preconceptions. Naturally, this process, initiated by post-Stalinist literature, could not be confined within literary bounds. The insistence on the discussion of truthfulness was prepared by the whole recent development of public opinion. But for that very reason, the writers and critics who had first taken up the problem immediately became the focus of public attention.

A great number of readers entered the discussion of truthfulness in literature initiated by Vladimir Pomerantsev. Many expressed their thanks to the author. As N. Shchennikov of Kuibyshev wrote, "Here is a bold, truthful, just comment, unprecedented in our Soviet literature, of a simple honest man who long ago observed the outrageous nature [of our life], grew indignant, felt the passionate wish to express himself, but could not. Perhaps he knew too little, perhaps he did not find the words. And here, finally, it has poured out! Many, many thanks! Everyone who thinks and loves the truth will appreciate it."[17]

Vladimir Dudintsev spoke of Pomerantsev's article at a writers' conference. "In my opinion the greatest service of Comrade Pomerantsev consists in the fact that he for the first time has shouted out the need for truthfulness, has appealed to our conscience."[18] The inertia of untruthfulness was, according to Dudintsev, not only a problem of literature but a sickness of society as a whole.[19] The problematical nature of the issue raised by Pomerantsev was contagious, and it soon stimulated an oblique approach to the question of overcoming the legacy of the past, to the problem of public guilt and public responsibility. The chief consideration here was the conscious aspiration to set out on the difficult path of self-examination in both a public and a private dimension. Typical of readers' reactions to Pomerantsev's article was this comment in one letter: "Having read the article 'On Truthfulness in Literature,' I intend to take a new attitude to work, a bolder and more dedicated attitude."[20]

But here was no mere question of personal opinion, of personal choice alone. One reader, G. Shchukin, shared his doubts in a letter to Pomerantsev.

> The truthfulness of the writer does not depend on the question whether he has understood its necessity or not. I am somehow sure that neither your article nor many others like it will change the nature of our literature. So long as our literature is afflicted by a premeditated

position assigning it the task of educating public opinion and turning the role of the writer into the attainment of fame and fortune, so long as any premeditated position prevails here, then there will be no literature of which we can be proud. The whole question, however, has more to do with politics than with literature.[21]

The controversy that Pomerantsev's article had initiated soon developed into a discussion of public problems, acquired a clearly political nuance, and revealed issues that had been maturing in the minds of thinking people for some time. Judging by readers' letters, many of them were especially concerned not to allow the discussion to degenerate to the level of the material issues of everyday life. In the words of a Moscow student, "The behavior of a schoolchild who gives his mother the right change after his trip to the store cannot be considered truthfulness. Truthfulness we must understand not only as the proper reflection of life today, but we must consider those problems that are perhaps not evident to everyone."[22]

Our contemporary reader of Pomerantsev's article, accustomed to the battle of the newspapers since the dawn of glasnost, might well not understand the heat of the passions engulfing the author, the journal, and its editor, Alexander Tvardovskii. In fact, at first glance Pomerantsev's article, and those like it in other journals, contained nothing that contradicted the officially pronounced ideological and political principles. The government itself at that time voiced the summons to struggle against the "embellishment of life," against the whitewashing of problems. Tvardovskii emphasized in his own letter to the Central Committee (July 1954) that "*Novyi mir* follows no special editorial policy apart from the desire to work in the spirit of the well-known directives of the party in questions of literature. The editors are obliged to abide by the party's guidelines on the necessity of boldly criticizing our [Soviet] shortcomings, including those in literature, in proportion to their ability and understanding, honestly and in good conscience."[23]

The order of the Central Committee, however, originating as a resolution of the presidium of the Union of Soviet Writers—"On the Errors of *Novyi mir*" (August 1954)—made it clear that Tvardovskii and his journal had mistaken their mandate and worked in too critical a fashion.[24] This was the first warning—and not only to *Novyi mir* but to all who were willing to share the new ethical principles of the journal.

A similar fate overtook writers addressing another subject, bureaucracy. Unlike official criticism of bureaucratism, confined in general to subsidiary issues—red tape, deception, etc.—the literary treatment advanced at once to a qualitatively different level, to the problem of the *nomenklatura* itself—that is, the party's control of appointments and nominations. One of the first examples was Leonid Zorin's play *Gosti* (Guests) in the journal *Theater* (1954, No. 2). One of the leading characters of the play was utterly unlike the boring but generally inoffensive and perfunctory bureaucrat. The chief antagonist of the hero says to him: "I know that you and your friends are not just paper pushers. I know that you are very capable, and, of course, it threatens me."[25] And he prepares to struggle against his fate: "I know that I am no genius but an ordinary middle-aged man already somewhat defeated by life. Still, I have not forgotten how to think, to feel, to hope. There is in this life one special law: guests come and go, but the host, the boss, remains."[26] But who is here the guest and who the host? The author leaves this question open. Zorin's play nevertheless put the party ideologues on guard. A whole series of devastating commentaries appeared, the common tone of which clearly indicated a well organized campaign. They hastened to declare the play "slanderous," "ideologically vicious," "false," "suffering from an absence of real-life conflicts," a "deceptive exposé," etc.[27]

Zorin's play served nevertheless as one of the seminal literary productions giving rise to a new form of public initiative—campaigns of letters addressed to the leadership. One of these letters was written by Andrei Sakharov, who later recalled:

> I don't remember exactly what it was about, but the play, written in the midst of the "thaw," offended the new Soviet party bureaucracy. . . . It was not worth my getting started in my epistolary habit [his letter to Khrushchev in defense of Zorin—E.Z.], it was not appropriate, but I yielded to impulse. On the other hand, I had to begin somewhere. And to speak out against the "new class," to use Djilas's terminology, was not so bad. This was my first letter to Khrushchev and my first letter outside my own field of work. I hardly remember how it ended. It seems that I got some kind of formal reply from the Central Committee.[28]

These were the first glimmerings of a new social consciousness formed independently of the old, prepackaged style of thinking, when it seemed that everything handed down from above or done at the instance of the authorities was irreproachably correct and infallible. It was a tough struggle, however, to reject all that had for so long been thus preordained, even to entertain doubts about it, and the new consciousness was full of paradoxes. There were divergences of attitudes, feelings of inner protest, lack of agreement between private opinion and official opinion. It may be that it was in the 1950s that private opinion emerged as a social phenomenon, an independent public opinion. It was in great part a response to a literature that, in spite of all the concerted attacks of official criticism, remained in the best sense of the term literature. It was a literature capable not only of affirming previously mastered values but of changing them as well, of subjecting them to doubt, of raising again the question what is true and what is false in this world.

An engineer, I. Efimov from Minsk, wrote to Alexander Tvardovskii:

> In February of this year I read the [critical] article of Bubennov on [Vasilii] Grossman's novel *Za pravoe delo* (For Justice). Not having enough time to read all of the new fiction, I have followed the rule not to waste time on those works given a negative evaluation in *Pravda*, and for thirty years I have not had occasion to put *Pravda*'s reviews to the test. . . . *Pravda* along with the classics of Marxism has formed not only our consciousness but our taste in the arts. So having read recently the devastating review of the novel *For Justice* not in some run-of-the-mill paper but in *Pravda*, and not by some anonymity but by a member of the editorial board of *Novyi mir*, which published it, was it worth my time to read an "ideologically vicious" novel of "gray" heroes? But wait. Vacationing recently in a sanatorium with a poor library, I picked up an issue of *Novyi mir* and began leafing through *For Justice*. Instead of merely leafing through it, I was soon unable to tear myself away from it except for meals and the obligatory sanatorium treatment. How is it that I, a middle-aged engineer, long a reader of fiction sanctioned by the authority of *Pravda*, was gripped by this insipid and brittle work and read it with satisfaction not once but twice? I can only explain it to myself by the fact that for the first time in many years I stumbled onto a book in which people are represented as they really are in life and not by some preconceived scheme of positive people and negative people.[29]

This was one characteristic position. As readers' letters demonstrate, however, far from everyone seemed ready to welcome the candid discussion initiated by literature and journalism in the 1950s. Fedor Abramov commented with his characteristic irony on this situation. "To write the truth is easier than to write untruth, but it is harder to publish it. But publishing it is not the most difficult thing. Harder yet is when your fellow writers and readers have grown up amid discreet silences and literary embellishments and, having become unaccustomed to the full truth, consider it inappropriate for art, consider it too stark, too crude and unvarnished, too damaging of the desirable impression."[30]

Some people were troubled, not being able to fit the new fictional characters into the categories of positive and negative. Some grew indignant, not finding in their reading the leading role of the party. For example, if the party played the leading role, then all obstacles should be surmountable. The party was viewed as the single force securing the necessary stability in society. One reader, exemplifying this attitude, wrote of Anatolii Zlobin's essay, "Mesiats v piatom raione" (A Month in District Five): "The author selects an isolated fact in the construction of a grand edifice and does not show the many other sides of the problem. Was there really at such a great construction site not one honest, principled communist? The essay altogether overlooks the party organization as an organ of supervision of the administration. And so it is not clear how in the end the poor state of affairs [described in the essay—H.R.] was remedied."[31]

The author of this and similar letters could imagine a remedy of such a situation only as a result of the intervention of the party organs. The leading role of the party was conceived as the presence of the party worker in the necessary place at the necessary time. As the party, in the conception of such people, was always on guard, any shortcomings, blunders, or mistakes looked like an annoying oversight of the vigilant party eye, an offensive but easily managed misunderstanding.

After 1953 the mass media began to show increased interest in readers' feedback. Some papers and journals began to reserve special columns for the publication of readers' letters. The volume of this correspondence began to be considered a matter of prestige. This new phenomenon reached massive proportions and was the subject of much imitation.

When the editor of the Voroshilovgrad Province [present name, Lugansk—H.R.] paper discovered that the editorial board had received fewer letters in 1953 than in 1952, he decided at once to correct matters. He assigned the correspondents to stir up twenty-five letters each. A witness describes what developed thereafter.

> The reporters got excited. They began to telephone the editorial offices one after the other. "Explain, please, the idea behind this new campaign." "On what subjects does the paper especially want letters?" And the editors answered: "On any subject whatever. It's not for publication, it's for keeping score." For three days, it was bedlam! The volume of letters grew rapidly. Figuring out the real idea behind this bureaucratic impulse, some of the reporters resorted to imaginative methods. One of them in the Belovodsk District procured twenty-six letters in a day. They were all written in the same hand and on the same subject. "We are

repairing the tractors ahead of schedule." "The quota was overfulfilled by cooperative efforts."[32]

The public began to imitate these methods, and it often took strange forms.

In February 1955 the elections to the supreme soviets of the union republics and the localities took place. As usual, these elections offered a single candidate per position. If the form of the elections thus continued without any change of procedure, a considerable change took place in the behavior of the electorate. Observers from the Central Committee reported that several candidates to the Supreme Soviet of the Russian Federation "received a substantial number of negative votes," and "several candidates of rural and village soviets were rejected" by the voters.[33] Comments had sometimes been scrawled on the ballots beside a candidate's name, for example "aristocrat," "bureaucrat," or "undeserving."[34] The Central Committee compiled accounts of the longer comments. There were positive remarks among them. "I gladly vote for the might of our beloved Fatherland." "Long live peace throughout the world."[35] The upper echelons of the party were interested, however, chiefly in comments of the other kind. Not long before the elections, in February 1955, G.M. Malenkov was replaced as premier of the government by N.A. Bulganin. The people reacted at once to this news, using the anonymity of their ballot. "They gobbled up Malenkov, who is next?" "I vote against the reorganization of the government. If Malenkov couldn't cope with it, then Bulganin can't handle it either."[36]

As the comments on the electoral ballots make clear, however, the people were less interested in intrigues in the corridors of power than in their own material problems. "What kind of faith can the voters have in the government when as long ago as 1930 the newspapers promised that people in the Soviet Union would soon cease to have to live in basements? This is deception. Until the present day people continue to take shelter in underground lodging in dreadful poverty. At the same time we have a new bourgeois class worse than the former landowners." "Everywhere it is said and written that we are prosperous and have everything, while in fact we have nothing. It is empty chatter. . . . What has become of consumer goods? We have to stand in line all day. Are we under blockade? The truth is that abroad they have everything, and here at home we have only rubbish."[37] In Leningrad, Chkalov, Vladimir, Cheliabinsk, and other cities there were cases of voters refusing to vote "on the grounds of poor living conditions and the indifference of local Soviet organs to the problem."[38]

The dissatisfaction sprang from the obvious gap between the standard of living of the simple people and that of those called the servants of the people, that is, the party workers, deputies, and other privileged strata of the population. This reaction reflects the sense of social injustice and the universal aspiration of the common Russian masses to implement the "black repartition" (*chernyi peredel'*), that is, to take from the rich and give to the poor. At the same time this antagonism of the simple people to the elite illustrates in everyday form the conflict that Leonid Zorin described in the play *Gosti*. If the line between guests and hosts or bosses remained unclear in the play, for the people there was no doubt whatever about it. The real hosts or bosses were the so-called servants of the people.

There is an opinion that the years between the death of Stalin and the Twentieth Party Congress (1956) were a kind of interlude, when the society was more or less stationary. Judging by developments on the surface of Soviet life, it seems so. A more perceptive view finds the beginnings of great changes as, recalling his own feelings, Ilia Ehren-burg described them.

> The years 1954–1955 seem a tense prologue in a book of stormy escapades, unexpected turning points, dramatic events. However, it was not that way. In my personal life that time was not at all dull. My heart thawed out, and it was as if I began to live anew. These were not colorless years in the life of the country. The beginning of the just evaluation of the injustices of the past was not accidental. It did not depend either on good intentions or on the temperament of one or another of the political figures. Critical thought simply spilled out, stimulating the wish to find out about one thing, to examine another. The 1940s were gradually liberated from preconceived characterizations fastened on them from adolescence, and adolescents learned to judge cautiously.[39]

The journalist Anatolii Zlobin, considering some years ago the question why people prefer to avoid the painful problems of reality, confirmed the beginning of a new public consciousness during these years. "We began to speak of our shortcomings at full voice."[40]

Chapter 16

The Repudiation of the GULAG

The movement toward an open society, some signs of which could be seen in the 1950s, was a response both to elemental urges and to conscious political decisions made at the time. Among the latter the most important was undoubtedly the decision to liberate and rehabilitate political prisoners. Even years later, this was the development remembered by contemporaries (above all by the intelligentsia) not only as the chief political step of the post-Stalinist leadership but one that in some fashion expiated its past and future sins. At the time it seemed that the doors of the prisons and the camps were opened exclusively by the goodwill of the authorities. This fact seemed so dramatically obvious that few people considered the real reasons behind such a decisive step.

The question of the number of Stalin's victims is still disputed among scholars and journalists, and the figures vary from several million to tens of millions.[1] If we consider only the political prisoners, then our best approach to a realistic figure is the work of V.P. Popov, whose estimates are based on the records of the Ministry of Internal Affairs. Popov calculates that a total of 4.1 million political prisoners were detained between 1921 and 1953.[2] The gross population of the camps, colonies, and prisons (that is, the GULAG as a whole) at the time of Stalin's death in March 1953 was 2,526,000 people serving time for various kinds of crimes. This was the figure reported by L.P. Beria to the Presidium of the Central Committee on 26 March 1953.[3] Here was a whole society living as if in another state, one to which Alexander Solzhenitsyn assigned the special name GULAG Archipelago, the name of an amazing country, "geographically distributed as an archipelago, though psychologically frozen into a continent—an almost invisible, almost intangible country inhabited by convicts. The archipelago was sculpted into a strip of dots on the map surrounded by another country into whose cities it penetrated and over whose streets it hovered, and still few people guessed its existence, though many had heard of it vaguely. Only its inhabitants knew all about it."[4]

This state within a state operated at an ever increasing financial loss. The GULAG did not pay for itself. The low cost of convict labor was obvious, but the productivity of labor working under such conditions was far from high. The average cost of maintaining convict labor on a construction site, for example, was higher than the average wage of free laborers.[5] In view of the fact that the maintenance of the camps and colonies did not pay the costs of the exploitation of convict labor, the GULAG received subsidies every year from the state budget. In 1952 this subsidy amounted to 16.4 percent of the cost of operation; in the first half of 1953, to 10.8 percent of cost.[6]

Moreover, the GULAG represented not only economic losses. In the course of time it became a source of social tension. The Ministry of Internal Affairs reported "massive disobedience" as well as revolts and uprisings in the camps and colonies in 1953–1954.[7] The most significant of these in the summer of 1953 occurred in special camp No. 2 in Norilsk and in special camp No. 6 in Vorkuta. In May and June 1954, the greatest uprising in the GULAG system occurred in special camp No. 4 in Karaganda Province (the Kengir uprising in Kazakhstan). The situation acquired an explosive character, and the authorities could not fail to take it into account.

In addition, the new leadership of the country had to consider the factor of international prestige. The image of a democratic country, as the whole Soviet press represented the Soviet state, was hardly compatible with the enormous army of political prisoners, which not even openly despotic countries maintained on such a scale. Moreover, rehabilitation of political prisoners might bring a great political gain by enhancing faith in the authorities both inside the country and in the international arena. It must be admitted that in spite of the urgent necessity of the amnesty and rehabilitations, they represented a principled departure from the policy of the past few decades. The fact of initiative from on high prompted by considerations of common sense obscured for a time disagreements and antagonism within the ruling circles.

The first reforms of the GULAG system did not affect political prisoners. Beria took the initiative on 27 March 1953 to declare a broad amnesty that liberated 1,181,264 people from prisons and camps.[8] It included those sentenced for five years or less—that is, for nonpolitical crimes, typically for theft—and encompassed many former collective farmers and women with children. Of course, among so enormous a number of people there was naturally a substantial group of common criminals, and local authorities soon began to complain of disturbances and crimes associated with their sudden appearance in conventional society. Thus according to the Amur Province party committee, long lines of former convicts on their way home pillaged several snack bars (*bufety*) at railroad stations along their route. At one of these they chased away the police detachment and held the whole station in their hands for over two hours, forcing the authorities to resort to firearms to restore order.[9] "A mood of panic provoked by the sharp increase in instances of violence committed by the criminal element prompted among a substantial part of the population a good deal of dissatisfaction with the policy of amnestying clearly dissolute and criminal types."[10]

There was a completely different reaction, especially in intelligentsia circles, to the decision to stop the purges and start the rehabilitations of those condemned in the fabricated affairs of the postwar years. In April 1953 the rehabilitation of those implicated in the doctors' plot took place, and the Central Committee decision of 1952 to proceed against the Mingrelian nationalist organization in Georgia was canceled. In September 1953, an order of the Presidium of the Supreme Soviet abolished the special tribunals of the Ministry of Internal Affairs and other extrajudicial purge organs (the infamous troikas), which had in the recent past handed out punishments without any judicial investigation or procedure.

In 1954 the process of rehabilitation of those involved in the political trials of the late 1940s and early 1950s began. On 30 April the Supreme Court rehabilitated people implicated in the "Leningrad affair."[11] From 1954 to 1 January 1956 the Party Control Committee restored to party membership more than 170 persons who had been expelled during the Leningrad affair.[12] A review of the criminal culpability of the members of the Jewish Antifascist Committee was instituted in 1955, after which the military collegium of the Supreme Court rescinded the sentence imposed on those convicted.

On the other hand, not one of the political trials of the 1930s was subjected to similar investigation, and only a few of the accused in these trials were rehabilitated in the 1950s and 1960s, while the chief among them (G.E. Zinoviev, L.V. Kamenev, N.I. Bukharin, A.I. Rykov, and others) were rehabilitated only in 1988 and 1989. The distinguishing feature of the rehabilitations of the 1950s was the refusal to review any of the party purges from the 1930s. The party spoke of the violation of socialist legality, of Leninist norms of party life and of particular abuses, but the principal responsibility for the illegal acts and palpable crimes was ascribed by tradition either to the security organs or to individual persons in the leadership. Between the death of Stalin and the Twentieth Party Congress (February 1956), the Party Control Committee rehabilitated 5,456 previously expelled party members "on the grounds of unfounded political accusations" and reinstated them as members.[13]

After the Twentieth Party Congress, when the process of rehabilitations acquired a massive character, Anna Akhmatova observed somewhat grimly, "Now that the convicts are returning, there are two Russias, and they are glaring at each other—the ones who went to the camps and the ones who sent them to the camps."[14] The historian Iu.P. Sharapov agreed and disagreed with Akhmatova. "The great poet was right and wrong. Akhamatova was wrong in that she did not mention a third Russia, that which neither went nor sent. This Russia also existed. Tens of millions of Soviet people between the 1930s and 1950s lived and worked on one side of the barbed wire and tens of millions on the other. Soviet society did not consist only of the convicts on the one side and the executioners and informers on the other."[15]

In fact the situation was often a thoroughly confused conglomerate of ironic dramas and broken fates. Among the victims were former informers and executioners, and among the loyal camp guards were genuine executioners and potentially honest people deluded by a perverse conception of dutiful service. Behind all this tangle of human destinies was a tragedy of whole generations. It was the inspiration of the moral quests of the 1960s, and it was one of the sources of the schism of generations aggravating the eternal antagonism of fathers and sons. The GULAG became a painful question joining the moral issues of guilt and responsibility. The GULAG was that one reality to which the young could not reconcile themselves; and the older generation did not find the moral absolutism of youth to be a satisfactory judgment on its relationship to the GULAG.

The well-known scholar B.V. Raushenbakh, who spent several years in the camps, wrote about the sharply different perceptions of camp life on the part of those viewing it from within and those viewing it from without. These views were hardly congruent, because the person falling into the net of the GULAG underwent a psychological dislocation, an adjustment to a new reality, as the frightful began to be perceived as natural.[16] Similar processes of adjustment were characteristic of society as a whole. If a part of this society accepted the GULAG as its normal lot, it also underwent a psychological dislocation—that is, it too embraced an alien dimension of reality.

Rehabilitation obscured this distinction. Although the psychological alienation of the refugees from the GULAG was overcome only with difficulty, the difficulty was a natural part of rehabilitation itself. The conventional part of the population found the unfortunates from the GULAG to be shy and embarrassed. Rehabilitation was in fact more like an expiation of sins, a product of an exalted mercifulness. It was, however, liberation, and those benefiting from it did not at first feel its incompleteness.

The former convict A.P. Borisov describes how people felt as they left the "zone."

> When the convict walks out the gates, he suddenly discovers that he is not followed by an escort of guards, and he doesn't hear the usual orders, "Don't turn around!" Freedom! After long years in the zone we had completely forgotten the sense of orientation to freedom, and we likely behaved in a strange way. The liberated convict held himself apart from people and took refuge in nature. I eagerly hugged and kissed every birch and every poplar. The rustle of falling leaves was to me the sweetest music and brought tears to my eyes. The thought of bread was nothing to me. The immediate thought was that I could read books and newspapers and spend hours listening to the quiet.[17]

At the moment of liberation, freedom was perceived as the most treasured value, obscuring the serious problems of readjustment. In the course of time, however, such apparently secondary problems became primary. It was not so much a matter of subsistence as one of social status. The newcomers were not always hired at their former place of work. In fact, it was rather the exception than the rule. Entrance into higher educational institutions was practically out of the question, and in almost any department of life or work a convict's record was viewed with suspicion.

V.L. Zhevtun described this problem from his own experience. He was arrested as a sixteen-year-old adolescent and spent eight years in captivity. After liberation he was able to have his case reviewed, and he was completely rehabilitated. It altered his fate very little, however. In spite of all his efforts, he was not admitted to higher education on account of his past, and he worked as a coal stoker on a locomotive.

I am not bitter. All is well that ends well. But the real tragedy is that until the present time there are people who went through all of that hell and have not found their place in life. Some, rejected by society, have sought solace in religion, trying to found new faiths to allow them to forget reality for a time and to satisfy their spiritual needs. The multiplicity of different sects active at the present time is no accident. They arose in response to the wasted and crippled life of people who have lost their faith in society. Others sought oblivion in vodka. For a person living in normal conditions it is hard to imagine what vodka means for someone utterly rejected. It is everything. It induces forgetfulness of the past. It stops one from thinking about the unknown that lies ahead. There is freedom in it, a little corner of happiness to surrender oneself to. My own saviors were always books. They helped me to survive the worst and to preserve my faith in people.[18]

This letter is from the beginning of the 1960s, when a massive rehabilitation had already taken place and a monument had been planned to the victims of the purges. The problems of the former convicts, however, were greater than the hopes of ever resolving them. D.I. Markelov of Kerch raised and answered the question for himself.

When will we former convicts, not guilty of anything, ever be fully rehabilitated? I have resolved the question for myself: Never. My fate? My future? It has already been determined. In words: trust. In fact: suspicion. In the hearts of the powers that be: eternal suspicion. But that no longer bothers me. The more important problem is settled: my children can respond without fear on that line in the questionnaires: "Who is your father?" They can write boldly and honestly: "reserve officer, soldier in the Great Patriotic War, communist since 1931."[19]

Thus the problem of outcasts in Soviet society served to refresh—and to plague—the memory of the people. A confession of the complete innocence of the victims would not mean simply lifting the burden of guilt but transferring it onto those who created the illegal system and those who in one degree or another accepted the illegal order of things. The burden of responsibility in this case would fall on everyone outside the camps, even if obliquely. Not everyone was ready to accept such a burden, especially those who were accustomed to identifying public enemies. Such people were capable of changing the definition of enemies but not of rejecting the concept altogether, which would have required greater moral sophistication. The masses' perception of the sore spots of Soviet reality, always oriented toward the search for malefactors, was not prepared for a sudden change of orientation. Not yet accepting the innocence of the victims, they were capable only of moving from the confidence that the entire purge was justified to considering whether mistakes might have been made. Public opinion was shocked by the accounts of the perversion of the trials that had taken place in the country, when Stalin's crimes were treated as acts of just retribution. In fact, the comprehension of these matters was for a long time deliberately discouraged. The subject of the camps was taboo.

The first breach in this wall of silence was cut only in 1963, when *Novyi mir* published Alexander Solzhenitsyn's *One Day in the Life of Ivan Denisovich*. This was the first generally accessible information on camp life to see the light—nearly ten years after the decisions on rehabilitation were made. Ten years of silence could not but leave their mark, especially on the development of public opinion, which by this time had divided into two camps. One grounded its outlook in the sentiments of the thaw and supported norms of socialist legality. The other continued to subscribe to the mythical justice of the GULAG system. If their paths did not diverge entirely, they did not in any event converge. Some saw the key to progressive change in working inside the system, or they at least averted their attention from the newly evolving facts of the past. Others, placed by the system itself in the role of unacceptable outcasts, increasingly rejected it altogether. The sources of Soviet dissent lie in this reflex of rejection of the system, a movement seeking sustenance outside the public order, trying to influence the transformation of the system. This is its distinction, its special conception, but also the source of its tragic quality: it was condemned to an extraneous status in society.

Rehabilitation resolved some sociopolitical problems of the period, but at the same time it brought new ones, prompting the thinking element of the population to look with different eyes on the country's past and future. There were now undoubted grounds to reevaluate the Soviet legacy honestly and without preconceptions. In spite of all the difficulties and the conflict of views, this was undeniably a step from permanent civil war toward civil peace.

Chapter 17

Turning to the Individual: The Paths from Above and Below

When we speak of de-Stalinization, we usually have in mind the conspicuous changes in the political life of the society in the 1950s and 1960s. This idea is in part appropriate, but it diverts attention from the deeper political processes that formed the nature of the thaw. The thaw was not born suddenly and without antecedents. It developed quietly on its own, naturally although unexpectedly. The very term *thaw* expresses what people anticipated, their feelings rather than their rational prognoses. It was a very personal conception; and the public, accustomed to thinking exclusively in terms of social issues, suddenly began to discover a new value, the individual.

In order to focus on this factor, we need go no further than the reference point of March 1953, when the nearly mystical fear of the idol confronted the common knowledge of his inevitably human fate. Here was a turning point, or rather the anticipation of a turning point, the development of which had yet to take shape. It first materialized in cultural life, in a new literature, theater, music, and painting. It was precisely in the arts that the new motif of individualism cried out at full voice, fighting for its own status in the face of the customary priority granted the social over the personal and the private.

Personal life had been perceived as a kind of accessory to the production process. Although the era of revolutionary romanticism, when people suspended the indulgence of their feelings until the victory of the world revolution was won, had long since passed, its legacy persisted in a whole system of informal norms of personal behavior. Private life was considered public. Party committees and trade unions followed the moral temper of their members with an eagle eye, intervening in family conflicts, love affairs in the workplace, and even common gossip. Yet in spite of everything, people lived their own lives, following their own rationale, and the lives that they were supposed to lead, proceeding from the officially approved set of values, were largely confined to books and movie screens.

This was the custom. Therefore, when reality began gradually and timidly to appear in literature and film, when people began to appear as they were rather than as they were supposed to be, it provoked a complex reaction. Formerly when the hero began to turn aside from production problems and concern himself with private life, the reader naturally excluded him from the number of positive personalities. Thus, a reader in Novosibirsk, G. Mareichev, noted that in Aleksandr Bek's story, "Novyi profil" (A Different Kind), while the hero Vasia turns all his attention to a problem in the technology of metallurgy, his girlfriend Nadia "devotes insufficient attention to production" and nourishes feelings "of another kind" for the hero. "This means that Nadia is not at all concerned about [metallurgy]," as the vigilant reader wrote, "that she loves neither Vasia nor production. If she loved him, she would share his enthusiasm."[1]

This reader's response might be regarded as a mere curiosity but for one circumstance: it reflects in extreme form the straight-and-narrow logic of the stereotypes of contemporary thinking. It exhibits in pure form the primitive conscience typical of the masses in those years. Views of this kind were already provoking protests. The thinking reader did not respond to heroes who "loved [the forge] more than their wives" and openly approved books in which real life was not masked by schematic clichés.[2] "We are sick of the same old novels, stories, and plays, always alike, virtually identical, with artificial themes, without live conflicts except those concerned with production," wrote V. Oskotskii of Leningrad. "And cinematography is worse yet. Instead of films about our daily life they give us an excess of foreign pulp, 'Tarzan,' for example. . . . Of course, it's easier to produce historical biography in films or to make grand spectacles. Easier here means safer. But we don't have on the screen the contemporary person, the individual."[3]

Readers found the character that they were seeking in the works of Vasilii Grossman, Vera Panova, Ilia Ehrenburg, and Emmanuil Kazakevich. Kazakevich's little story, "Serdtse druga" (The Heart of a Friend), published in Novyi mir, unexpectedly prompted stormy indignation from the vigilantes of morality. The ground for sharp criticism—the author was reproached for nothing less than carnality, the debasing of Soviet womanhood, and other such sins—was a single episode, the rendezvous of the hero, Captain Akimov, and the teacher, Natasha, treated by Kazakevich in a fashion perhaps more natural than was usual in the canons of Soviet literature. Whole pedagogical institutes protested. As the director of one school in Moscow wrote, "You, Comrade Kazakevich, have treated with unceremonious disrespect the Soviet teacher, who has always given her best, under the leadership of the party, for the education of Soviet patriots. Against an otherwise positive background the teacher Natasha is such a pathetic and lonely person that she is accessible only for the satisfaction of the purely masculine passions of occasionally perverse Soviet officers."[4] The author was given practical advice—for example, the suggestion to "complete" the story by rewriting the disputed scene in a positive fashion or eliminating it.[5]

But there was an entirely opposite reaction as well. "They are accusing you of carnality," the reader V. Boitsov wrote to Kazakevich, "and I, for example, sincerely rejoiced at your courage, for intimate relations are usually represented in books by an ellipsis, whereas it is the duty of the writer to instruct the youth seriously and to treat the intimate relations of people with respect."[6] The issue grew larger. Does the individual generally have the right to a private life, always and in all circumstances? Notwithstanding the apparently rhetorical nature of the question, it elicited extremely sharp disagreements.

"In the days of the Great Patriotic War, the patriotic Soviet writer did not think of dumplings and parties nor of love stories," wrote A. Ostapenko from Vinnitsa. "His whole thought was devoted to our beloved country, the beloved Soviet Army, to the great and wise I.V. Stalin."[7] But many of those who had been at the front thought otherwise. The man at the front remained quite human, although the war brought its inhuman adjustments into normal human life. Life continued, nevertheless, according to the former soldier Iu. Golovtsov from Tallin, as he expressed himself to his invisible opponent. "Yes, love during the war was often painful, disturbing, a source of jealousy, and you will find, if you speak of it honestly with former Soviet soldiers, that it was often necessary to struggle with the feeling of love."[8]

The perception of the right to a private life soon elicited a lively reaction, especially among young people. A movement for internal liberation soon began, as there could be no open society without it. Too many disputed questions lay across this path—questions of ethical philosophy and of personal intimacy, of the stereotypes of the past and established norms of behavior—to admit of quick and stable solutions inspired by the new outlook. But the process gained strength and became so conspicuous that indignant public opinion alone could not stop it. An official reaction soon began, chiefly in response to the summons of public opinion.

At the Second Congress of Soviet Writers (1954), the "problem of the individual" resounded in a series of literary themes. The official literary leadership, having pronounced in its time on the issues of "the positive and the negative," on "the typical and the atypical," on "the disputed and the undisputed," decided to speak its piece on "production and the individual." "In the center of the literary portrayal of our contemporary life," said Konstantin Simonov at the congress, "we must place those people who stand at the center of our life today, people of creativity, ordinary people who nevertheless exemplify a heroic spirit. To portray these people *only at work* . . . would be to represent them in a one-sided fashion. If work is the center of their life, it is not their whole life. . . . How many party secretaries in our novels, stories, novellas are deprived of sleep, of meals, of medical care, not to speak of love and happiness, and all in the name of this unimaginable severity of the primacy of public interests over private interests?"[9] Simonov did not attack the primacy of public interests, "the reality of life,"[10] but tried to formulate a more flexible junction of public and private principles. "Public activity, work as creativity, becomes in great part the private affair of the individual, and his private life reflects the role of public interests."[11]

Alexei Surkov, one of the leaders of the Writers' Union, gave particular examples. He named Vsevolod Kochetov, author of the novel *Zhurbiny* (The Zhurbins), as a writer who combined the correct blend of the private and the public, and Ilia Ehrenburg (*Ottepel'* [The Thaw]) and Vera Panova (*Vremena goda* [Seasons of the Year]) as authors who failed to do so. Of what were these authors guilty in Surkov's opinion? "The flaw lies in the fact that in spite of the objective laws of literary method [socialist realism—E.Z.], they stood on the shifting sands of solipsism and opposed to the lawful development of the public personality the arbitrariness of the author's subjective conceptions of Soviet people as individuals whose private life is strictly distinguished from their social and economic life."[12] This was the kind of evaluation given to those authors and books that in the opinion of the majority of readers approached literature in a fashion characterized by officialdom as abstract solipsism.

This taboo extended to the treatment of that sensitive juncture where the individual came into contact with the state system. This relationship was always characterized by the subjection of the individual to a dual mechanism of control, by the state from above and by the collective from below. The restricted range of choice in personal behavior emphasized group interests and narrowed the scope of individual development to a series of public services. Service was the obligation of everyone, and it assumed the absorption of the individual into the life of the nation. Here was the source of speaking "in the name of" some group, thereby identifying oneself with one or another collective.

The readers' letters to newspapers and journals of the 1950s reveal one characteristic feature. Those letters standing on conservative positions were usually written in the name of a collective or begin with such words as "I, like the whole Soviet people," "we, Soviet youth," Soviet teachers," etc. On the other hand, letters taking issue with the official position were as a rule submitted by individuals. They contain in embryo that same disputed personal outlook that was in the process of breaking with the traditional corporate style of thinking. Thus it was less regulated, administered, less subject to ideological or any other kind of review. The public service principle did not disappear. Rather it came to be consciously inspired by individual choice. In a broader perspective it became one of the constituent elements of the whole system of intrastate relations in the process of rejecting traditional paternalism and making the transition to the bases of a democratic power structure.

This perspective departed entirely from the course of modernization planned by the government. The leaders of the country after Stalin's death embraced the policy of enhanced social programs, trying to transfer the economic center of gravity from forced industrialization to those spheres of production that served the demands of popular well-being (light industry, agriculture, residential construction). They worked out a broad system of social security, introduced passports in the peasant villages, shortened the work day, increased vacation time, and built more vacation facilities and sanatoria for factory workers. Popular programs of this magnitude were hitherto unknown in the country. Government policy, it seemed, did in fact turn its face to the people, to the attainment of that very better life that resounded so often from speakers' platforms, and to the ordinary family. Why then do we continue to this day not merely to ignore but to scorn what was done for the people in the 1950s? What is this, elementary human ingratitude, or did revenues not support the solution of social problems by the more demanding standards of our own time?

The answers to this and similar questions lay beyond the range of the individual's conceptions and of his social functions at that time. Since the individual was considered merely an appendage of state policy, then his place in the system of social relations could not change, however substantial the content of social policy. Substituting initiative for doles but preserving the passive role of the people in the processes of public administration, it was impossible to achieve the desired levels of output and material investments in the consumer economy. Some time later, when the economic policy of the 1970s led predictably into a blind alley, the chairman of a collective farm explained the problem. "If we didn't work before because we knew that they would not in any event give us anything, we don't work now because we know that they *will* give it in any event."[13]

The position of the leaders was defined by the principle of state socialism, the blind adherence to which lowered the idea of the turn to the individual to the level of cheap charity. "Now we have built many homes with bathrooms and refrigerators, we have declared war on insufficient living space and every kind of consumer deficit, and we are concerned a hundred times more about the human being. Homes in the vicinity of the factory must be constructed along with the factory, and all kinds of goods must be available in every little town. Yes, it is necessary," wrote Vladimir Pomerantsev, and he added, "Yes, we will live well. And nevertheless, while working for a prosperous material life, we must remain above material life."[14]

Vladimir Dudintsev shared these concerns of Vladimir Pomerantsev entirely. As he explained in a teachers' conference in Leningrad, "Across from my home is a balcony. It always had a Spartan appearance, there was no sign of consumer goods. It was not clear what the inhabitants lived on. But suddenly after the order of the party and the government to emphasize the construction of balconies, there are pretty curtains, fat cats, and foxtrots from morning till evening! . . . There are people who misunderstood the turn to material prosperity, who threw out the baby [of good cultural values—H.R.] with the bathwater [of Stalinist dross—H.R.] and the most precious feature of the man who doesn't hurry off to the dance but dreams of overturning the world and, like Archimedes, seeks a support. Suddenly, all of that idealism is devalued."[15]

The fear of materialism, *of philistinism,* more characteristic of the revolutionary romanticism of the 1920s, revived in the 1950s, and, in spite of its shrill character, nevertheless had a rational basis. The protest, be it ever so extreme, against the *slide into materialism,* not merely against such modest phenomena as foxtrots and house plants, the characteristic symbols of philistine psychology, signified a serious problem. The chief point of it was that the turn to the individual and the turn to material well-being were not perfectly identical.

The social policy of the 1950s, never mind its failure, in fact bypassed those processes of the cultural maturation of society that gradually developed below. The recognition of the unique value of the human personality, the quests and passions that occupy social thought, on the one hand, and the attachment of the authorities to the old, objective approach to mankind, on the other hand, led in time not only to the divergence of these two paths to the further evolution of society but to different perceptions of the chief political and moral problem of the 1950s—the problem of overcoming the Stalinist legacy.

Chapter 18

The Decision on the Cult of Personality and Its Social Impact

It remains mysterious to whom belongs the dubious idea of reckoning the political accounts of whole decades under the rubric of the "cult of personality." What we know for certain is that this new term in the authorities' lexicon in no sense signified the propagation of a new theory. Its use was clearly tentative, an effort to put into words the refusal of the new leaders to engage in ritual reverence of the deceased leader.

The question was raised at the first meeting of the Central Committee Presidium (10 March 1953) after Stalin's funeral, when G.M. Malenkov spoke critically of the national press. "We consider it necessary to put an end to the politics of the cult of personality."[1] Secretary P.N. Pospelov was charged with overseeing this issue in the media, and N.S. Khrushchev was given the more specific responsibility for dealing with comments devoted to the memory of Stalin.[2] Thus in the beginning the whole question of overcoming the tradition of apotheosis consisted merely of revising propaganda.

There was evidently a strong inclination in the Central Committee to limit the Stalinist cult, as Malenkov elaborated on the issue several months later in the July 1953 plenum. "It is not only a question of propaganda. The question of the cult of personality is directly related to the question of collective leadership."[3] Thus one more step was taken in the direction of changing the bases of party life. "You should know, comrades," Malenkov said at the plenum, "that Comrade Stalin's cult of personality acquired pathological forms and dimensions in the everyday practice of leadership. The methods of collective work were discarded, criticism and self-criticism were absent from our highest level of leadership. We do not have the right to hide from you that such a monstrous cult of personality led to his categorical and individual decisions and in the last years began to do serious damage to the business of leading the party and the country."[4]

The plenum heard the factual particulars, how Stalin alone made notoriously mistaken decisions with the silent consent of his lieutenants. His initiative in raising taxes on the village and the idea of constructing the Turkmen Canal without taking economic factors into account were recalled. The scientific substance of several of his theories was subjected to doubt. Malenkov, for example, said that the idea of the exchange of products between city and village was proposed in Stalin's work *The Economic Problems of Socialism in the USSR* "without sufficient analysis and economic foundation" and that as a consequence "for years it prevented the solution of the most important problems of the exchange of goods."[5]

The most important of Stalin's mistakes, if we follow the logic of discussion at the plenum, was the Beria phenomenon (the plenum had assembled above all in order to deal with the issue of Beria, who had just been arrested). Beria's intrigues were, according to Malenkov, "the result of the inadequate vigilance of the Central Committee, including that of Comrade Stalin. Beria discovered the human weaknesses of Stalin, and who doesn't have such weaknesses? He [Beria] exploited them cunningly and successfully for a considerable length of time."[6] Kaganovich added: "He cunningly worked his way into Comrade Stalin's confidence."[7] And Khrushchev: "He clawed his way with his dirty paws into Comrade Stalin's mind and imposed his opinion on Comrade Stalin."[8]

Thus the Beria phenomenon was explained as the consequence of Stalin's human weaknesses. The participants in the plenum were of one mind on this question. The party leaders were not so unanimous about Beria himself. In this question, the evolution of their opinion required some time. The development of their logic is obvious if we follow the characteristics that their speeches at the plenum attributed to Beria. Malenkov: "[he] violated and subverted the unity of our Central Committee, [he was] an enemy of the party and the people, a degenerate and criminally dissipated person."[9] Khrushchev: "a cunning person, a clever careerist, not a communist, a provocateur, an adventurer, a scoundrel and intriguer."[10] Molotov: "an agent of an alien camp, an agent of the class enemy, a provocateur."[11] Kaganovich: "a counterrevolutionary fascist conspirator, a spy of international proportions."[12]

It is easy to observe how, step by step, from speech to speech, the denunciation of Beria grew ever harsher. At the same time the leaders' general conception of the Beria phenomenon developed gradually, defining the relationship of the party to the problem ever more distinctly. It was construed fundamentally by the motif of alienation. Beria was declared in the beginning to be an *internal enemy*, later to be *an agent of international imperialism*. Denounced as an *alien*, a person of the other camp, Beria was excluded from the category of *us* and relegated to the ranks of *them*. Here is the source of the evaluation of Beria's personality as exclusively negative (degenerate, intriguer, morally dissolute person, etc.). The coherence of the characterization was broken by a single circumstance: until recently the alien had been considered their own man and even as one of the first among them. The contradiction was resolved with the help of the idea of "our fault," which consisted chiefly of the confession of insufficient vigilance. This explanation was soon accompanied, however, by a mitigating factor— that is, the special talents of the alien, who masked himself cleverly and wormed his way into the confidence of the others. Their mistake was thus the product of the malevolent schemes of the alien, and the general responsibility for the whole affair was thus thrust onto him as the uniquely guilty party. The motif of alienation played another important role. It exonerated from criticism not only his former colleagues but the system as a whole. The activity of the alien bore an extrasystemic character, one hostile to the system itself.

The guilt of Stalin, displaced now onto the intrigues of Beria, was also treated as extrasystemic—that is, as independent of the laws of politics. It was declared a matter of human flaws. Stalin was thus distinguished from Stalinism, the leader from the system. The entire subsequent attack on the cult of Stalin would be founded on this distinction. It would be an attack on the name, on the icon, but it would not engage the factors that gave birth to the phenomenon, the political etiology.

Strictly speaking, the criticism of Stalin had to avoid the model of the attack on Beria. Stalin could not be considered, for example, a foreign spy. He could not be thrust out of the parameters of the system. He remained *inseparable* from it. Stalin was intrinsic to the system bearing his name, and this factor defined the limits beyond which the measures taken against the cult of personality could not go. The criticism always stopped at the threshold of intrasystemic analysis. Therein lies the key to the enigmatic instability, to the fits and starts, of the whole history of the struggle against the cult of personality.

An adequate assessment of the Stalin phenomenon required a different kind of logic, another mental perspective, one simply beyond the reach of the people belonging to the system. A new view of the matter might appear only from without or gradually develop on the basis of the internal evolution of politics, but its advocates had to be people relatively free of the whole complex of sins of the past. In the formative stage questions relating in any way to the name of Stalin were not discussed beyond the bounds of a narrow circle of party faithful. Everything said at the July 1953 Central Committee plenum, all the arguments and disagreements, remained for the common people a secret under seven seals.

When the term *cult of personality* first appeared in the press, most people did not perceive it as the portent of a major shift of policy. Only the acutely sensitive caught the new accents on the motive forces of history, on the role of personality among the popular masses, on the party and its leaders. On 10 June 1953, *Pravda* published an article addressed to party propagandists under the headline "The Communist Party Is the Leading Force of the Soviet People." The article was devoted to the task of overcoming subjective approaches in the conception of the role of the party and of individual personalities in the history of society. It mentioned the harmful influence of the cult of personality and made the point that Marx, Engels, and Lenin had spoken against it. Even the name of Stalin was mentioned among the *early* ranks of those struggling against the cult, but his name was surrounded by a protective taboo, and criticism of the cult was treated positively as a stage of transition to collective leadership.

There was a clear and deliberate reason behind this positive reference. Public opinion after the death of Stalin anticipated changes for the better (as it had just after the war) but also sought stability, continuity of the general course of the new leadership in Stalinist policies. Taking account of this outlook, the leaders of the party were obliged to act in general as the heirs of Stalin.

Nevertheless, the question arose what part of the legacy to reject. It first resounded on high, though a particular conception of it formed slowly, step by step, losing its way in the contradictions of public well-being and personal responsibility. A distinct stimulant of constructive reflection was the Beria affair. His was the first name to which the idea of the cult of personality was attached. The question was soon posed more broadly. What conditions make possible the emergence of people who concentrate in their hands unlimited power? It was suggested that "the monopoly position of the Communist Party" might have its "shady features." These "shady features" were represented as the penetration of the party by enemies and adventurists, "cunningly masked as communists" and using "the authority and position of the ruling party for their own corrupt interests."[13]

What was the point of all this verbal probing and searching? It seemed that an alternative to strict centralization and party monopoly might be provided only by movement along a path to democracy. Logic, however, is not always compatible with political reality. The answer to this question had more to do with the spirit of the times than with political logic. "Revolutionary vigilance is our weapon against all enemies. We will always keep this weapon sharp, always ready for battle. And thus we will hope to bring to naught the intrigues of our enemies."[14]

Calls to increase revolutionary vigilance in the past were usually followed by extraordinary measures, the strengthening of party and government controls. In 1953, the situation took a different turn. There were no new waves of persecution. Moreover, after the condemnation of Beria, the motif of vigilance generally disappeared from the press. At the same time, the cult of personality ceased to be mentioned. The process of examining the past was halted.

The public was thus given the dose of truth that the leaders deemed appropriate. At the heights of power they presumed that the ministration of truth and justice was part of the competence of the leadership. At that level they knew what was better for the people and what was worse, what to allow and what to forbid. There was a firm certainty that many things accessible to the understanding of the leaders would undoubtedly be misunderstood by the people. Worse yet, if the people began to take an active role in public life, the results would, of course, be unfortunate. In order to cross the line dividing society into the omniscient leaders and the ignorant masses, the studied caution of a Malenkov would not suffice. What was needed was a breakthrough, a leap into the unknown, something of which Khrushchev alone proved capable. But that came later.

For a while the prohibition on mentioning Stalin's name in relation to the cult of personality preserved relative unanimity among the leadership. The phenomenon of the cult was viewed as a kind of sickness that struck the party apparatus. "What it was accepted to call the 'cult of personality,'" Malenkov wrote much later, "consisted above all of the assertion and self-assertion of a leader flawless in word and deed without regard to the question whether he is right or wrong—or malevolent."[15] If that were true, how could the intolerable nature of the situation be represented as the confidential affair of the leadership? Nevertheless, the leadership shared the illusion that the subject of Stalin could be relegated to silence, and this illusion led to a development that they did not foresee.

On the eve of International Women's Day, 8 March, in one of the student dormitories it was a tradition to show the film "Chlen pravitelstva" (Member of the Government). In the final scene of the film, Stalin enters a large hall to the thunderous applause of a crowd. In 1954, as soon as Stalin appeared on the screen the audience in this dormitory stood and began to applaud. These students were not Stalin fanatics. This behavior in any event was prompted by other feelings. The contrast between the publicity formerly surrounding Stalin's name and the sudden regime of silence was so artificial that it seemed immoral.

"When the name of Stalin disappeared from the press and then the formula 'cult of personality' quickly appeared, it wounded people's moral sense, the sense of justice," explained I.A. Dedkov, then a student at Moscow State University, later a well-known journalist, critic, and publicist. "How could it be? He filled all the newspapers, everyone prayed for him. And who were the first to pray? All of these authorities, the leaders of the country. Why did they earlier shout 'hurrah' and now they are quiet? This was done immorally. It was not natural."[16]

On 5 March 1954 Dedkov approached the professor in his first class before the lecture began and proposed that the class stand for a moment in honor of Stalin's memory. And the class stood up. "This was a rather bold move," said Dedkov, "because it ran counter to the current. Although at the same time a critical outlook on Stalin was steadily developing. Very quickly, even among my own companions."[17]

They had not even thought at the time of such conceptions as Stalin and Stalinism, but, moved by moral intuition, they stood for overcoming the legacy of Stalin, and the result was more constructive and more profound than the measures taken by the government against the cult. The task seemed at first glance simple, but different social forces approached it with different moral criteria and a different degree of receptiveness to future political changes. Some were prepared to surrender the memory of Stalin to public opinion, leaving the political regime essentially untouched though somewhat modernized. Others proceeded from doubts about the man and did not consider criticism of Stalin an adequate reform. Rather they set out at once on another and higher level of perception of public problems and the possibility of resolving them. As the culmination of these trends loomed in the Twentieth Party Congress, the leadership of the country and that part of the public that succeeded in working out a reserve of revised ideas approached the projected reforms with a different degree of preparedness and the changes in store with a different perspective.

The last day of the Twentieth Party Congress, 25 February 1956, was a historical milestone. It was then that Khrushchev shocked the majority of the delegates with his speech "On the Cult of Personality and Its Consequences" [the famous/notorious "secret speech"—H.R.]. Although the meeting was closed and the delegates were warned about the confidentiality of the proceedings, the secrets long surrounding the name of Stalin were soon known everywhere. The documents of the Twentieth Congress have special significance. They embodied in fact the first serious attempt to examine the essence of the Stalinist era, to draw lessons from it, to assess its history, and to identify those responsible for it.

The personal factor acquired a special significance, and the negative manifestations of socialist construction in practice were attributed to the decisive influence of Stalin's character flaws. His policies were divided into two periods, the positive one (the struggle with the opposition, the period of industrialization and collectivization, and the Great Patriotic War) and the negative one, when, to put it simply, Stalin's character was corrupted. Thus a distinct era appeared in Soviet history, *the era of the cult of personality*. Its chronological limits were not defined sufficiently clearly, but the beginning date was sometime in the late 1930s. The period as a whole was viewed as something like an appendix to a healthy historical organism, a kind of zigzag, a fortuitous misunderstanding.

So the shadow of Stalin once more disturbed the minds and souls of his contemporaries. The first word of truth on Stalin was for them shattering, notwithstanding the fact that most of the particulars had long been anticipated by the restoration of conventional legality. Most striking were the facts and figures and the names of those slandered, persecuted, and consigned to oblivion. Among them were well-known political personalities, outstanding scientists, military leaders, and artists. They were the flower of society, its intellectual elite, thousands of simple, honest people, people dedicated to the party. And beside this national tragedy was the name that for years had embodied all the success and the triumphs, all that had been attained at the price of enormous pressure on the whole people. "At the closed session of 25 February during the report by Khrushchev several delegates fell into a faint," Ilia Ehrenburg later recalled. "I won't hide it. When I read the speech, I was shaken, as it was not spoken in a circle of friends of one of Stalin's victims but by the first secretary of the party. February 25, 1956 was for me and for all of my contemporaries a big day."[18]

The content of the Twentieth Party Congress gradually became known to the party at large and subsequently to the public as a whole. It was no accident that 1956 is fixed in the memory of Russian society as a turning point, a milestone. The reactions to it, however, were quite varied. Confusion stimulated in some minds the development of thought. Others it simply left disoriented. In one of the opinion polls of the 1960s, the public was queried about its attitudes toward the different events of the time, and one particular answer was characteristic: "The worst was the series of events surrounding the criticism of Stalin and the work of the party in that period. No other event in my life hit me so hard, not even the disasters of the first years of the war with fascist Germany."[19] Another testimony, of a party member's initial reaction to Khrushchev's speech, evinced similar feelings.

A week has already passed since the time when our party organization was acquainted in detail with the materials of the Twentieth Party Congress on the cult of personality, and I have spent the whole time under the impression that they made. . . . In the first days I was irritated that we are passing judgment on a deceased person, and I wanted Iosif Vissarionovich Stalin to remain in our memory as a just and honest man, as he was portrayed for us for more than three decades. . . . And now that we have found out about his most serious faults, it is difficult, very difficult to extinguish in the heart that great love that was so strongly rooted in our whole organism.[20]

On 5 March 1956 students in Tbilisi went out into the streets to lay flowers at the monument to Stalin on the third anniversary of his death. Their gesture in honor of Stalin turned into a protest against the decisions of the Twentieth Party Congress. The demonstrations and meetings continued for five days, and on the evening of 9 March tanks were brought into the city to restore order.

The events in Tbilisi are in their way an index of the incompetence, the lack of sufficient deliberation, with which the whole anti-Stalinist campaign was conducted. By any serious reckoning it was the result of the utter neglect of social psychology. The time chosen for the decisive exposé of Stalin virtually coincided with the anniversary of his death. A coincidence of this kind, even if not deliberate, if only accidental, can provoke a psychological reaction of rejection of the best intentions. That was just the kind of reaction that Khrushchev confronted in March 1956.

The party apparatus reacted quite unexpectedly to the new line. It demonstrated the unambiguous desire to put the brakes on the new campaign, observing the party line in a purely ritual fashion. Judging by the number of questions from lower to higher party organizations, the party members were more concerned about outward forms of expression than about the analysis of what had taken place. What should be done with the portraits of Stalin? Could Stalin's works be used in propaganda and in teaching? Were his works still considered among the classics of Marxism-Leninism? Party committees responded to many such questions, but as no special instructions had been prepared for the eventuality of a confused reaction to an unplanned speech, confusion was inevitable.

The portraits were taken down in official buildings but not without a good deal of resistance. The director of one factory shop would not consent to remove his own portrait of Stalin. When he went home and told his wife, she advised him at once: "Go and take it down yourself, or they will arrest you and put you in prison for cult of personality."[21] Such fears may be perceived now as naive, but their appearance at that time was quite conspicuous. People often did not distinguish the new campaign from the past practice of struggle with enemies of the people in spite of the fact that there was not a hint of the methods common to such campaigns in the past. Fear was alive and well, nourishing and supporting the psychology of the bystander: "We are little people."

But this was only one slice of opinion. There was another reaction, a very lively one, to the exposé of Stalin's crimes. Many people did not accept, for example, the concept of Stalin's personal guilt as a perfectly satisfactory explanation. The general attitude of the doubters was expressed, it seems, by a letter addressed at the time to the journal *Communist*: "They say that the policy of the party was right, and yet Stalin was wrong. But who was in charge of this policy for decades? Stalin. Who formulated the basic political positions? Stalin. The two propositions are incompatible."[22] The logic of this kind of reasoning led to other questions: "Why could the members of the Politburo of the Central Committee, old communists and loyal students of Lenin, not correct Stalin in good time?"[23] "If all the members of the Politburo, the Central Committee, and the government saw that Stalin was making incorrect decisions, why did they not re-

THE CULT OF PERSONALITY AND ITS SOCIAL IMPACT 187

move him from the post?" "Were the members of the Politburo such cowards and the party too impotent to take the place of Stalin?"[24]

To a certain extent the answer to these questions was given in the reflections of one of the participants in the discussion of the Twentieth Congress at the Gorky Institute of World Literature.

> It seems to me that as a result of historical causes there was in the party and the government a stratum of people for whom the cult of personality was beneficial, who got along well with it. Now they are pronouncing big words and they consider how they can maintain themselves in their positions. . . . There were people who led thousands of honest citizens to their destruction and there were people who saw it all. . . . If all of these people remain at their posts, and if they are entrusted with carrying out the decisions of the Twentieth Congress, it would be pure self-deception on our part.[25]

Others carried their personal inquiries further and even took specific steps bringing them into direct confrontation with the authorities. A worker at an electric power station in Arkhangelsk Province who was found in possession of a letter that he planned to send to Khrushchev was arrested by the organs of state security. The content of the letter was characterized as anti-Soviet.

> Nikita Sergeevich! We . . . thank you for finding in yourself the courage to tell the truth to the whole people and to reveal facts that give us grounds for trusting you and the government. We hold Lenin and his teachings in holy esteem and consider that in the present circumstances we are obliged to act as Lenin taught: all power to the Soviets, that is, to the local soviets of workers' deputies. Only in this fashion can we come to communism. If your speech and respect for Lenin are not hypocritical, then send us the government's guarantee that the police and security agents will not bother us delegates and agitators. In the contrary case incidents may arise and, it may be, even bloodletting, for which you will be held responsible. We think that we are entitled to an answer without superfluous delay and red tape.[26]

The letter naturally did not reach the addressee. This is an isolated example, and the public reaction to Khrushchev's report was more often expressed in doubts, reflections, and questions rather than in willingness to proceed with any practical action.

In a variety of party meetings after the discussion of Khrushchev's report special resolutions were passed as if to develop the decisions of the congress. Thus the communists at the Stalin Metallurgical Factory in Leningrad resolved to ask the Central Committee to transfer Stalin's body out of the mausoleum and to remove his name from their factory.[27] A party meeting in Chkalovsk region issued a similar resolution: "In view of the fact that during the last period of his work Stalin made a series of serious mistakes bordering on crimes, the party meeting, expressing the will of communists, asks the Central Committee to transfer the body of Stalin out of the mausoleum and to order the removal of his portraits."[28] Other party organizations made similar proposals.[29] One party meeting in Leningrad heard the suggestion "to subject Stalin posthumously to a party court."[30] (Only four of 750 people, however, voted for the resolution.) The casualness with which some party workers were prepared to judge their recent idol did not always garner the support of their colleagues and gives us ground to doubt the genuineness of such impulses, all the more since after Khrushchev's speech, it was not only safe but actually obligatory to criticize Stalin.

To criticize the new leadership with Khrushchev at its head was another matter. At a party meeting of the Latvian Committee of State Security one of the communists suggested that the reasons given by Khrushchev for the rise of the cult of personality "could not be recognized as persuasive," and he proposed his own conception of the problem: "the cult of personality became possible as a result of the irresponsibility of members of the Central Committee and the Politburo."[31] The party committee expelled him for this suggestion, but its decision was not supported by a higher instance of party authority, and he was simply reprimanded.[32]

There was also a grassroots reaction of disagreement with the criticism of Stalin. After a meeting at the university in Vologda a handwritten note was found: "Idle chatter. Stalin is with us. Komsomol (Communist Youth League)."[33] The soldiers said to each other, "Stalin is alive in the memory of the people, we went into battle and died in his name." One of them elaborated.

> I was reading the confidential letter of the Central Committee [on the cult of personality—E.Z.] and got angry at its contents. . . . I cannot easily believe all the facts that are laid out in the letter. Stalin did much for the Soviet state, and we must not belittle his services. He transformed our country from backwardness into an advanced industrial power. Thanks to Stalin we won the war. . . . Stalin raised me from childhood in his ideas, and I will not reject these ideas now. I had and will have the best opinion of Stalin. . . . I am angry about what the letter revealed. . . . If he was guilty of anything, it was only that he trusted

Beria and shot many honest Soviet people. . . . But for Stalin, we might not have a Soviet state but a republic of the bourgeois type.[34]

The logic of the arguments proposed by this soldier was rather widespread among those who did not accept the decisions on the cult of personality. As information reaching the Central Committee indicates, the former soldiers remained the most conservative in their perceptions of Stalin. The bulk of the favorable reactions to Khrushchev's speech came from the artistic intelligentsia and the students.

The journalist O.P. Latsis recalls the impression that Khrushchev's report made on him and his fellow students at Moscow State University.

His speech, all of our lack of preparation for it and our inexperience notwithstanding, was striking for its simplicity and absence of cunning. He said that the great genius was a great malefactor, and that was that. We believed that he was a great malefactor, as the facts were irresistible. But it provoked more objections and doubts. How could it be in our country, in our party, in our revolution? How was it compatible with socialism? The reduction of all these questions to an issue of personality was deliberately misleading. This was not some kind of renegade personality but the leader whom we had followed. Two questions arose at once: how could it happen, and where were the guarantees that it would not be repeated? There was no answer either to the one or to the other. We demanded the formation of such guarantees, and nobody responded. It was all reduced to the replacement of one person by another, but we understood that this was no guarantee.[35]

Doubts gave rise to reflection and reflection to more questions. Meetings took place, informal discussions, and arguments. Ilia Ehrenburg recalls it.

They spoke of Stalin everywhere, in every apartment, at work, in the cafeterias, in the metro. One Muscovite would say to another, "Well, what do you think?" He didn't expect an answer, there was no explanation of the past. After dinner the head of the family would repeat what he had heard at a meeting. Kids listened. They knew that Stalin was a wise genius . . . and suddenly they heard that Stalin killed his close friends . . . that he believed firmly in the word of Hitler, approving the nonaggression pact. A son or daughter would ask: "Papa, how could you have known nothing?"[36]

One discussion led to another, the wave of public concern grew wider and deeper. The leadership of the country was not prepared for such a sweep of events. "After the Twentieth Congress, when people began to raise all kinds of issues, we were not prepared to respond," as the secretary of the Moscow party committee, E.A. Furtseva, confessed at a local meeting.[37] The decision was made to suspend temporarily the public reading of Khrushchev's report. When questions were raised about the reasons, it was usually explained, first, that it was to avoid the intrigues of Western propaganda and, second, that it was for the conduct of more conscientious preparatory work among communists, who had on several occasions taken "incorrect positions on unhealthy opinions."[38]

Some responses to the widespread criticism of the cult of personality were considered excessive. They led, on the one hand, to an elementary mania for meetings and, on the other, to efforts to subvert authority. Some of the excesses occurred for logical reasons. If the party, for example, spoke out against the deification of leaders, then why do we still have monuments to living people in the leadership? Why are cities, collective farms, and enterprises named for them?

A special situation began to take shape in society. In removing Stalin from his pedestal, Khrushchev had dispelled the aura of inviolability around the leading political personality and his entourage in general. The system of fear was broken (here was an undoubted service of the new leadership), and the former perfect impunity of the supreme power was no longer intact. Khrushchev thus brought himself willy-nilly under the fixed gaze—examination—of his fellow citizens. While all of the institutional power structure remained the same, this new outlook undoubtedly altered the internal balance of power. People were now in possession of the right not only to expect changes for the better but to demand them. The new situation at the grass roots formed an atmosphere of impatience, which, on the one hand, stimulated the authorities to undertake decisive measures, but, on the other, increased the risk of turning the course of reform into the pulp of populism. As subsequent developments illustrated, the government did not succeed in avoiding this danger.

Chapter 19

Public Opinion and the "Hungarian Syndrome"

Noticeable changes were taking place in the country. Above all, the public atmosphere was changing; a modest liberation of society was proceeding. The Soviet Union opened up to the world. International contacts and exchanges developed, trips of Soviet delegations abroad and of foreigners to the Soviet Union became an ordinary phenomenon. One such occasion was the World Youth and Student Festival in Moscow. But the most substantive change was that the life of the people inside the country was palpably different: it no longer resembled so much a one-way street, and it actively embraced new forms of open social intercourse. On the wave of public élan new forms of literature, painting, and the theater were born. The experimental theater Sovremennik (Contemporary) evoked open discussion, a reborn avant-garde defended its right to interpret the world, and literature and journalism—nearly indistinguishable—became an active part of everyday life, forcing everyone to choose this or that side of the barricades. The processes of emotional and cultural liberation and rebirth, which had been gestating for decades, suddenly burst forth with a mighty impulse and a new face.

A critical glance backward at the year 1956 is almost like stumbling into the present. People began to react more sharply to the problems of their own time. The volume of readers' mail to the newspapers and journals increased. A major theme of this correspondence was the cult of personality. Some demanded that the past should not be stirred up; others wished to pursue the issue to its end. But the most important questions had to do with the past and with expectations of the future.

The past demanded a substantive analysis. In 1955 and 1956 the journal *Voprosy istorii* (Problems of History, chief editor: A.M. Pankratova) published a series of articles and documents designed to broaden the rigidly circumscribed perspective of the *Short History of the Bolshevik Party* [the infamously Stalinist account published in 1938—H.R.] and to formulate historical questions in the spirit of the new era. These materials, as well as the journal as a whole, were subjected to such severe criticism that Pankratova felt compelled to send the Central Committee in August 1956 a special note challenging the accusations against the journal. "The incorrect attitude to our journal is a significant problem," she wrote. "The discipline of history and the other social sciences have accumulated a great many serious mistakes and shortcomings intolerable in the light of the decisions of the Twentieth Party Congress. Yet our efforts to speak out against these mistakes and shortcomings have run into resistance."[1]

The resistance, both direct and oblique, was encountered not only by the editors of the journal and its contributors. Unanimity was formerly the official norm, and any deviation from the norm was perceived as hostile intrigues and subversion of the foundations, whether it had to do with scholarly discussion or the fashions of youth.

The big blow of the vigilantes of morality among youth was delivered to the so-called *stiliagi*, that is, the young people smitten by the new Western styles of fashion. They were easily identified by their appearance, their dress (narrow pants and wide neckties) and hair styles in particular, and especially by their musical tastes. They were inordinately fond of jazz, which Soviet ideologues considered unwholesome. "Today they play jazz, and tomorrow they will betray their country," as the captions under cartoons maintained. Their addiction to fashion was ridiculed and derided in cartoons and newspaper columns. It could also exclude them from the Communist Youth League or ruin their careers, and such fates were not rare. According to the more categorical judgments, "From the *stiliag* to crime the distance is microscopic."[2]

At the same time there were efforts to see beyond mere appearance and to overcome crude views of the outward signs of sound judgment or the lack of it. One of the researchers at the Institute of Public Opinion commented on the question in *Komsomol'skaia pravda* (Communist Youth League Pravda).

> I don't consider the *stiliagi* to be those who dress fashionably (narrow pants do not make a *stiliag*) but those who along with narrow pants

narrow their honor and their conscience. These people parade their scorn for work, for life, for all that is holy. By themselves they are not frightening. There are few of them, and they can be swept into the garbage at any moment. But they set a bad example in idleness, dandyism, and dissipation and have a bad influence on youth. Like a case of the flu, the frightening thing is the risk of complications. The complications of the *stiliagi* I consider parasitism, hooliganism, and banditism.[3]

In disputes of this kind something new appeared in Soviet life: a *public opinion* that was earlier confined chiefly to private and confidential conversations became open and genuinely public. It was as if the society had suddenly discovered the right of free speech, and, true to Russian tradition, literature and journalism again assumed the role of social commentary.

Novyi mir began to publish in 1956 V.D. Dudintsev's novel, *Ne khlebom edinym* (Not by Bread Alone). It related the conflicts of a young engineer and inventor, Lopatkin, and his confrontations with the bureaucratic apparatus in the person of the factory director Drozdov: the complex and sometimes dramatic fate of an unconventional personality in a world of truculent traditions. Of course, Dudintsev understood perfectly well that his book was a challenge to the spirit of the time, and the editorial staff of the journal took full account of the fact that it was publishing a far from inoffensive work. Still, scarcely any of them imagined the explosive public reaction that the novel provoked. They received more than six hundred letters about it. No other literary production prior to that time had such an impact. Lines formed in libraries to read it, and copies of the journal were passed from hand to hand.

"The first discussion of the novel [at the Writers' Union in October 1956—E.Z.]," recalls Dudintsev, "drew so many people that the horseback police were called. People climbed up the water pipes on the outside of the building in order to listen to the proceedings through a second-story window."[4] And there was plenty to hear. It began on a neutral note in the spirit of support of the Twentieth Party Congress. Then it turned gradually, in great part thanks to the fervor of the student gallery, into ever more severe criticism of the bureaucratic apparatus.[5] Everyone present recalled especially the intervention of Konstantin Paustovskii. "I don't intend to speak of the literary merits or flaws of Dudintsev's novel. That is not the point now. The novel is a major public event, and that is its significance. This is the first battle with the Drozdovs."[6] This speech was reproduced over and over again, distributed by the early purveyors of *samizdat,* and later confiscated in police searches as an anti-Soviet document.[7]

The social significance of the novel, its antibureaucratic thrust, was at once appreciated by readers, who were not intimidated by the negative reviews that appeared at first in the newspapers *Izvestia* and *Literary Gazette.*[8] The engineer A. Shcherbakov addressed himself to *Izvestia.*

> I disagree entirely with your assessment, and I consider the appearance . . . of the novel in our press to be an important development. . . . It summons us to struggle with the bureaucrats and careerists at all levels, including the ministries and the tyrants in academic and scientific life, and allows us to feel (it is strange that you didn't notice it), along with all the bureaucracy and the red tape, a province of life where they don't belong.[9]

Taking issue with those who were ready to explain conflicts in the novel as survivals of the past, one reader reasoned otherwise. "Please, the old and senile types of the past forty years of Soviet power have died off. And here is a new species that is not even considering dying out but, on the contrary, is forcing many others to worry about their own modest position in society."[10] Another reader continued the same thought: "Leaders of this kind have taken their place in their lounge chairs, and they are afraid that criticism will bounce them out of their accustomed sinecures."[11] The conclusion drawn in many of the letters to *Novyi mir* was that the bureaucrats would never surrender their positions willingly. So a struggle was foreseen, a confrontation with those who personified bureaucratic power, one of Dudintsev's principal ideas. "It's necessary! Say it louder!" wrote P. Kuznetsov from Tagil [Urals]. "We hear you, and we will do something. We are speaking out against our monopolists of power. They multiplied a good deal during the cult of personality. But our meetings are growing interesting, and we do not fear the struggle."[12]

The public opinion forming around Dudintsev's novel reflected not only readiness for a fight but formulated demands as if it were an informal social institute. In the main these demands concerned changes in the established order, which it was traditionally considered possible to criticize by reference to the principle "from the top down," that is, when initiated by the higher authorities. The speeches, proposals, and demands now being heard naturally provoked nervousness among employees of the apparatus, especially those in its lower and middle ranks. A variety of local authorities forbade libraries to give Dudintsev's novel to readers, and in several cities scheduled discussions of it were suddenly canceled. But the dynamism of public reaction had already been set in motion. People felt that in the atmosphere surrounding the novel "some kind of intangible mechanism was at work. People would come up and say, 'Do you know about it? Have you read it?' And people who had never read *Novyi mir* ran their legs off looking for [the issues containing] the novel."[13]

At Leningrad University, the tone of the discussion was clear. "We won't speak of the literary power of this work; let us speak of how we are going to struggle with the Drozdovs."[14] The students of Leningrad University then sent a letter to Moscow University with an appeal: "Let us unite in common cause against the Drozdovs."[15]

Official criticism of the novel reproached the author for slander, for the atypical nature of the character that he chose to portray, for political immaturity, etc., and some readers shared these sentiments. Such accusations, however, were based on a broader concern than the work of a single author. It was a question of admissible limits, of the bounds in which public opinion should be confined in order to avoid excessive conflict with the authorities. As an employee of the Central Committee observed, evidently speaking only for himself, "Let them generalize as Azhaev did.[16] Or as Malyshkin[17] has an old man say of a teapot, 'That is what Soviet power is like, it can't even make a decent teapot.' That we will allow. But we cannot allow individual people to have influence over youth. We must be united. That is the present situation."[18] So the bar on the high jump of criticism was supposed to be lowered to the level of the teapot. But that was obviously not the present situation.

Lev Kopelev described the development of events after this point. "At the very time . . . when the most important item for us was to discuss Dudintsev's [serialized] novel, in particular the question whether it would subsequently be published as a book, during those very hours in Budapest they overthrew a cast-iron statue of Stalin and marched in a demonstration to the monument of the Polish General Bem, who had fought for the freedom of Hungary [in the revolution of 1848–1849—H.R.]. A real people's revolution was under way there."[19]

Thus the internal life of the country was inscribed into an international context. The Hungarian question became for the Soviet leadership a kind of index of the volatility of the political crisis at home. It was thus perceived as the prospective model of development of the public movement in the Soviet Union, threatening to repeat the lessons of Budapest in a Soviet variant. A mood of panic spread among party functionaries in the fall and winter of 1956, and rumors were afloat that a secret list of communists had been composed for a future settling of accounts.[20] The rumors supplemented the newspaper reports, whose photos must have been selected for their shock effect. The Soviet press presented a picture of bloody counterrevolution against which background the introduction of Soviet forces into Budapest appeared not an illegal act trampling on the norms of international law but virtually an act of salvation.

Such images, however, fell far short of persuading everyone. The party informers recorded "unhealthy facts and hostile pronouncements" on the developments in Hungary.[21] One worker from Stalingrad was quoted as sympathetic to the Hungarians.

> I consider that they are doing the right thing to go on strike. They don't want our kind of regime, they don't like collective farms and socialism. Evidently they want to live on a grander scale, and they are doing right, [they want] freedom for their people. Not like among us, where everyone is intimidated. We can only dawdle, we can't do anything. You can see that they have a leader who knows how to organize the whole people, and they have begun to act, but we are too afraid to get organized. If anyone speaks out, he is instantly taken away. They don't want to live as we do, and you see that our leaders take our produce and send it to them, knowing that our people will put up with anything.[22]

In the laconic terms of a worker from Omsk, "In Hungary they are sick of socialism, they are turning to capitalism."[23] In several Soviet cities leaflets appeared calling for support of the Hungarian people and condemning the Soviet armed intervention. In Barnaul (southwest Siberia), for example, during the night of 6–7 November ten such leaflets were found.

> Citizens! Friends! It is time to act! Down with the Central Committee of the Communist Party, which for thirty-nine years has led the people of Russia to unmitigated poverty! Join the ranks of the Union of Liberation of the Peoples of Russia! Death to the oppressors, to the base extortioners! For the happiness of the people of Russia against the savage Central Committee of the Communist Party! . . . Read it and pass it on.[24]

During a demonstration on the anniversary of the October Revolution, a student in Yaroslavl unfurled a handwritten banner reading "We demand the withdrawal of Soviet troops from Hungary!" After his detention by the security organs, he explained that he wrote it himself without anyone's prompting "in order to determine whether there is democracy in the USSR or not."[25] But on the whole the manifestations of open protest against the Soviet intervention in Hungary were few and isolated. People of course discussed the matter, but the discussion did not reach beyond circles of close friends.

The Hungarian crisis was at the same time a crisis of Khrushchev's "new course." The Budapest autumn put him to the test, disclosing the most vulnerable points of the incipient political reform and threatening its successful continuation. A major question stood across the path of progressive political reforms, the question of the attitude of the Soviet leadership and the political opposition to each other. The open existence of opposition could serve as a guarantor of the irreversible nature of progressive reforms. Intervention in Hungary, however, and the events following it in the USSR showed that, under the present power structure, the legalization of opposition was out of the question. The leaders who had attained their posts in a struggle with various kinds of opposition and deviation in the 1920s and 1930s perceived the very idea of opposition as unconditionally hostile and thus liable to destruction—if possible, at the moment of its conception. Among those who managed the fate of the country in the 1940s, not one would have advocated any other principle.

The uprising in Budapest was a turning point in the development of domestic reform, demonstrating to the whole world the limits of Khrushchev's liberalization. The leadership of the country hastened to take measures of intimidation designed to block the development of a Soviet version of the Hungarian events.

In December 1956 the Central Committee addressed to all members of the party a confidential letter, the title of which speaks for itself: "On the strengthening of the political work of party organizations among the masses and preempting the attacks of hostile, anti-Soviet elements." The letter included a detailed list of "risk groups," especially those subject to the influence of alien ideology, among which first place was occupied by the artistic intelligentsia and student bodies. The spirit and the phraseology of the letter were familiar and might easily have come from the most fervent witch-hunts of the 1930s and 1940s. Especially expressive was the conclusion in which the Central Committee considered it appropriate to emphasize that "there cannot be two opinions about our manner of combating the enemy rabble. The dictatorship of the proletariat must deal with anti-Soviet elements mercilessly."[26] There was a degree of reserve in the letter. It spoke of "parts of the Soviet people" who "sometimes do not exhibit sufficient political maturity," but "such people may not be lumped together in a single category with enemy elements."[27] It remained only to distinguish between the two kinds.

The first victim in the campaign against the Hungarian syndrome was the national intelligentsia, above all, the writers: Dudintsev, the author of the novel *Not by Bread Alone;* the authors of the almanac *Literary Moscow* [Margarita Aliger and others—H.R.]; Boris Pasternak, the author of *Doctor Zhivago.* Ehrenburg characterized the campaign as follows.

> The attacks on the writers had nothing to do with criticism of their literary works but with the change in the political situation. People tried not to recall the Twentieth Party Congress, and of course they could not foresee the Twenty-Second. The youth were intimidated, and students had ceased to speak their thoughts at meetings. They spoke only among themselves. The fear that forced people to be silent under Stalin had disappeared. It was replaced by more ordinary fears. If you speak out too much, you will be sent to work far from Moscow.[28]

Unpleasant memories returned: of the campaigns against cosmopolitanism, against kowtowing before the West, and against various phenomena considered bourgeois. In May 1957 there was a meeting of party leaders and writers—directors of the Union of Writers—the first in a series of traditional "historical meetings," as the propaganda termed them, between the leadership of the country and the intelligentsia. The writer Veniamin Kaverin, present at the first such meeting, later recalled that the artistic intelligentsia still hoped that Khrushchev would use his authority to support the liberal trend of literature.[29] But it turned out quite otherwise. Khrushchev began to speak of Stalin, reproaching the writers for understanding only one side of the criticism of the cult of personality. "Stalin occupies an appropriate place in Soviet history," Khrushchev explained. "He had great shortcomings, but Stalin was loyal to Marxism-Leninism, a devoted and staunch revolutionary. Our party and people will remember Stalin and give him his due."[30] Signaling in such an unambiguous fashion the principal ideological criteria, Khrushchev turned to their particular implications. "However incoherent Khrushchev's speech was," wrote Veniamin Kaverin, "his thought was perfectly clear. . . . It smelled of arrests, especially as he said that the 'revolt in Hungary would not have happened if two or three windbags had been thrown in prison in time.' "[31]

Alexander Tvardovskii characterized the situation in 1957 as "the dissipation of the last illusions."[32] This was a turning point, a retreat, alarming not only by virtue of that fact but because it threatened fundamentally all the important achievements of recent years, the freedom of the press, relative and limited but better than before. The watchword of 1957 was the restoration of unanimity of thought. Of freedom of speech, of glasnost, there was not a word. And without glasnost, of course, there was no healthy public opinion.

In the absence of free speech, public opinion inevitably returned to the catacomb level, and thus the Soviet dissident movement arose, fundamentally oppositionist in its attitude to the government and its policy. Driven underground, the dissident movement concentrated the energy of its thoughts and deeds in the political and juridical sphere, gradually turning into a movement to support legal rights. The open opposition of the dissident movement and its uncompromising character cut it off from mainstream political life, condemning it to the path of solitary opposition. Such a fate was characteristic not only of dissent. The public atmosphere itself and the conduct of the authorities prompted people to choose the path of individual resistance, some forms of which did not necessarily exhibit the qualities of dissent.

Igor Dedkov recalls his feelings of the time.

> It was just at that time that I came to the conclusion that every attempt at organized opposition was doomed to failure. Because everything was controlled, every step, even in the provinces where I lived. I remember that my colleagues from Moscow came to me in a ferment of ideas and plans. And I said no! The only way that I considered then possible was the way of individual, spiritual, moral resistance. Only on an individual basis. Because every other way was blocked. I felt it literally physically. If an ordinary provincial student, who simply writes and receives letters, is so surrounded [by security agents—H.R.], it means one of two things. Either [the agents] have nothing to do, or their numbers suffice for any task whatever.[33]

After 1957 the contacts of Soviet citizens with the outside world were again more restricted. While trying to block the development of public opinion that they did not approve, however, the Soviet authorities could not foresee everything, and 1957 is remembered by contemporaries not only as a time of disappointment but as a time of new discovery. The vehicle of this discovery was the Moscow Festival of Youth and Students. The decision to hold it in Moscow was made, naturally, before the tightening of the screws of cultural policy. By the time of the cultural crackdown, it was too late to cancel the occasion. As a result the residents of Moscow witnessed during the festival a great deal that was new and unexpected.

Most unexpected was the holiday appearance of the city. The streets of Moscow were for the first time decked out in multicolored flags rather than the customary red one, and Pablo Picasso's doves of peace replaced the customary hammer and sickle as the symbol of the festival. The program of the festival included three artistic exhibits, each of which featured pictures by the "abstractionists," artists who were not recognized by Soviet artistic canons. For many people, this was the first opportunity to view abstract painting. "Perhaps from our contemporary viewpoint, this was not a first-class exhibit," recalled one of the viewers, "but the mere spirit of free communication, simply of unfettering, that prevailed there, the fact of an exhibit of paintings that we were previously forbidden in principle to see—that was the important thing."[34]

In addition, the Moscow festival to a significant degree rehabilitated jazz, previously condemned to the underground. Jazz musicians came to Moscow from the United States, Italy, and Poland. A modest jazz festival was organized. All of these events, literally stunning to the young people of Moscow, formed an especially festive spirit. It was a real holiday, a holiday of discovery and of socializing. The jazz musician Alexei Kozlov remembers these days.

> The city was abuzz night and day. Crowds of foreigners strolled about Moscow, many Americans among them. We were so surprised. They had nothing in common with the caricatures of them in *Krokodil* [the Soviet satirical magazine—E.Z.] and in the drawings of [Herluf] Bidstrup. Those were either fat cats with cigars in their teeth or filthy tramps in pants full of holes and a baggy hat. And these were entirely different: simple, friendly, robust, full of smiles, all with short haircuts, and in blue pants that we later learned to call jeans.[35]

Many participants in those events later assessed the Moscow festival as a kind of turning point in the development of their own view of the world. The contact with another culture, the very idea of a multiplicity of models of the world reflected in a variety of artistic styles, contrasted sharply with the customary monocultural thought and the oppressive monotony of official Soviet art. And if the political significance of the festival soon became the property of propaganda, the spirit of the occasion was long remembered, at least in Moscow.

The year 1957 did not put an end to the history of the thaw, but it clearly suggested that public opinion and the intentions of the authorities were far from compatible. As after the war, the government proved unprepared for an open dialogue with the public. Public opinion was as formerly assigned a role summed up in two words: approve and support.

But the spirit of society already exhibited changes that were irreversible. People could not yet say openly all that they thought about the government, about the present and the future of the country, but they ceased to be afraid of each other, and so they acquired for the first time the opportunity to socialize freely, though only, it is true, in a narrow circle of friends. "Under Stalin, when informing was the norm, social life outside the workplace was reduced to a minimum," related Liudmila Alekseeva, author of *The History of Dissent in the USSR.* "In Moscow there was scarcely a house where unfamiliar people were welcome. . . . When the terror of unwarranted arrests passed, people began to visit each other, taking pleasure in the mere fact of being together."[36]

New forms of social life arose among neighbors and friends, who began to spend time in conversation in the kitchen. As the soldiers after the war found release in the "blue Danubes," the intelligentsia of the 1950s and 1960s sought out their intellectual friends and enemies in the kitchen. A great many anecdotes were spawned in the kitchen,[37] a characteristic sign of the times. They were told and retold by people who no longer feared imprisonment on account of them. There were favorite songs accompanied by guitar. Society began to warm up and thaw out. It is true that matters did not develop much farther at that time. But no rigorous return to the past was possible. Russia paused again halfway through the course, as it had already done more than once, on the route to reform.

Conclusion

Historical analogies can be deceptive, but they are often useful. In any event, an attentive and impartial examination of the past sometimes spares the statesmen of the present the repetition of the most futile paradigms of discarded policy. Notwithstanding the caprices of historical fate, the experience of the past sometimes suggests how to avoid dangerous confrontations with unexpected obstacles, including those that have stood as an insurmountable barrier across the path of Russian reform.

Let us consider the factor of timing, the choice of the most favorable moment for the introduction of reform. Obviously, such a moment must involve the common consent of the government and the public. In the postwar period, there was no such moment. The Stalinist regime was determined to restore the essentials of the prewar order, and the public, dreading above all reforms that would make matters worse, consented to "temporary difficulties" as the lesser of two evils. Thus the government, counting on the people's patience, let slip the two opportunities most favorable for reform, one in 1945–1946 and another in 1956.

The authorities were concerned, of course, to maintain themselves and their power, and the different leaders were concerned to pursue policies enhancing their own positions in the government. As both their conservative nature and their rivalry with each other militated against systemic reform, the demand for progressive change devolved upon other elements of society. In the absence of a parliamentary tradition, the most conspicuous support of reform came from the literary intelligentsia. The activism of the literary movement, however, frightened the authorities, who then stiffened their opposition to reform.

Malenkov's efforts perhaps held out the promise of something better. Had he been allowed to develop his program more fully, he might well have inaugurated a variant of what Mikhail Gefter called the "prosperous police state." And once the genie was out of the bottle, it would have been necessary to adjust politics to new conditions of life. A road to pluralism might have been opened, one taking public opinion into account and inaugurating a new distribution of power.

We must not make the mistake, however, of thinking that the strangulation of reform in the 1950s and 1960s was the work of the party-state apparatus alone. Behind the reform efforts social interests always stood, and the success of the reforms depended on the social milieu that stood to benefit by them. Society was divided both against itself and against the nomenklatura as well. Both the one and the other were intimidated by "mental arresting devices," those unimpeachable invocations of the liturgy of Stalinist socialism. As a consequence, neither the party elite nor the general public was rich in reformist ideas. New ideas, more humanistic values, were present— and persistent—in embryo, and they were destined to grow, but they faced enormous odds. Few people had the courage to raise the question of the fundamental rectitude of socialism. No one attacked in public the basic values of state property, collective farms, and industrial giants. The most progressive ideas of the time did not overstep the bounds of socialist ideology, and the development of public opinion proceeded fundamentally from the slogan "back to Lenin."

Finally, these lost opportunities did not pass, alas, without other losses, the saddest of which were the losses of human life and of humane values. The thaw proceeded from admirable moral impulses, from faith in ideals, many of them laudable and later lost. If we are to build a better future, our society must cure itself of the disease of hate. In order to do so, it must return to its past, where there were not only missed opportunities but real evocations of the human spirit on which inspired people might be able to found a political and cultural renaissance.

Notes

List of Abbreviations

GARF—Gosudarstvennyi arkhiv Rossiiskoi federatsii
RGALI—Rossiiskii gosudarstvennyi arkhiv literatury i iskusstva
RTsKhIDNI—Rossiiskii tsentr khraneniia i izucheniia dokumentov novoi istorii
TsKhSD—Tsentr khraneniia sovremennoi dokumentatsii
d.   = delo: volume
f.   = fond: record group
l.   = list: page
ll. = listy: pages
op. = opis′: inventory

Translator's Introduction

1. The one development of the period that scholars have probed more deeply is the series of policy debates that eventuated in the alleged defeat of A.A. Zhdanov. Perhaps the best example is Werner G. Hahn, *Postwar Soviet Politics: The Fall of Zhdanov and the Defeat of Moderation, 1946–1953* (Ithaca, NY, 1982).

2. Alexander Werth, *Russia: The Post-War Years* (New York, 1971), ix.

3. Roger W. Pethybridge, *A History of Postwar Russia* (New York, 1966), 15.

4. The new Russian historiography is admirably covered in two volumes by Robert W. Davies, *Soviet History in the Gorbachev Revolution* (Bloomington, IN, 1989) and *Soviet History in the Yeltsin Era* (Basingstoke, UK, 1997).

Introduction

1. Aleksandr Zinoviev, *Homo sovieticus,* trans. Charles Janson (London, 1985).

2. Mikhail Geller, *Cogs in the Soviet Wheel: The Formation of Soviet Man,* trans. David Floyd (London, 1988).

3. Vera S. Dunham, *In Stalin's Time: Middleclass Values in Soviet Fiction* (New York, 1976).

4. Seweryn Bialer, *Stalin's Successors: Leadership, Stability and Change in the Soviet Union* (Cambridge, UK, 1980); Dietrich Beyrau and Ivo Bock, eds., *Das Tauwetter und die Folgen* (Bremen, 1988); Donald A. Filtzer, *The Khrushchev Era: De-Stalinisation and the Limits of Reform in the USSR, 1953–1964* (Basingstoke, UK, 1993); O.L. Leibovich, *Reforma i modernizatsiia v 1953–1964 gg.* (Perm, 1993); James G. Richter, *Khrushchev's Double Bind: International Pressures and Domestic Coalition Politics* (Baltimore, 1994).

5. Timothy Dunmore, *Soviet Politics, 1945–1953* (London, 1984); Werner G. Hahn, *Postwar Soviet Politics: The Fall of Zhdanov and the Defeat of Moderation, 1946–1953* (London, 1982); Alexander Werth, *Russia: The Postwar Years* (New York, 1971).

6. N.V. Romanovskii, *Liki stalinizma, 1945–1953 gg.* (Moscow, 1995).

7. Susan J. Linz, ed., *The Impact of World War II on the Soviet Union* (Totowa, NJ, 1985); John Garrard and Carol Garrard, eds., *World War II and the Soviet People* (New York, 1993); M.M. Narinskii et al., eds., *Kholodnaia voina: Novye podkhody, novye dokumenty* (Moscow, 1995).

8. Vladimir Shlapentokh, *Public and Private Life of the Soviet People: Changing Values in Post-Stalin Russia* (New York, 1989).

9. Karl Schlögel, *Der renitente Held: Arbeiterprotest in der Sowjetunion, 1953–1983* (Hamburg, 1984); Donald A. Filtzer, *Soviet Workers and De-Stalinization: The Consolidation of the Modern System of Soviet Production Relations, 1953–1964* (New York, 1992).

10. I.M. Volkov, *Trudovoi podvig sovetskogo krest'ianstva v poslevoennye gody: Kolkhozy SSSR v 1946–1950 gg.* (Moscow, 1972); V.P. Popov, *Rossiiskaia derevnia posle voiny (iiun' 1945–mart 1953 gg.)* (Moscow, 1991); O.M. Verbitskaia, *Rossiiskoe krest'ianstvo: Ot Stalina k Khrushchevu* (Moscow, 1992).

11. Vladimir Shlapentokh, *Soviet Intellectuals and Political Power: The Post-Stalin Era* (Princeton, 1990); Hans Gunter, ed., *The Culture of the Stalin Period* (Basingstoke, UK, 1990); Edith R. Frankel, *Novyi Mir: Case Study in the Politics of Literature, 1952–1958* (Cambridge, UK, 1981); Dietrich Beyrau, *Intelligenz und Dissens: Die russischen Bildungsschichten in der Sowjetunion, 1917–1985* (Göttingen, 1993); Liudmila Alekseeva, *Soviet Dissent: Contemporary Movements for National, Religious, and Human Rights,* trans. Carol Pearce and John Glad (Middletown, CT, 1985); D.L. Babichenko, *Pisateli i tsenzory: Sovetskaia literatura 1940–kh godov pod politicheskim kontrolem TsK* (Moscow, 1994).

12. The bulk of the diaries and memoirs of the period are by people in the academic or artistic professions—writers, poets, and scholars—e.g., G.A. Arbatov, *The System: An Insider's Life in Soviet Politics* (New York, 1992); Fedor M. Burlatskii, *Vozhdi i sovetniki: O Khrushcheve, Andropove i ne tol'ko o nikh* (Moscow, 1990); Emmanuil Kazakevich, *Slushaia vremia: Dnevniki, zapisnye knizhki, pis'ma* (Moscow, 1990); Lev Kopelev, *To Be Preserved Forever,* trans. and ed. Anthony Austin (Philadelphia, 1977); idem, *Utoli moia pechali: Memuary* (Moscow, 1991); Vladimir Lakshin, *"Novy mir" vo vremena Khrushcheva: Dnevnik i poputnoe, 1953–1964* (Moscow, 1991); Zdenek Mlynarzh [Zdeněk Mlynař], *Moroz udaril iz Kremlia* (Moscow, 1992); Valentin V. Ovechkin, *Stat'i, dnevniki, pis'ma* (Moscow, 1972); David Samoilov, *Pamiatnye zapiski* (Moscow, 1995); Andrei Sakharov, *Memoirs,* trans. Richard Lourie (London, 1990); Konstantin M. Simonov, *Glazami cheloveka moego pokoleniia: Razmyshleniia o I.V. Staline* (Moscow, 1988); Aleksandr T. Tvardovskii, "Iz zapisnykh knizhek, 1953–1960," *Znamia,* 1989, Nos. 7–9; Kornei I. Chukovskii, *Dnevnik, 1930–1969 gg.* (Moscow, 1995); Ilia G. Erenburg, *Sobranie sochinenii,* 9 vols. (Moscow, 1962–1967).

Chapter 1: The Social Psychology of the War

1. Ales' Adamovich, Ianka Bryl', and Vladimir Kolesnik, *Out of the Fire,* trans. Angelia Graf and Nina Belenkaia (Moscow, 1980); Ales' Adamovich and Daniil Granin, *A Book of the*

Blockade, trans. Hilda Perham (Moscow, 1983); Svetlana Aleksievich, *War's Unwomanly Face* (Moscow, 1988).

2. Grigorii Ia. Baklanov, *Piad'zemli: Povest'* (Moscow, 1960); Vasil'Bykau (Bykov), *Dozhit' do rassveta; Obelisk; Povesti* (Moscow, 1973); idem, *Poiti i ne vernut'sia* (Moscow, 1979); Viktor Nekrasov, *Front-Line Stalingrad,* trans. David Floyd (London, 1962); Viacheslav Kondrat'ev, *Sashka: Povesti i rasskazy* (Moscow, 1981).

3. Konstantin M. Simonov, *Pis'ma o voine, 1943–1979* (Moscow, 1990).

4. Sergei Alekseev, "Ne poteriat' by . . . : Razmyshleniia o nastoiashchem, k kotorym primeshany grust' ob utratakh proshlogo i trevoga za nashe budushchee," *Sovetskaia kul'tura,* 13 December 1990.

5. Lev Voitolovskii, *Ocherki kollektivnoi psikhologii,* Part I (Petrograd, 1924), 49.

6. Gabriel' Tard, *Obshchestvennoe mnenie i tolpa* (Moscow, 1902), 160.

7. Mikhail Gefter, "V predchuvstvii proshlogo," *Vek XX i mir,* 1990, No. 9: 34.

8. "Ukradennaia pobeda," *Komsomol'skaia pravda,* 5 May 1990.

9. Ibid.

10. "Shel soldat. . . . ," ibid., 27 April 1990.

11. "Paradoksy frontovoi nostal'gii," *Literaturnaia gazeta,* 5 May 1990, 9.

12. "Vysota voiny," ibid., 19 June 1992, 1.

13. "Paradoksy frontovoi nostal'gii," 9.

14. Simonov, *Pis'ma o voine: 1943–1979 gg.,* 80–81.

15. "Stalin umer vchera. . . . ," A.A. Protashchik, ed., *Inogo ne dano* (Moscow, 1988), 305 [Author's emphasis—E.Z.].

16. "Ot anti-Stalina k ne-Stalinu: Neproidennyi put'," *Osmyslit' kul't Stalina* (Moscow, 1989), 501.

17. "Ukradennaia pobeda," *Komsomol'skaia pravda,* 5 May 1990.

18. *Pamiatnye zapiski* (Moscow, 1995), 210.

19. SMERSH' = SMERt' (death) + SHpionam (to spies), the organ of counter-intelligence at the front.

20. Interview with Boris Kondrat'ev; personal archive of the author.

21. "Voina, kotoruiu ne znali: Iz dnevnika, prokommentirovannogo samym avtorom 45 let spustia," *Sovetskaia kul'tura,* 5 May 1990.

22. "Glazami cheloveka moego pokoleniia: Razmyshleniia o I.V. Staline," *Znamia,* 1988, No. 3: 48.

23. Ibid.

24. *Stat'i, dnevniki, pis'ma* (Moscow, 1972), 203.

Chapter 2: The Victory and The Victors

1. B.N. Ponomarev, *Istoriia SSSR s drevneishikh vremen do nashikh dnei,* 11 vols. (Moscow, 1966–1980), 11: 47. [As the ruble of the time was a controlled currency not traded in world financial markets, its real value is impossible to determine, and hence it hardly makes sense to try to give an equivalent dollar value for the sum cited here.—H.R.]

2. Not even the formerly secret information recently put at the disposal of historians on the demographic composition of the population during and after the war has clarified the situation fully. The indices of the birth and death rates of the population held in different offices of the government (for example, the Central Statistical Administration of the USSR and the Ministry of Health) often not only fail to coincide but contradict each other. The most detailed examination of the problem is in V.P. Popov, "Prichiny sokrashcheniia chislennosti naseleniia RSFSR posle Velikoi otechestvennoi voiny," *Sotsiologichcskie issledovaniia,* 1994, No. 10, 76–79.

3. The human losses evaluated here to determine the demographic balance include: (a) those dying as a consequence of the military or other action of the enemy; (b) those dying as a result of the higher level of mortality during the war in the rear, in the regions abutting the front, and in the occupied territory; (c) those people from the population of the USSR on 22 June 1941 who left the territory of the country during the war and did not return before its conclusion (not including POWs and displaced persons).

4. E.M. Andreev et al., *Naselenie Sovetskogo Soiuza, 1922–1991 gg.* (Moscow, 1993), 73.

5. Ibid., 77.

6. Ibid., 121–34.

7. Iu.V. Argutiunian, *Sovetskoe krest'ianstvo v gody Velikoi otechestvennoi voiny* (Moscow, 1963), 318.

8. Popov, "Prichiny sokrashcheniia chislennosti naseleniia RSFSR posle Velikoi otechestvennoi voiny," 91.

9. Andreev et al., *Naselenie Sovetskogo Soiuza, 1922–1991*, 53, 70.

10. Dokladnaia zapiska upolnomochenogo Komissii partiinogo kontrolia pri TsK VKP(b) po Gor'kovskoi oblasti "O neudovletvoritel'nom kul'turno-bytovom obsluzhivanii i proizvodstvennykh usloviakh rabochikh-podrostkov na riade predpriitii Gor'kovskoi oblasti, 11 June 1945; RTsKhIDNI, f. 17, op. 122, d. 103, l. 77.

11. Ibid.

12. *Istoriia SSSR s drevneishikh vremen,* 11: 53.

13. Ibid., 56.

14. Informatsiia Organizatsionno-instruktorskogo otdela TsK VKP(b) o vypolnenii postanovleniia TsK VKP(b) ot 25 avgusta 1945 g. "O rabote mestnykh partiinykh organizatsii i sovetskikh organov po ustroistvu demobilizovannykh iz deistvuiushchei armii," 11 March 1946; RTsKhIDNI, f. 17, op. 122, d. 145, l. 193.

15. Ibid., l. 194.

16. Ibid.

17. Boguslav Shnaider, "Neizvestnaia voina," *Voprosy istorii,* 1995, No. 1: 110.

18. Dokladnaia zapiska zaveduiushchego otdelom Upravleniia Kadrov TsK VKP(b) Petrova "O neobkhodimosti perestroiki dela lechebnoi pomoshchi invalidam Otechestvennoi voiny," 25 April 1945; RTsKhIDNI, f. 17, op. 117, d. 511, l. 107.

19. Ibid., 108.

20. Mikhail Gefter, "Stalin umer vchera. . . . ," in A.A. Protashchik, ed., *Inogo ne dano* (Moscow, 1988), 305.

21. One of the first problems of the deliberate division of Soviet society into different interest groups after the war was described by Vera S. Dunham, *In Stalin's Time: Middleclass Values in Soviet Fiction* (Cambridge, MA, 1976), 12.

22. For all of the differences in the historical conditions of the two wars, that of 1812 and that of 1941–1945, they had similar sociopsychological consequences: the awakening of the spirit of freedom, the aspirations of the people for a better life as a reward for the victory, the birth of progressive political ideas among the intelligentsia and others. There was also some parallel in the moods of the peasantry in favor of the abolition of serfdom in the earlier case and of the abolition of the collective farm in the second. Both wars also provided an impetus for reevaluation of political values in the minds of social groups participating in the power structure, some representatives of which gradually formed conservative and reformist wings. [That is, they were opposed to the radical storm and stress approach to economic planning and expansion, in favor of emphasizing consumer industry rather than the capital goods industries—in Soviet parlance, Group B and Group A respectively—and committed to economic concessions for the peasantry.—H.R.] This wing of the administration was characterized by a wish to turn from the idea of autocratic power—the *vozhd'*, leader, Stalin—to power limited to some degree by the influence of democratic institutions.

23. Emmanuil Kazakevich, *Slushaia vremia: Dnevniki, zapisnye knizhki, pis'ma* (Moscow, 1990), 259.
24. RGALI, f. 631, op. 15, d. 737, l. 86.
25. Interview with V.L. Kondrat'ev; author's personal archive.
26. Viacheslav Kondrat'ev, "Ne tol'ko o svoem pokolenii," *Kommunist*, 1990, No. 7: 115.
27. Viktor Smirnov, "Zaulki: Povest'," *Roman-gazeta*, 1989, No. 3–4: 8.
28. Viacheslav Kondrat'ev, "Paradoksy frontovoi nostal'gii," *Literaturnaia gazeta*, 9 May 1990, 9.
29. Kazakevich, *Slushaia vremia*, 28.
30. *Pravda*, 9 May 1945.
31. Ibid.
32. Ibid., 10 May 1945.
33. Ibid., 25 May 1945.
34. Ibid., 27 June 1945.

Chapter 3: "How To Live after the War"?

1. Fedor Abramov, "A liudi zhdut, zhdut peremen: Iz dnevnikovykh i rabochikh zapisei," *Izvestia*, 3 February 1990.
2. Georgii Fedotov, "Rossiia i svoboda," *Znamia*, 1989, No. 12: 214.
3. Viktor Nekrasov, "Tragediia moego pokoleniia. *V okopakh Stalingrada:* Do i posle," *Literaturnaia gazeta*, 12 September 1990, 15.
4. Cited in "Dnevniki vesti ne razreshalos'," *Sovetskaia kul'tura*, 25 April 1990.
5. Fedotov, "Rossiia i svoboda," 198.
6. Mikhail Gefter, "Stalin umer vchera. . . . ," in A.A. Protashchik, ed., *Inogo ne dano* (Moscow, 1988), 305.
7. Emmanuil Kazakevich, *Slushaia vremia: Dnevniki, zapisnye knizhki, pis'ma* (Moscow, 1990), 316.
8. Boris Galin, "V odnom naselennom punkte: Rasskaz propagandista," *Novyi mir*, 1947, No. 11: 162–63.
9. K.M. Simonov, *Sobranie sochinenii*, 6 vols. (Moscow, 1966–1970), 3: 124.
10. RGALI, f. 631, op. 15, d. 737, ll. 86–87.
11. Cited in "Shel soldat. . . . ," *Komsomol'skaia pravda*, 28 April 1990.
12. Cited in Elizar Mal'tsev, "Ne izmeniaia sebe," *Literaturnaia gazeta*, 18 February 1987, 8.
13. Vladislav Serikov, "Dogovor po sovesti," *Roman-gazeta*, 1986, No. 7: 9.
14. Informatsiia Upravleniia propagandy i agitatsii TsK VKP(b) "O material'no-bytovom polozhenii rabochikh ugol'noi promyshlennosti Tul'skoi oblasti," January 1946; RTsKhIDNI, f. 17, op. 125, d. 421, ll. 2–3.
15. Informatsiia Upravleniia propagandy i agitatsii TsK VKP(b) o polozhenii del v Penzenskoi oblasti v sviazi s podgotovkoi k vyboram v Verkhovnyi Sovet SSSR, January 1946; ibid., d. 420, l. 40.
16. Ibid.
17. Ibid.
18. Informatsiia Upravleniia propagandy i agitatsii TsK VKP(b) o podgotovke k prazdnovaniiu 29oi godovshchiny Oktiabr'skoi revoliutsii, November 1946; ibid., d. 421, l. 102.
19. Dokladnaia zapiska zaveduiushchego otdelom Upravleniia kadrov TsK VKP(b) Borodina o polozhenii del na tankovom zavode v gorode Omske, 18 September 1945; ibid., op. 117, d. 530, ll. 37–38.
20. Iurii Aksiutin, "Pochemu Stalin dal'neishemu sotrudnichestvu s soiuznikami posle

pobedy predpochel konfrontatsiiu s nimi: Nekotorye sotsial'no-psikhologicheskie aspekty
vozniknoveniia kholodnoi voiny," in M.M. Narinskii et al., eds., *Kholodnaia voina: Novye
podkhody, novye dokumenty* (Moscow, 1995), 52–53.

21. Vyderzhki iz pisem rabochikh zavodov g. Omska, zaderzhannykh Voennoi tsenzuroi
NKGB SSSR, 19 September 1945; RTsKhIDNI, f. 17, op. 117, d. 530, l. 54.

22. Ibid., l. 57.

23. Postanovlenie Sekretariata TsK VKP(b) "O meropriiatiiakh po uluchsheniiu
massovo-politicheskoi raboty i material'no-bytovogo obsluzhivaniia rabochikh zavodov No.
22, 174 i 179," 4 August 1945; ibid., ll. 11–12.

24. I.M. Volkov, *Trudovoi podvig sovetskogo krest'ianstva v poslevoennye gody: Kolkhozy SSSR v
1946–1950 godakh* (Moscow, 1972), 21.

25. Ibid.

26. V.F. Zima, *Golod v SSSR 1946–1947 godov: Proiskhozhdenie i posledstviia* (Moscow,
1996), 159.

27. Svodka pisem, postupivshikh v gazetu "Pravda" o banditizme, vorovstve i
khuliganstve, 17 November 1945 g.; RTsKhIDNI, f. 17, op. 122, d. 118, l. 92.

28. Ibid., ll. 92–93.

29. Ibid., l. 93.

30. Dokladnaia zapiska upolnomochennogo Komissii partiinogo kontrolia pri TsK
VKP(b) po Vladimirskoi oblasti Shkol'nikova "O neudovletvoritel'noi rabote organov
militsii, suda i prokuratury Vladimirskoi oblasti v bor'be s khuliganstvom, krazhami,
grabezhami i drugimi prestupleniiami," 12 December 1945 g.; ibid., d. 103, l. 217.

31. Ibid.

32. Dokladnaia zapiska ministra vnutrennikh del SSSR S. Kruglova o sostoianii
ugolovnoi prestupnosti v SSSR v 1948 g., 18 January 1949; GARF, f. 9401, op. 2, d. 234, l. 20.

33. Dokladnaia zapiska ministra vnutrennikh del SSSR S. Kruglova o sostoianii
ugolovnoi prestupnosti v SSSR za 1947 g., 4 February 1948; ibid., d. 199, l. 184.

34. Ibid.

35. Informatsiia Upravleniia po proverke partiinykh organov TsK VKP(b) "O faktakh
uvelicheniia prestupnosti i khuliganstva," 10 February 1947; RTsKhIDNI, f. 17, op. 122, d.
289, ll. 1–6.

Chapter 4: The Famine of 1946–1947

1. *Sel'skoe khoziaistvo SSSR: Statisticheskii sbornik* (Moscow, 1971), 152.

2. V.F. Zima, *Golod v SSSR 1946–1947 godov: Proiskhozhdenie i posledstviia* (Moscow,
1996), 20.

3. *Istoriia Velikoi Otechestvennoi voiny Sovetskogo Soiuza, 1941–1945*, 6 vols. (Moscow,
1960–1965), 6: 411–12.

4. Soobshchenie Soveta Ministrov SSSR i Tsentral'nogo Komiteta VKP(b). Protokol
No. 54 zasedaniia Politbiuro TsK VKP(b), 6 September 1946; RTsKhIDNI, f. 17, op. 3, d.
1061, ll. 12–13.

5. Ibid., l. 16.

6. Ibid., ll. 12–13.

7. "V Sovete Ministrov SSSR," *Pravda*, 16 September 1946.

8. Politicheskaia informatsiia o provedennykh meropriiatiiakh i politicheskikh
nastroeniiakh sredi trudiashchikhsia g. Moskvy i oblasti v sviazi s postanovleniem Soveta
Ministrov SSSR i TsK VKP(b), 6 September 1946; RTsKhIDNI, f. 17, op. 121, d. 524, ll. 8–11.

9. Ibid., l. 9.

10. Ibid., l. 11.

11. Ibid., l. 10.

12. Ibid., l. 9.

13. Svodka voprosov, zadavaemykh po sobraniiakh gorodskikh partiinykh aktivov v sviazi s Soobshcheniem Soveta Ministrov SSSR i TsK VKP(b) ob uvelichenii paikovykh tsen na produkty pitaniia i snizhenii kommercheskikh tsen na produkty i promyshlennye tovary, 16 September 1946; and ll. 28–31.

14. Zima, *Golod v SSSR 1946–1947 godov*, 149.

15. Svodka voprosov, zadavaemykh na sobraniiakh gorodskikh partiinykh aktivov. . . . , RTsKhIDNI, f. 17, op. 121, d. 524, l. 31.

16. Dokladnaia zapiska Moskovskogo gorodskogo komiteta VKP(b) "Politicheskie nastroeniia sredi trudiashchikhsia goroda Moskvy," September 1946; ibid., l. 12.

17. Ibid., l. 11.

18. Ibid., ll. 12–13.

19. Ibid., ll. 13–14.

20. Dokladnaia zapiska N.S. Patolicheva A.A. Zhdanovu "O gorodskikh sobraniiakh partiinykh aktivov po raz''iasneniiu Soobshcheniia Soveta Ministrov SSSR i TsK VKP(b) o povyshenii paikovykh tsen," 14 September 1946; ibid., l. 26.

21. "V Sovete Ministrov SSSR," *Pravda*, 14 September 1946.

22. Dokladnaia zapiska N.S. Patolicheva I.V. Stalinu "O sobraniiakh rabochikh i sluzhashchikh na predpriiatiiakh i v uchrezhdeniiakh po raz''iasneniiu soobshcheniia Soveta Ministrov SSSR ob izmenenii tsen na produkty pitaniia i promyshlennye tovary," 21 September 1946; RTsKhIDNI, f. 17, op. 121, d. 524, l. 56.

23. Ibid., l. 57.

24. Informatsiia VTsSPS "Vyskazyvaniia rabochikh i sluzhashchikh po povodu izmeneniia tsen," 20 September 1946; ibid., l. 62.

25. Dokladnaia zapiska N.S. Patolicheva I.V. Staliny "O sobraniiakh rabochikh i sluzhashchikh. . . ," ibid., l. 57.

26. Ibid.

27. Ibid., l. 52.

28. Postanovlenie Soveta Ministrov SSSR i TsK VKP(b) "O zapreshchenii povysheniia zarabotnoi platy i norm prodovol'stvennogo i promtovarnogo snabzheniia," 16 September 1946; ibid., f. 17, op. 3, d. 1062, l. 11.

29. Postanovlenie Soveta Ministrov SSSR i TsK VKP(b) "Ob ekonomii v raskhodovanii khleba," 27 September 1946; ibid., ll. 21–23.

30. Postanovlenie Soveta Ministrov SSSR i TsK VKP(b) "O dopolnitel'nykh merakh po ekonomii v raskhodovanii khleba i usilenii kontrolia za rabotoi Ministerstva torgovli i ego organov, 18 October 1946; ibid., l. 41.

31. Ibid.

32. Informatsiia Upravleniia po proverke partiinykh organov TsK VKP(b) "O nastroeniiakh i vyskazyvaniiakh naseleniia v sviazi s postanovleniem Soveta Ministrov SSSR i TsK VKP(b) 'Ob ekonomii v raskhodovaniia khleba,' " 2 October 1946; ibid., f. 17, op. 122, d. 188, l. 9.

33. Ibid., l. 11.

34. Ibid., l. 20.

35. Ibid., ll. 9–12.

36. Informatsiia Upravleniia po proverke partiinykh organov TsK VKP(b) "O nekotorykh voprosakh v rabote promyshlennykh predpriiatii, sovkhozov i MTS v sviazi s provedeniem v zhizn' postanovleniia Soveta Ministrov SSSR i TsK VKP(b) 'Ob ekonomii v raskhodovanii khleba,' " 29 October 1946; ibid., ll. 22–23.

37. Ibid., l. 24.

38. Informatsiia Upravleniia po proverke partiinykh organov TsK VKP(b) "O

nastroeniiakh i vyskazyvaniiakh naseleniia v sviazi s provedeniem v zhizn' postanovleniia Soveta Ministrov SSSR i TsK VKP(b) 'Ob ekonomii v raskhodovanii khleba,' " 4 October 1946; ibid., l. 17.

39. Zima, *Golod v SSSR 1946–1947 godov*, 11.

40. Ibid., 168.

41. Dokladnaia zapiska "O prodovol'stvennykh zatrudneniiakh v nekotorykh raionakh Kaluzhskoi oblasti," 31 January 1947; RTsKhIDNI, f. 17, op. 122, d. 220, l. 58.

42. [The term *unit/units* in this quotation is my translation of the Soviet Russian term *trudoden'/trudodni*. In Soviet parlance, the technical term "workday/workdays" (*trudoden'/trudodni*) is significant in two inherently related senses. On the one hand it designates what the name obviously implies, a day spent working in the collective fields, that is, in the fields belonging to the collective farm as a whole, as opposed to the private garden plots allowed each peasant household. It also designates a unit of income distributed to peasant households at the end of the harvest after all collective obligations have been met. That is, when all collective expenses have been paid—for seed grain, farm machinery rental, fees for community construction projects, and the like—the remainder of the harvest is divided among the peasant households in proportion to the number of workdays accumulated by each of them in working in the collective fields (as opposed to private garden plots).—H.R.]

43. Ibid., ll. 58–59.

44. Informatsiia o polozhenii del na predpriiatiiakh g. Mariupolia, 1947; ibid., l. 119.

45. Vyderzhki iz pisem, iskhodiashchikh ot naseleniia Voronezhskoi i Stalingradskoi oblastei (prilozhenie k dokladnoi zapiske L.P. Beria), 31 December 1946; TsKhSD, f. 89, perechen' 57, dokument 20, l. 9.

46. Ibid., l. 10.

47. Ibid., l. 12.

48. Zima, *Golod v SSSR 1946–1947 godov*, 99.

49. Ibid., 116.

50. V.P. Popov, "Gosudarstvennyi terror v sovetskoi Rossii, 1923–1953 gg.," *Otechestvennye arkhivy*, 1992, No. 2: 27.

51. Informatsiia Upravleniia po proverke partiinykh organov TsK VKP(b), 12 June 1947; RTsKhIDNI, f. 17, op. 122, d. 289, l. 17.

52. Informatsiia Novosibirskogo obkoma VKP(b) o politicheskikh nastroeniiakh naseleniia Novosibirskoi oblasti, 16 March 1948; ibid., d. 306, l. 19.

Chapter 5: The Currency Reform of 1947

1. Pis'mo narkoma finansov SSSR A.G. Zvereva narkomam finansov soiuznykh i avtonomnykh respublik "O vypuske Gosudarstvennogo zaima vostanovleniia i razvitiia narodnogo khoziaistva SSSR," March 1946; RTsKhIDNI, f. 17, op. 125, d. 424, l. 10.

2. Ibid.

3. Informatsiia Upravleniia propagandy i agitatsii TsK VKP(b) "O politicheskikh nastroeniiakh trudiashchikhsia Cheliabinskoi oblasti," September 1947; ibid., d. 518, l. 7.

4. Ibid.; and ibid., d. 425, l. 3.

5. Ibid., d. 517, l. 7.

6. A.G. Zverev, *Zapiski ministra* (Moscow, 1973), 273.

7. Ibid., 235.

8. Viacheslav Kondrat'ev, *Krasnye vorota: Povest', roman* (Moscow, 1988), 146.

9. Iurii Aksenov and Aleksei Uliukaev, "O prostykh resheniiakh neprostykh problem," *Kommunist*, 1990, No. 6: 83.

10. Ibid., 80.

11. Ibid.

12. Aleksei Uliukaev and Iurii Aksenov, "Legendy ob odnoi reforme," *Nedelia*, 1990, No. 19: 16.

Chapter 6: The State and the Peasant

1. The order was issued by the Council of People's Commissars and the Central Committee of the Communist Party 13 April 1942: "O povyshenii dlia kolkhoznikov obiazatel'nogo minimuma trudodnei." According to this order the obligatory minimum of workdays was raised to 150 in the cotton-raising regions [chiefly in Central Asia—H.R.], to 100 in the regions north of the black-soil belt, and to 120 in the remainder of the country. It had previously been 100, 60, and 80 in these areas respectively. At the same time an obligatory minimum of 50 workdays was established for adolescents between the ages of 12 and 16. [On the term *trudodni*/workdays, see chapter 4, n. 42.—H.R.]

2. For details, see V.P. Popov, *Rossiiskaia derevnia posle voiny (iiun' 1945–mart 1953): Sbornik dokumentov* (Moscow, 1993), 153, 159–66.

3. O.M. Verbitskaia, *Rossiiskoe krest'ianstvo: Ot Stalina k Khrushchevu* (Moscow, 1992), 137; V.F. Zima, *Golod v SSSR 1946–1947 godov: Proiskhozhdenie i posledstviia* (Moscow, 1996), 44.

4. Popov, *Rossiiskaia derevnia posle voiny*, 160–61.

5. Vyderzhki iz pisem kolkhoznikov Stavropol'skogo kraia, zaderzhannykh Voennoi tsenzuroi i punktami politicheskogo kontrolia MGB SSSR, 10 July 1946; RTsKhIDNI, f. 17, op. 121, d. 547, ll. 14–15.

6. Dokladnaia zapiska instruktora Sel'skokhoziaistvennogo otdela TsK VKP(b) "Ob obstanovke v kolkhozakh i neobkhodimosti ozhivleniia partiino-massovoi i kul'turnoi raboty v derevne," 18 July 1945; ibid., op. 117, d. 527, l. 90.

7. Informatsiia Organizatsionno-instruktorskogo otdela TsK VKP(b) "O nekotorykh politicheskikh nastroeniiakh derevni," 3 July 1945; ibid., op. 122, d. 122, l. 28.

8. Ibid.

9. In similarly obligatory letters industrial enterprises were required to endorse their assigned production quotas. These rituals were a form of propaganda, labor discipline, and consciousness enhancement.

10. Informatsiia Organizatsionno-instruktorskogo otdela TsK VKP(b) "O nekotorykh politicheskikh nastroeniiakh derevni," 3 July 1945, l. 27.

11. Ibid., ll. 27, 29.

12. Ibid., l. 29.

13. Ibid.

14. Ibid., l. 28.

15. Dokladnaia zapiska instruktora Sel'skokhoziaistvennogo otdela TsK VKP(b) "Ob obstanovke v kolkhozakh i neobkhodimosti ozhivleniia partiino-massovoi i kul'turnoi raboty v derevne," 18 July 1945, l. 92.

16. Informatsiia Organizatsionno-instruktorskogo otdela TsK VKP(b) "O nekotorykh politicheskikh nastroeniiakh derevni," 3 July 1945, l. 28.

17. Dokladnaia zapiska Narkomata gosudarstvennoi bezopastnosti Buriat-Mongol'skoi ASSR "O finansovo-khoziaistvennom sostoianii kolkhozov Buriat-Mongol'skoi ASSR," 10 July 1945; RTsKhIDNI, f. 17, op. 117, d. 528, l. 120.

18. Ibid., l. 121.

19. Ibid.

20. Dokladnaia zapiska instruktora Sel'skokhoziaistvennogo otdela TsK VKP(b) "Ob obstanovke v kolkhozakh i neobkhodimosti ozhivleniia partiino-massovoi i kul'turnoi raboty v derevne," 18 July 1945, l. 94.

214 NOTES TO CHAPTER 6

21. Informatsiia Upravleniia propagandy i agitatsii TsK VKP(b) "O khode repatriatsii, ob ustroistve na rabotu repatriirovannykh sovetskikh grazhdan i ob organizatsii politicheskoi raboty s nimi," 27 July 1945; RTsKhIDNI, f. 17, op. 117, d. 533, l. 20.

22. Ibid.

23. Ibid., l. 19.

24. Informatsiia Organizatsionno-instruktorskogo otdela TsK VKP(b) "O nekotorykh politicheskikh nastroeniiakh v derevne," 3 July 1945, l. 28.

25. The burden of taxation on the peasant economy was determined on the basis of so-called income norms, varying according to each head of livestock and every hundred hectares [1 hectare = 2.47 acres—H.R.] of cultivated land. The income norms were in fact defined arbitrarily and by no means corresponded to the real income of the peasant family. The peasants paid taxes in kind (with agricultural products) as well as in money. In the summer of 1946 the Council of Ministers of the USSR published an order raising average income norms in the agriculture economy (for details, see Zima, *Golod v SSSR 1946–1947 godov: Proiskhozhdenie i posledstviia*, 45–46).

26. Vyderzhki iz pisem kolkhoznikov Penzenskoi i Riazanskoi oblastei, zaderzhannykh Voennoi tsenzuroi MGB SSSR, 25 July 1946; RTsKhIDNI, f. 17, op. 121, d. 547, l. 6.

27. Ibid., l. 5.

28. Doklad Ministerstva sel'skogo khoziaistva i zagotovok SSSR "O nedostatkakh v sel'skom khoziaistve i merakh po uluchsheniiu del v kolkhozakh i sovkhozakh," July 1953; TsKhSD, f. 5, op. 30, d. 20, l. 12.

29. Popov, *Rossiiskaia derevnia posle voiny (iiun' 1945–mart 1953): Sbornik dokumentov*, 64.

30. The historian V.F. Zima analyzed the letters and complaints that peasants sent to the Presidium of the Supreme Soviet of the USSR. He found that a few dozen requests for revisions of tax burdens and obligatory deliveries were granted, while the bulk of them were stamped "examined and refused." Zima, *Golod v SSSR 1946–1947 godov*, 199.

31. Ibid., 180.

32. Informatsiia Novosibirskogo obkoma VKP(b) "O politicheskikh nastroeniiakh naseleniia Novosibirskoi oblasti," 16 March 1948; RTsKhIDNI, f. 17, op. 122, d. 306, l. 17.

33. Ibid.

34. Ibid.

35. Doklad Ministerstva sel'skogo khoziaistva i zagotovok SSSR "O nedostatkakh v sel'skom khoziaistve i merakh po uluchsheniiu del v kolkhozakh i sovkhozakh," July 1953, l. 9.

36. Informatsiia Novosibirskogo obkoma VKP(b) o politicheskikh nastroeniiakh kolkhoznikov v sviazi s provedeniem v zhizn' Ukaza Prezidiuma Verkhovnogo Soveta SSSR ot 2 iiunia 1948 g., 21 June 1948; RTsKhIDNI, f. 17, op. 122, d. 306, l. 35.

37. Ibid., l. 36.

38. Ibid.

39. Informatsiia Moskovskogo Komiteta VKP(b) ob obshchikh sobraniiakh kolkhoznikov, posviashchennykh provedeniiu v zhizn' Ukaza Prezidiuma Verkhovnogo Soveta SSSR ot 2 iiunia 1948 g., July 1948; ibid., d. 315, l. 4.

40. Informatsiia Iaroslavskogo obkoma VKP(b) o khode realizatsii Ukaza Prezidiuma Verkhovnogo Soveta SSSR ot iiunia 1948 g.; ibid., l. 97.

41. Information of a similar kind came in from Novosibirsk, Cheliabinsk, Moscow, Kostroma, and other provinces; RTsKhIDNI, f. 17, op. 122, dd. 306, 315.

42. Informatsiia Novosibirskogo obkoma VKP(b) o sobraniiakh kolkhoznikov po provedeniiu v zhizn' Ukaza Prezidiuma Verkhovnogo Soveta SSSR ot 2 iiunia 1948 g., 18 June 1948; ibid., d. 314, l. 138.

43. Ibid.

44. Zima, *Golod v SSSR 1946–1947 godov*, 188.

45. Informatsiia Novosibirskogo obkoma VKP(b) o politicheskikh nastroeniiakh

kolkhoznikov v sviazi s provedeniem v zhizn' Ukaza Prezidiuma Verkhovnogo Soveta SSSR ot 2 iiunia 1948 g., 18 June 1948, l. 36.

Chapter 7: Religion and Politics

1. The problems of other confessions are not examined in this chapter, as the policy of the state in reference to non-Orthodox sects remained practically unchanged during and after the war.

2. Dokladnaia zapiska o rabote Soveta po delam religioznykh kul'tov pri Sovete Ministrov SSSR za 1948 g. i pervyi kvartal 1949 g.; RTsKhIDNI, f. 17, op. 132, d. 111, l. 46.

3. Spravka Soveta po delam Russkoi pravoslavnoi tserkvi "O pravoslavnykh monastyriakh v SSSR," January 1951; ibid., d. 497, l. 19.

4. Informatsiia Soveta po delam Russkoi pravoslavnoi tserkvi pri Sovete Ministrov SSSR "O sostoianii russkoi pravoslavnoi tserkvi," August 1946; ibid., d. 407, l. 66.

5. Ibid., l. 67.

6. Doklad Soveta po delam Russkoi pravoslavnoi tserkvi pri Sovete Ministrov SSSR o svoei deiatel'nosti za 1946 god, 1947; ibid., d. 407, l. 3.

7. Informatsiia Organizatsionno-instruktorskogo otdela TsK VKP(b) "Ob otnoshenii nekotorykh chlenov partii k predstaviteliam religioznykh kul'tov," 14 February 1945; ibid., op. 122, d. 122, l. 13.

8. Informatsiia Upravleniia po proverke partiinykh organov TsK VKP(b) "Ob usilenii deiatel'nosti predstavitelei religioznykh kul'tov," 2 August 1946; ibid., d. 188, l. 4.

9. Ibid.

10. Ibid.

11. Ibid., l. 5.

12. Doklad Soveta po delam Russkoi pravoslavnoi tserkvi pri Sovete Ministrov SSSR o svoei deiatel'nosti za 1946 god, 1947, ll. 12–13.

13. Informatsiia Organizatsionno-instruktorskogo otdela TsK VKP(b) "Ob otnoshenii nekotorykh chlenov partii k predstaviteliam religioznykh kul'tov," l. 13.

14. Ibid., l. 12.

15. Informatsiia Upravleniia po proverke partiinykh organov TsK VKP(B) "Ob usilenii deiatel'nosti predstavitelei religioznykh kul'tov," l. 5.

16. Ibid., l. 6.

17. Informatsiia Organizationno-instruktorskogo otdela TsK VKP(b) "Ob otnoshenii nekotorykh chlenov partii k predstaviteliam religioznykh kul'tov," l. 13.

18. Informatsiia o vyskazyvaniiakh naseleniia v sviazi s opublikovaniem materialov o Pomestnom sobore Russkoi pravoslavnoi tserkvi, 10 February 1945; RTsKhIDNI, f. 17, op. 122, d. 122, l. 9.

19. Ibid., l. 10.

20. Informatsiia Organizatsionno-instruktorskogo otdela TsK VKP(b) "Ob otnoshenii nekotorykh chlenov partii k predstaviteliam religioznykh kul'tov," l. 12.

21. Informatsiia Organizatsionno-instruktorskogo otdela TsK VKP(B) "O nekotorykh otklikakh po povodu Pomestnogo sobora Russkoi pravoslavnoi tserkvi," 9 March 1945; RTsKhIDNI, f. 17, op. 122, d. 122, l. 17.

22. Ibid.

23. Informatsiia o vyskazyvaniiakh naseleniia v sviazi s opublikovaniem materialov o Pomestnom sobore Russkoi pravoslavnoi tserkvi, l. 9.

24. Doklad Soveta po delam russkoi pravoslavnoi tserkvi o svoei deiatel'nosti za 1946 god, l. 10.

25. Informatsiia o vyskazyvaniiakh naseleniia v sviazi s opublikovaniem materialov o

Pomestnom sobore Russkoi pravoslavnoi tserkvi, l. 9.

26. Ibid. See also: Informatsiia Organizatsionno-instruktorskogo otdela TsK VKP(b) "O nekotorykh otklikakh po povodu Pomestnogo sobora Russkoi pravoslavnoi tserkvi," l. 17.

27. Informatsiia o vyskazyvaniiakh naseleniia v sviazi s opublikovaniem materialov o Pomestnom sobore Russkoi pravoslavnoi tserkvi, ll. 10–11.

28. Informatsiia Organizatsionno-instruktorskogo otdela TsK VKP(b) "O nekotorykh otklikakh po povodu Pomestnogo sobora Russkoi pravoslavnoi tserkvi," l. 17.

29. Informatsiia o vyskazyvaniiakh naseleniia v sviazi s opublikovaniem materialov o Pomestnom sobore Russkoi pravoslavnoi tserkvi," l. 10.

30. Dokladnaia zapiska o rabote Soveta po delam religioznykh kul'tov pri Sovete Ministrov SSSR za 1948 g. i pervyi kvartal 1949 g.; RTsKhIDNI, f. 17, op. 132, d. 111, l. 46.

31. Spravka Soveta po delam Russkoi pravoslavnoi tserkvi pri Sovete Ministrov SSSR "O pravoslavnykh monastyriakh v SSSR," January 1950; ibid., d. 497, l. 19.

32. Postanovlenie TsK VKP(b) "O nepravil'noi linii v rabote Soveta po delam Russkoi pravoslavnoi tserkvi pri Sovete Ministrov SSSR," Protokol zasedaniia Orgbiuro TsK VKP(b) ot 28 fevralia 1949 g.; ibid., op. 118, d. 323, l. 224.

33. Ibid.

34. Ibid., l. 225.

Chapter 8: The Political Temper of the Masses, 1945–1948

1. "Svodka donesenii mestnykh organov NKVD ob antisovetskikh i khuliganskikh pro-iavleniiakh v period podgotovki k vyboram v Verkhovnyi Sovet Soiuza SSR za dekabr' 1945–ianvar' 1946, 27 ianvar' 1946"; V.A. Kozlov, ed., *Neizvestnaia Rossiia: XX vek*, 4 vols. (Moscow, 1992–1993), 4: 468–75.

2. Ibid., 468–71.

3. Informatsiia o podgotovke k vyboram v Verkhovnyi Sovet SSSR po Novgorodskoi oblasti, January 1946; RTsKhIDNI, f. 17, op. 125, d. 420, l. 32. The digests of public attitudes in other provinces contain similar data.

4. Informatsiia o podgotovke k vyboram v Verkhovnyi Sovet SSSR po Voronezhskoi oblasti, January 1946; ibid., l. 18.

5. Ibid.

6. Informatsiia o podgotovke k vyboram v Verkhovnyi Sovet SSSR po Penzenskoi oblasti, January 1946; ibid., l. 41.

7. Ibid.

8. Informatsiia o podgotovke k vyboram v Verkhovnyi Sovet SSSR po Voronezhskoi oblasti, January 1946; ibid., l. 18.

9. Informatsiia o podgotovke k vyboram v Verkhovnyi Sovet SSSR po Krymskoi avtonomnoi oblasti, January 1946; ibid., l. 29.

10. Informatsiia o podgotovke k vyboram v Verkhovnyi Sovet SSSR po Penzenskoi oblasti, January 1946; ibid., l. 41.

11. Informatsiia o podgotovke k vyboram v Verkhovnyi Sovet SSSR po Novgorodskoi oblasti, January 1946; ibid., l. 33.

12. Informatsiia Upravleniia po proverke partiinykh organov TsK VKP(b) "O voprosakh, zadannykh trudiashchimisia na sobraniiakh, lektsiiakh i besedakh," 9 January 1947; ibid., op. 122, d. 289, l. 9.

13. Informatsiia o podgotovke k vyboram v Verkhovnyi Sovet SSSR po Penzenskoi oblasti, January 1946; ibid., op. 125, d. 420, l. 41.

14. Ibid.

15. Dokladnaia zapiska Upravleniia propagandy i agitatsii TsK VKP(b) "O politicheskikh nastroeniiakh trudiashchikhsia v gorodakh Cheliabinskoi oblasti," September

1947; ibid., d. 518, l. 7.

16. Reshenie partiinogo komiteta Ivanovskogo melanzhevogo kombinata, January 1946; ibid., op. 122, d. 131, l. 14.

17. Dokladnaia zapiska Upravleniia propagandy i agitatsii TsK VKP(b) "O politicheskikh nastroeniiakh trudiashchikhsia v gorodakh Cheliabinskoi oblasti," ll. 9–10.

18. Informatsionnoe soobshchenie Sverdlovskogo obkoma VKP(b) "O politicheskikh nastroeniiakh trudiashchikhsia gorodov Sverdlovskoi oblasti," 13 September 1947; ibid., d. 289, l. 37.

19. Informatsiia Upravleniia po proverke partiinykh organov TsK VKP(b) "O politicheskikh nastroeniiakh gorodov i promyshlennykh tsentrov," 19 August 1947; ibid., l. 60.

20. Dokladnaia zapiska Upravleniia propagandy i agitatsii TsK VKP(b) "O politicheskikh nastroeniiakh trudiashchikhsia Cheliabinskoi oblasti," l. 9.

21. Informatsionnoe soobshchenie Pskovskogo obkoma VKP(b) "O politicheskikh nastroeniiakh naseleniia Pskovskoi oblasti," 15 July 1948; ibid, d. 306, l. 41.

22. Informatsiia Upravleniia o proverke partiinykh organov TsK VKP(b) "O politicheskikh nastroeniiakh naseleniia gorodov i promyshlennykh tsentrov," l. 60.

23. Information on similar incidents is found in the proceedings of different divisions of the Central Committee, for example, ibid., d. 122, l. 28 and op. 125, d. 420, l. 32.

24. *Spravochnik KPSS* (Moscow, 1978), 243.

25. Informatsionnye materialy otdela partiinykh, profsoiuznykh i komsomol'skikh organov TsK VKP(b), podgotovlennye k XIX s''ezdu partii, 17 September 1951; RTsKhIDNI, f. 17, op. 131, d. 284, l. 90.

26. Here and following, the source of the information is Spravka po proverke partiinykh organov TsK VKP(b) "K voprosu o rabote partii v poslevoennoe vremia," 1947; ibid., op. 122, d. 291, l. 131.

27. Zapiska Organizatsionno-instruktorskogo otdela TsK VKP(b) "O nekotorykh otritsatel'nykh iavleniiakh sredi raionnykh rabotnikov," 30 May 1946; ibid., d. 130, l. 21.

28. Ibid., l. 22.

29. Informatsionnoe soobshchenie Sverdlovskogo obkoma VKP(b) "O politicheskikh nastroeniiakh trudiashchikhsia gorodov Sverdlovskoi oblasti," 13 September 1947; ibid., d. 289, ll. 26–27.

30. Informatsiia Upravleniia po proverke partiinykh organov TsK VKP(b) "O politicheskikh nastroeniiakh naseleniia gorodov i promyshlennykh tsentrov," 19 August 1947; ibid., l. 62.

31. The question of the wisdom of rejecting the Marshall Plan arose in various audiences. See, for example, ibid., op. 125, d. 517, ll. 33–34 and op. 122, d. 289, l. 34.

32. Informatsiia "O politicheskikh nastroeniiakh trudiashchikhsia v gorodakh Cheliabinskoi oblasti," September 1947; ibid., op. 125, d. 518, l. 12.

33. Dokladnaia zapiska sekretaria TsK VKP(b) A.A. Kuznetsova I.V. Stalinu, 10 October 1947; ibid., op. 121, d. 639, l. 106.

34. Ibid., l. 107.

35. Cited in N.V. Romanovskii, *Liki stalinizma, 1945–1953 gg.* (Moscow, 1995), 43.

36. Dokladnaia zapiska nachal'nika Upravleniia propagandy i agitatsii TsK VKP(b) G.F. Aleksandrova sekretariu TsK VKP(b) A.A. Zhdanovu, September 1946; RTsKhIDNI, f. 17, op. 125, d. 425, l. 4.

37. Informatsiia Otdela propagandy i agitatsii TsK VKP(b) "O sostoianii agitatsionno-propagandistskoi raboty v Primorskoi kraevoi partorganizatsii," November 1950; ibid., op. 132, d. 289, l. 91.

38. David Samoilov, *Pamiatnye zapiski* (Moscow, 1995), 160.

39. Zdeněk Mlynař, *Moroz udaril iz Kremlia* (Moscow, 1992), 21. [The author's name is

spelled here, unlike in phonetic Russian transliteration, as in the original Czech.—H.R.]

40. Sigmund Freud, *Civilization and Its Discontents*, trans. James Strachey (New York, 1962), 24.

41. Nikolai Simonov, *Voenno-promyshlennyi kompleks SSSR v 1920–1950-e gody: tempy ekonomicheskogo rosta, struktura, organizatsiia proizvodstva i upravlenie* (Moscow, 1996), 329.

42. Ibid., 209.

43. Ibid., 210.

44. Informatsiia Upravleniia po proverke partiinykh organov TsK VKP(b) "O voprosakh, zadannykh trudiashchimisia na sobraniiakh, lektsiiakh i besedakh," 9 January 1947; RTsKhIDNI, f. 17, op. 122, d. 289, ll. 9–12.

Chapter 9: The Intelligentsia and the Intellectual Mavericks

1. Konstitutsiia SSSR: Proekt; RTsKhIDNI, f. 17, op. 125, d. 379, l. 56.

2. Predlozheniia ob izmenenii k dopolnenii teksta Konstitutsii SSSR, postupivshie v Redaktsionnuiu komissiiu i ne priniatye, 1946; ibid., ll. 41–49.

3. Cited in *Izvestia*, 16 June 1992.

4. A.Ia. Gurevich, " 'Put' priamoi, kak Nevskii prospekt,' ili ispoved' istorika," *Odissei*, 1992, 10 [an annual—E.Z.].

5. Informatsionnye materialy Upravleniia propagandy i agitatsii TsK VKP(b), 1946; RTsKhIDNI, f. 17, op. 125, d. 454, ll. 1–2.

6. Cited in N.V. Romanovskii, *Liki stalinizma, 1945–1953 gg.* (Moscow, 1995), 94.

7. Cited in V.P. Popov, *Rossiiskaia derevnia posle voiny, iiun' 1945–mart 1953 gg.: Sbornik dokumentov* (Moscow, 1993), 105.

8. "Iz istorii bor'by s lysenkovshchinoi," *Izvestia TsK KPSS*, 1991, Nos. 4–5.

9. Ibid., No. 4: 125.

10. Ibid., 131.

11. Ibid., 133.

12. Ibid., 134.

13. Vera S. Dunham, *In Stalin's Time: Middleclass Values in Soviet Fiction* (New York, 1976) [see Zubkova's introduction—H.R.].

14. David Samoilov, *Pamiatnye zapiski* (Moscow, 1995), 142–43.

15. Ibid., 154.

16. Ibid., 344.

17. Konstantin Simonov, "Glazami cheloveka moego pokoleniia," *Znamia*, 1988, No. 3: 49.

18. Polozhenie o zhurnale "Oktiabr'," 28 November 1945; RTsKhIDNI, f. 17, op. 117, d. 571, ll. 193–97.

19. Stenogramma soveshchaniia v TsK VKP(b) po voprosam kino, 26 April 1946; ibid., op. 125, d. 378, l. 44.

20. Pis'mo slushatelei 2–go kursa Vysshei partiinoi shkoly pri TsK VKP(b) G.M. Malenkovu i M.A. Suslovu, July 1950; ibid., op. 132, d. 278, ll. 129–30.

21. Ibid., l. 130.

Chapter 10: The Crisis of Postwar Expectations

1. GARF, f. 7676, op. 9, d. 888, l. 237; op. 11, d. 189, l. 97.

2. Dokladnaia zapiska "O khode vosstanovleniia zhilishchno-kommunal'nogo khoziaistva v gorodakh, razrushennykh nemetskimi zakhvatchikami," 12 June 1947; RTsKhIDNI, f. 17, op. 122, d. 220, l. 170.

3. Dokladnaia zapiska ministra gosudarstvennogo kontrolia RSFSR A. Dedova o polozhenii s zhil'em v riade oblastei respubliki, 27 October 1956; TsKhSD, f. 5, op. 32, d. 39, l. 127.

4. Informatsiia Upravleniia propagandy i agitatsii TsK VKP(b) "O nedostatkakh massovo-politicheskoi raboty sredi shakhterov," February 1948; RTsKhIDNI, f. 17, op. 125, d. 596, l. 42.

5. Ibid., l. 45.

6. Informatsiia Upravleniia po proverke partiinykh organov TsK VKP(b) o polozhenii na shakhtakh Kuzbassa, 11 November 1947; ibid., op. 122, d. 220, ll. 215–16.

7. Informatsiia Upravleniia propagandy i agitatsii TsK VKP(b) "O sostoianii massovo-politicheskoi i kul'turno-prosvetitel'skoi raboty sredi rabochikh i sluzhashchikh chernoi metallurgii," February 1948; ibid., op. 125, d. 596, l. 56.

8. Informatsiia Upravleniia propagandy i agitatsii TsK VKP(b) "O politicheskikh nastroeniiakh trudiashchikhsia v gorodakh Cheliabinskoi oblasti," September 1947; ibid., d. 518, l. 10.

9. Dokladnaia zapiska ministra ugol'noi promyshlennosti zapadnykh raionov SSSR A. Zasiad'ko sekretariu TsK VKP(b) A. Kuznetsovu, 8 December 1947; ibid., op. 122, d. 220, l. 211.

10. Ibid.

11. V.N. Zemskov, "Chernye dyry istorii," *Raduga*, 1990, No. 6: 47.

12. Ibid.

13. [In the Soviet Union, the term passport described what was effectively a personal identity paper like the French *carte d'identité* or the German *Personalausweis*. There is no equivalent document in the Anglo-Saxon world. It was necessary to have such a passport in order to get a job, get a room in a hotel, etc., but peasants were not issued passports. Hence what might be regarded in the English-speaking world as an offensive intrusion into privacy was for the Russian peasants a considerable disadvantage. For travel abroad, the Soviet government issued another document, the external passport.—H.R.]

14. B.N. Ponomarev et al., eds., *Istoriia SSSR s drevneishikh vremen do nashikh dnei*, 11 vols. (Moscow, 1966–1980), 11: 208.

15. Spravka Upravleniia po proverke partiinykh organov TsK VKP(b) "K voprosu o rabote partii v poslevoennoe vremia," 1947; RTsKhIDNI, f. 17, op. 122, d. 291, ll. 130–31.

16. A.A. Sheviakov, "Repatriatsiia sovetskogo mirnogo naseleniia i voennoplennykh, okazavshikhsia v okkupatsionnykh zonakh gosudarstv antigitlerovskoi koalitsii," in Iu.A. Poliakov et al., eds., *Naselenie Rossii v 1920–1950–e gody: Chislennost', poteri, migratsii* (Moscow, 1994), 210–11.

17. Informatsiia Upravleniia propagandy i agitatsii TsK VKP(b) "O khode repatriatsii, ob ustroistve na rabotu repatriirovannykh sovetskikh grazhdan i ob organizatsii politicheskoi raboty s nimi," 17 July 1945; RTsKhIDNI, f. 17, op. 117, d. 533, l. 17.

18. Ibid., l. 22.

19. V.N. Zemskov, "Spetsposelentsy, 1930–1959 gg.," in Poliakov et al., eds., *Naselenie Rossii v 1920–1950–e gody*, 158.

20. Dokladnaia zapiska ministra vnutrennikh del SSSR S. Kruglova o polozhenii spetsposelentsev, July 1946; GARF, f. 9401, op. 2, d. 138, l. 317.

21. Ibid., ll. 320, 382.

22. Dokladnaia zapiska ministra vnutrennikh del SSSR S. Kruglova o polozhenii spetspereselentsev s Severnogo Kavkaza, 31 January 1946; ibid., d. 134, l. 237.

23. A.N. Dugin, "Stalinizm: Legendy i fakty," *Slovo*, 1990, No. 7: 23.

24. "Vse my vyshli iz stalinskoi shineli: Diskussiia o sobytiiakh 1948 goda i ikh posledstviiakh," *Literaturnaia gazeta*, 21 March 1990, 14.

Chapter 11: The Birth of the Anti-Stalinist Youth Movement

1. Aleksandr Solzhenitsyn, "Arkhipelag GULAG, 1918–1936: Opyt khudozhestvennogo issledovaniia," *Novyi mir*, 1989, No. 8: 12.

2. Dokladnaia zapiska Cheliabinskogo oblastnogo komiteta VKP(b) "O krupnykh nedostatkakh v politiko-vospitatel'noi rabote sredi molodezhi vysshikh i srednikh uchebnykh zavedenii Cheliabinskoi oblasti," September 1946; RTsKhIDNI, f. 17, op. 125, d. 424, ll. 60–62.

3. Pavel Korchagin is a character in the novel of N.A. Ostrovskii, *Kak zakalialas' stal'* (How the Steel Was Tempered); Andrei Bolkonskii, Natasha Rostova, and Platon Karataev are characters in Leo Tolstoy's novel, *War and Peace;* Tat'iana Larina is from Alexander Pushkin's *Eugene Onegin;* Pavel Vlasov is from A.M. Gorkii's *Mat'* (Mother); Ostap Bender is from Il'ia Ilf and Evgenii Petrov, *Dvenadtsat' stul'ev* (The Twelve Chairs); Nekhliudov is from Leo Tolstoy's *Resurrection;* and Pechorin is from M.Iu. Lermontov's *Geroi nashego vremeni* (A Hero for Our Time).

4. Dokladnaia zapiska Cheliabinskogo oblastnogo komiteta VKP(b) "O krupnykh nedostatkakh v politiko-vospitatel'noi rabote sredi molodezhi," l. 69.

5. Ibid.

6. Ibid., l. 68.

7. Informatsionnoe pis'mo Glavnogo Politicheskogo Upravleniia Sovetskoi armii i Voenno-morskogo flota SSSR sekretariu TsK VKP(b) A.A. Zhdanovu, September 1946; ibid., ll. 54–55.

8. Dokladnaia zapiska Cheliabinskogo oblastnogo komiteta VKP(b) "O krupnykh nedostatkakh v politiko-vospitatel'noi rabote sredi molodezhi, l. 62.

9. Ibid., ll. 64–65.

10. Pis'mo iz Verkhovnogo Suda RSFSR sekretariu TsK VKP(b) A.A. Kuznetsovu, September 1946; ibid., l. 50.

11. Ibid.

12. Ernst Neizvestnyi, "Katakombnaia kul'tura i ofitsial'noe iskusstvo," *Literaturnaia gazeta,* 10 October 1990, 8.

13. Pis'mo iz Verkhovnogo Suda RSFSR sekretariu TsK VKP(b) A.A. Kuznetsovu, September 1946; RTsKhIDNI, f. 17, op. 125, d. 424, l. 51.

14. Anatolii Zhigulin, "Chernye kamni: Avtobiograficheskaia povest'," *Znamia,* 1988, No. 7: 21.

15. Ibid., 21–22.

16. Cited in Anton Antonov-Ovseenko, "Ne govorite roditeliam pro arest," *Moskovskii komsomolets,* 28 March 1990.

17. Zhigulin, "Chernye kamni," 21.

18. Pis'mo iz Verkhovnogo Suda RSFSR sekretariu TsK VKP(b) A.A. Kuznetsovu, September 1946; RTsKhIDNI, f. 17, op. 125, d. 424, l. 49.

19. Zhigulin, "Chernye kamni," 21.

20. Cited in Antonov-Ovseenko, "Ne govorite roditeliam pro arest."

Chapter 12: The Struggle with Dissent

1. See, for example, Stenogramma plenuma Vladimirskogo obkoma VKP(b) 31 January 1947; RTsKhIDNI, f. 17, op. 121, d. 572, l. 14; and N.V. Romanovskii, *Liki stalinizma, 1945–1953 gg.* (Moscow, 1995), 27.

2. In particular the confidential letters of the Central Committee of 18 January 1935, "Uroki sobytii, sviazannykh so zlodeiskim ubiistvom tovarishcha Kirova," and of 29 July 1936, "O terroristicheskoi deiatel'nosti trotskistsko-zinov'evskogo kontrrevoliutsionnogo bloka."

3. "Doklad sekretaria TsK VKP(b) A.A. Kuznetsova na sobranii rabotnikov apparata TsK VKP(b) po vyboram suda chesti, 29 sentiabria 1947 g.," *Istochnik,* 1994, No. 6: 74.

4. L.N. Voitolovskii, *Ocherki kollektivnoi psikhologii,* 2 vols. (Petrograd, 1925), 2: 75. [Author's emphasis—E.Z.]

5. N.G. Kliueva and G.I. Roskin were Soviet research scientists in oncology. They developed a medicine that they called *krutsin* to treat cancer. They had prepared the manuscript of a book scheduled to be published simultaneously in the USSR and the United States. The proposal to cooperate with American colleagues had initially been supported by the Central Committee, by A.A. Zhdanov in particular. The fact that the Central Committee had issued no specific decision to this effect, however, subsequently served as a pretext for the accusation of "antipatriotic and antistate conduct." The gist of the charge was that Kliueva and Roskin would have "deprived Soviet science of priority in this discovery [the cancer-fighting medicine] and have inflicted serious damage on the interests of the Soviet Union." *Kentavr,* 1994, No. 2: 66.

6. Zakrytoe pis'mo TsK VKP(b) "O dele professorov Kliuevoi i Roskina," 16 July 1947; ibid., 68.

7. Ibid.

8. The courts of honor instituted in 1947 were modeled on the officers' courts of honor in the Imperial Russian army. These latter were devoted to reinforcing discipline and raising the combat efficiency of the army. The new courts of honor were deputed to combat dissent in society and to discipline both the state and the party apparatus—that is, they were utilized to control public opinion and the conduct of the intelligentsia and the officials of government and party. The courts of honor were elected organs, and their competence was limited to issuing public reprimands and social censure, or alternatively, to remanding business to the investigative organs. The courts of honor were elected by the vote of the employees of the institute where the court sat, usually for a year.

9. Postanovlenie Soveta Ministrov SSSR i TsK VKP(b) "O sudakh chesti v ministerstvakh SSSR i tsentral'nykh vedomstvakh," 28 March 1947; *Istochnik,* 1994, No. 6: 69.

10. Ibid., 68.

11. Reshenie suda chesti ministerstva zdravookhraneniia Soiuza SSSR, 7 July 1947; *Kentavr,* 1994, No. 3: 114.

12. Informatsiia Upravleniia po proverke partiinykh organov TsK VKP(b) "O dopolnitel'nykh faktakh, kharakterizuiushchikh ugodnichestvo pered inostranshchinoi v kollektive rabotnikov Otdeleniia tekhnicheskikh nauk Akademii Nauk SSSR," 29 August 1947; RTsKhIDNI, f. 17, op. 122, d. 262, l. 205. [The name of the scientist identified here is given in the Russian text as Fol'k Odvist. He seems to be, in fact, Folke Karl Gustaf Odqvist (1899–?), a Swedish mechanical engineer (studied and taught at University of Stockholm) specializing in plastics and strength of materials more generally. Of course, the accuracy of the facts was in this case irrelevant to Stalin's purpose. *World Who's Who in Science* (Chicago, 1968), 1275.—H.R.]

13. Stenogramma vystupleniia sekretaria TsK VKP(b) A.A. Kuznetsova na soveshchanii rabotnikov Upravleniia kadrov TsK VKP(b), 14 July 1947; ibid., op. 121, d. 572, l. 141.

14. Spravka otdela Upravleniia kadrov TsK VKP(b) o provedenii partiinogo sobraniia vo Vserossiiskom soiuze kooperatsii invalidov v sviazi s zakrytym pis'mom TsK VKP(b) "O dele professorov Kliuevoi i Roskina," 11 August 1947; ibid., op. 122, d. 270, l. 8.

15. Stenogramma partiinogo sobraniia v Fizicheskom institute im. P.N. Lebedeva po obsuzhdeniiu zakrytogo pis'ma TsK VKP(b) "O dele professorov Kliuevoi i Roskina," 25 September 1947; ibid., d. 262, l. 33.

16. Ibid., l. 45.

17. Spravka otdela Upravleniia kadrov TsK VKP(b) o rezul'tatakh obsuzhdeniia zakrytogo pis'ma TsK VKP(b) "O dele professorov Kliuevoi i Roskina" na partiinom sobranii v ministerstve torgovli SSSR, 7 August 1947; ibid., d. 271, l. 21.

18. Informatsiia Upravleniia po proverke partiinykh organov TsK VKP(b) o khode obsuzhdeniia v partorganizatsiiakh zakrytogo pis'ma TsK VKP(b) "O dele professorov Kliuevoi i Roskina," 26 August 1947; ibid., d. 272, l. 21.

19. Informatsiia "O meropriiatiiakh, provedennykh rukovodstvom i partorganizatsiei ministerstva aviatsionnoi promyshlennosti SSSR v sviazi s zakrytym pis'mom TsK VKP(b) 'O dele professorov Kliuevoi i Roskina,' " 8 October 1947; ibid., d. 269, l. 51.

20. Informatsiia Upravleniia o proverke partiinykh organov TsK VKP(b) o khode obsuzhdeniia v partorganizatsiiakh zakrytogo pis'ma TsK, l. 29.

21. Vystuplenie sekretaria TsK VKP(b) A.A. Kuznetsova na zasedanii Orgbiuro TsK VKP(b) 15 oktiabria 1947 g.; ibid., op. 121, d. 640, l. 40.

22. Informatsiia otdela Upravleniia kadrov TsK VKP(b) o khode realizatsii zakrytogo pis'ma TsK VKP(b) "O dele professorov Kliuevoi i Roskina," 12 December 1947; ibid., op. 122. d. 269, ll. 187–88.

23. See *Voprosy filosofii*, 1947, No. 1.

24. Yurii Furmanov, "Uroki odnoi diskussii," *Sovetskaia kul'tura*, 12 March 1988.

25. Pis'mo G.F. Aleksandrova I.V. Stalinu i A.A. Zhdanovu, 11 July 1947; RTsKhIDNI, f. 17, op. 125, d. 492, l. 2.

26. Zapis' besedy upolnomochennykh TsK VKP(b) s zaveduiushchimi otdelami propagandy i agitatsii raionnykh komitetov VKP(b) Gor'kovskoi oblasti, 1947; ibid., l. 27.

27. Ibid., l. 28.

28. Dokladnaia zapiska Upravleniia propagandy i agitatsii TsK VKP(b) "O nedostatkakh v rabote po podboru i vospitaniiu agitatorov v Stalingradskoi oblastnoi partiinoi organizatsii," November 1947; ibid., l. 172. [We may surmise that the initials RKK were a mistaken reference to RKI (Raboche-krest'ianskaia inspektsiia/Workers' and Peasants' Inspectorate) or to RKKA (Raboche-krest'ianskaia krasnaia armiia/Workers' and Peasants' Red Army)—H.R.]

29. Informatsiia o nachale uchebnogo goda v sisteme partiinogo prosveshcheniia, 1948; ibid., op. 132, d. 103, l. 2.

30. "Za bol'shevistskuiu partiinost' literaturnoi kritiki," *Novyi mir*, 1948, No. 12: 193.

31. N.Ia. Marr (1865–1934) was a Soviet Russian linguist and specialist in the languages of the Caucasus. He advanced the so-called "new theory" of language. One of the fundamental ideas of this theory was the affirmation of the class character of language. The views of Marr long held sway in Soviet linguistics (and survived him), during which time all who did not share Marr's theory were subjected to persecution. The last attack on the opponents of Marr's ideas took place in 1948. [Marr's antagonists emphasized ethnic and cultural factors rather than Marxist principles of class consciousness in the evolution of language. Stalin eventually came down on their side.—H.R.]

32. Pis'mo L.F. Denisovoi v redaktsiiu gazety *Pravda*, 1950; RTsKhIDNI, f. 17, op. 132, d. 337, l. 287.

33. Otkliki na stat'i I.V. Stalina po voprosam iazykoznaniia, 1950; ibid., ll. 32, 33, 47.

34. Ibid., l. 16.

35. Ibid., l. 10.

36. Ibid., l. 15.

37. F.A. Abramov, *Priasliny: Trilogiia* (Leningrad, 1978), 491–92.

38. RTsKhIDNI, f. 17, op. 132, d. 550, l. 113.

39. Ibid., l. 162.

40. Ibid., l. 115.

41. Ibid., l. 169.

Chapter 13: The Wave of Repression, 1949–1953

1. V.P. Popov, "Gosudarstvennyi terror v sovetskoi Rossii, 1923–1953 gg. (Istochniki i ikh interpretatsiia)," *Otechestvennye arkhivy*, 1992, No. 2: 28.

2. Ibid., 29.

3. Ibid., 28.

4. Ibid.

5. "O tak nazyvaemom 'leningradskom dele,' " *Izvestia TsK KPSS*, 1989, No. 2: 128.

6. Reshenie Politbiuro TsK VKP(b) "Ob antipartiinykh deistviiakh chlena Politbiuro TsK VKP(b) t. Kuznetsova A.A. i kandidatov v chleny Politbiuro TsK VKP(b) tt. Rodionova M.N. i Popkova P.S.," 15 February 1949; RTsKhIDNI, f. 17, op. 3, d. 1074, l. 35.

7. "O tak nazyvaemom 'leningradskom dele,' " 131.

8. V.I. Demidov and V.A. Kutuzov, eds., *Leningradskoe delo* (Leningrad, 1990), 158.

9. Postanovlenie Politbiuro TsK VKP(b) "O nedostatkakh i oshibkakh TsK KP(b) Estonii," 7 March 1950; RTsKhIDNI, f. 17, op. 118, d. 745, ll. 3–5.

10. Ibid.

11. Ob''iasnitel'naia zapiska N. Karotamma predsedateliu komissii TsK VKP(b) po rassmotreniiu polozheniia v kompartii Estonii P. Ponomarenko, 21 December 1951; ibid., op. 131, d. 81, l. 327.

12. Dokladnaia zapiska chlenov komissii TsK VKP(b) P. Ponomarenko, M. Shkiriatova, E. Gromova po povodu polozheniia del v kompartii Estonii, 20 December 1951; ibid., ll. 403, 410.

13. Postanovlenie Politbiuro TsK VKP(b) "O vziatochnichestve v Gruzii i ob antipartiinoi gruppe t. Baramiia," 9 November 1951; ibid., op. 3, d. 1091, l. 73.

14. Postanovlenie Politbiuro TsK VKP(b) "Polozhenie v kompartii Gruzii," 27 March 1952; ibid., d. 1093, l. 37.

15. *Istochnik*, 1994, No. 4: 11.

16. The Jewish Antifascist Committee was founded in 1942 for the purpose of mobilizing Soviet and world opinion against the crimes of fascism. It was chaired by the director of the Jewish Theater in Moscow, S.M. Mikhoels.

17. V.P. Naumov et al., eds., *Nepravednyi sud: Poslednii stalinskii rasstrel: Stenogramma sudebnogo protsessa nad chlenami Evreiskogo antifashistskogo komiteta* (Moscow, 1994); G.V. Kostyrchenko, *V plenu u krasnogo faraona: Politicheskie presledovaniia evreev v SSSR v poslednee stalinskoe desiatiletie: Dokumental'noe issledovanie* (Moscow, 1994); Shimon Redlich, *Propaganda and Nationalism in Wartime Russia: The Jewish Antifascist Committee in the USSR, 1941–1948* (Boulder, CO, 1982); Jehoshua A. Gilboa, *The Black Years of Soviet Jewry, 1939–1953* (Boston, 1971); Benjamin Pinkus, *Jews of the Soviet Union* (New York, 1988).

18. Kostyrchenko, *V plenu u krasnogo faraona*, 60–61.

19. "O tak nazyvaemom 'dele Evreiskogo antifashistskogo komiteta,' " *Izvestia TsK KPSS*, 1989, No. 12: 40.

20. *Pravda*, 13 January 1953.

21. Svodka pisem-otklikov na soobshchenie TASS ob areste "gruppy vrachei-vreditelei," 1953; TsKhSD, f. 5, op. 16, d. 602, l. 14.

22. Ibid., l. 17.

23. Ibid., ll. 32–34.

24. Ibid., l. 30.

25. Ia.L. Rapoport, "Vospominaniia o 'dele vrachei,' " *Druzhba narodov*, 1988, No. 4: 224.

Chapter 14: The Evolution of Public Opinion

1. L.N. Voitolovskii, *Ocherki kollektivnoi psikhologii*, 2 vols. (Petrograd, 1925), 2: 75.

2. See, for example, Otto Latsis, "Skazki nashego vremeni," *Izvestia*, 15 April 1988.

3. Informatsiia Otdela propagandy i agitatsii TsK VKP(b) ob otklikakh trudiashchikhsia na snizhenie roznichnykh tsen, March 1949; RTsKhIDNI, f. 17, op. 132, d. 114, l. 27.

4. Ibid., l. 28.

5. Ibid., l. 27.

6. Ibid.

7. Programma VKP(b): Proekt; ibid., op. 125, d. 476, l. 190.

8. *Voprosy ekonomiki,* 1950, No. 10: 101.

9. Ibid., 106–08.

10. Informatsiia Otdela propagandy i agitatsii TsK VKP(b) "O nedostatkakh v provedenii sobranii rabochikh i sluzhashchikh na promyshlennykh predpriiatiiakh Tul'skoi
oblasti," August 1950; RTsKhIDNI, f. 17, op. 132, d. 291, l. 84.

11. Ibid., l. 85.

12. Ibid., l. 86.

13. Ibid., l. 87.

14. *Pravda,* 11 October 1952.

15. Zapiska I.M. Stul'nikova G.M. Malenkovu, 12 January 1950; RTsKhIDNI, f. 17, op.
132, d. 278, l. 6.

16. Ibid., l. 7.

17. Ibid., l. 10.

18. Anatolii Zlobin, "Ural'skie vstrechi," *Novyi mir,* 1953, No. 12: 194.

19. *Pravda,* 13 October 1952.

20. Ibid., 2 December 1952.

21. Iurii Sharapov, "Bez gneva i pristrastiia: Politicheskie zametki," *Moskovskie novosti,* 3
September 1989, 22.

22. Interview with P.V. Volobuev; author's personal archive.

23. Ibid.

24. N.S. Atarov, *Dal'niaia doroga: Literaturnyi portret V. Ovechkina* (Moscow, 1977), 101.

25. Ibid., 114.

26. Ibid.

27. Vladimir Dudintsev, "Obraz svobody," *Literaturnaia gazeta,* 8 May 1991, 9.

28. Ales' Adamovich, "Tikhoe imia," ibid., 18 October 1991, 4.

Chapter 15: The New Public Atmosphere

1. "Svidetel'stvuiu," *Argumenty i fakty,* 1988, No. 50: 3.

2. I.G. Erenburg, *Sobranie sochinenii,* 9 vols. (Moscow, 1962–1967), 9: 730.

3. Cited in *Nedelia,* 1989, No. 19.

4. Erenburg, *Sobranie sochinenii,* 9: 731.

5. A.D. Sakharov, "Vospominaniia," *Znamia,* 1990, No. 12: 34.

6. Pis'ma s predlozheniiami ob uvekovechivanii pamiati I.V. Stalina, March-July 1953;
TsKhSD, f. 5, op. 16, d. 593(a), ll. 6–16.

7. Ibid.

8. Ibid.

9. Interview with Iu.S. Apenchenko; author's personal archive.

10. Harrison Salisbury, *Moscow Journal: The End of Stalin* (Chicago, 1961), 349.

11. For details on the activity of L.P. Beriia and an assessment, see N.F. Nekrasov, ed.,
Beriia: Konets kar'ery (Moscow, 1991); Amy Knight, *Beria: Stalin's First Lieutenant* (Princeton,
1993); B.A. Starkov, "Sto dnei lubianskogo marshala," *Istochnik,* 1993, No. 4; O.V. Khlevniuk,
"L.P. Beriia: Predely istoricheskoi reabilitatsii," *Istoricheskie issledovaniia v Rossii: Tendentsii
poslednikh let* (Moscow, 1996); A.I. Kokurin and A.I. Pozharov, " 'Novyi kurs' L.P. Beriia 1953
g.," *Istoricheskii arkhiv,* 1996, No. 4.

12. *Pravda,* 6 and 9 August 1953.

13. *Izvestia TsK KPSS*, 1989, No. 6: 149.

14. Fedor Burlatskii, *Vozhdi i sovetniki* (Moscow, 1990), 27.

15. Cited in T.A. Lukovtseva, "Poisk putei obnovleniia obshchestva i sovetskaia literatura v 50–60kh godakh," *Voprosy istorii KPSS*, 1989, No. 1: 39.

16. F.A. Abramov, "Liudi kolkhoznoi derevni v poslevoennoi proze," *Novyi mir*, 1954, No. 4; M.A. Lifshits, "Dnevnik Marietty Shaginiana," ibid., No. 2; M.A. Shcheglov, " 'Russkii les' Leonida Leonova," ibid., No. 5.

17. Pis'mo N. Shchennikova V. Pomerantsevu, 1954; RGALI, f. 1702, op. 6, d. 72, l. 69.

18. Stenogramma chitatel'skoi konferentsii po obshuzhdeniiu stat'i V. Pomerantseva "Ob iskrennosti v literature," 12 February 1954; ibid., d. 77, l. 52.

19. Ibid.

20. Pis'mo v redaktsiiu zhurnala "Novyi mir" I. Ivannikova, December 1953; ibid., d. 72, l. 3.

21. Pis'mo G. Shchukina V. Pomerantsevu, December 1953; ibid., l. 21.

22. Stenogramma chitatel'skoi konferentsii po obsuzhdeniiu stat'i V. Pomerantseva "Ob iskrennosti v literature"; ibid., d. 77, l. 21.

23. Aleksandr Tvardovskii, "Iz rabochikh tetradei (1953–1960)," *Znamia*, 1989, No. 7: 139.

24. See *Novyi mir*, 1954, No. 8: 307.

25. Leonid Zorin, "Gosti; Ottepel', 1953–1957," *Stranitsy russkoi sovetskoi literatury* (Moscow, 1989), 119.

26. Ibid.

27. Ibid., 434–36.

28. Sakharov, "Vospominaniia," 59. [The reference here is to Milovan Djilas, *The New Class: An Analysis of the Communist System* (New York, 1957)—H.R.]

29. Pis'mo I. Efimova v redaktsiiu zhurnala "Novyi mir"; RGALI, f. 1702, op. 4, d. 317, l. 19.

30. Cited in "Ego sotvorennoe pole: Valentin Rasputin o Fedore Abramove," *Sovetskaia kul'tura*, 10 March 1987.

31. Iz chitatel'skoi pochty zhurnala "Novyi mir"; RGALI, f. 1702, op. 4, d. 391, l. 3.

32. *Pravda*, 11 January 1954.

33. Informatsiia otdela partiinykh organov po RSFSR TsK KPSS "Ob itogakh vyborov v Verkhovnyi Sovet RSFSR i mestnye sovety deputatov trudiashchikhsia," 4 March 1955; TsKhSD, f. 5, op. 32, d. 34, l. 7.

34. Ibid.

35. Informatsiia Moskovskogo komiteta KPSS o nadpisiakh na izbiratel'nykh biulleteniakh, sdelannykh izbirateliami v den' vyborov 27 fevralia 1955 g.; ibid., l. 15.

36. Ibid., l. 20.

37. Ibid., ll. 20, 23.

38. Informatsiia otdela partiinykh organov po RSFSR TsK KPSS "Ob itogakh vyborov . . . ," l. 9.

39. Ilia Erenburg, "Liudi, gody, zhizn'," *Ogonek*, 1987, No. 22: 23.

40. Anatolii Zlobin, "Posle soveshchaniia," *Novyi mir*, 1955, No. 7: 38.

Chapter 16: The Repudiation of the GULAG

1. Anton Antonov-Ovseenko, "Protivostoianie," *Literaturnaia gazeta*, 3 April 1991, 2; "Desiat' 'zheleznykh narkomov,' " *Komsomol'skaia pravda*, 19 September 1989; A.N. Dugin, "Stalinizm: Legendy i fakty," *Slovo*, 1990, No. 7; V.N. Zemskov, "GULAG: Istoriko-sotsiologicheskii aspekt," *SOTSIS*, Nos. 6, 7, and passim.

2. "Gosudarstvennyi terror v sovetskoi Rossii, 1923–1953: Istochniki i ikh inter-

pretatsiia," *Otechestvennye arkhivy*, 1992, No. 2: 27.

3. "Zapiska ministra vnutrennikh del SSSR L.P. Beriia v Prezidium TsK KPSS o neobkhodimosti provedeniia amnistii, 26 March 1953," *Istoricheskii arkhiv*, 1996, No. 4: 143.

4. Aleksandr Solzhenitsyn, "Arkhipelag GULAG," *Novyi mir*, 1989, No. 8: 8.

5. O.V. Khlevniuk, "L.P. Beriia: Predely istoricheskoi reabilitatsii," in G.A. Bordiugov, ed., *Istoricheskie issledovaniia v Rossii: Tendentsii poslednikh let* (Moscow, 1996), 151. For detail on the economic crisis in the GULAG, see Marta Kraveri (Marta Craveri) and O.V. Khlevniuk, "Krizis ekonomiki MVD (konets 1940kh–1950e gody)," *Cahiers du monde russe et soviétique*, 36 (1995): 179–90; G.M. Ivanova, "GULAG v ekonomicheskoi i politicheskoi zhizhi strany," in V.S. Lel'chuk and E.I. Pivovar, eds., *SSSR i kholodnaia voina* (Moscow, 1995), 203–48.

6. Ivanova, "GULAG v ekonomicheskoi i politicheskoi zhizni strany," 247.

7. *Otechestvennye arkhivy*, 1994, No. 4: 33. [The colonies were a mild regime of the camps, where the inhabitants were often simply confined to the immediate vicinity. They often consisted of specially qualified professional personnel assigned to work on projects of high priority, usually of military significance.—H.R.]

8. Ivanova, "GULAG v ekonomicheskoi i politicheskoi zhizni strany," 246.

9. Informatsiia Otdela partiinykh, profsoiuznykh i komsomol'skikh organov TsK KPSS "O khode vypolneniia postanovleniia Soveta Ministrov SSSR ot 30 maia 1953 g. 'Ob ustranenii nedostatkov v trudoustroistve osvobozhdennykh po amnistii grazhdan,' " 25 June 1953; TsKhSD, f. 5, l. 15, d. 402, l. 88.

10. Ibid., l. 89.

11. "O tak nazyvaemom 'leningradskom dele,' " *Izvestia TsK KPSS*, 1989, No. 2: 133.

12. Ibid., No. 11: 48.

13. Ibid., 41.

14. Cited in *Ogonek*, 1989, No. 11: 9.

15. Iu.P. Sharapov, "Bez gneva i pristrastiia: Politicheskie zametki," *Moskovskie novosti*, 3 September 1989, 22.

16. "Vse ne tak, rebiata," *Sovetskaia kul'tura*, 7 April 1990.

17. Pis'mo A.P. Borisova v redaktsiiu zhurnala "Novyi mir"; RGALI, f. 1702, op. 10, d. 2, l. 167.

18. Pis'mo V.L. Zhevtuna v redaktsiiu zhurnala "Novyi mir"; ibid., ll. 32, 32(ob).

19. Pis'mo D.I. Markelova v redaktsiiu zhurnala "Novyi mir"; ibid., ll. 155–56.

Chapter 17: Turning to the Individual

1. Pis'mo G. Mareicheva v redaktsiiu zhurnala "Novyi mir," 1951; RGALI, f. 1702, op. 6., d. 35, l. 82.

2. Pis'mo I. Efimova v redaktsiiu zhurnala "Novyi mir," 1953; ibid, op. 4, d. 317, ll. 19–20.

3. Pis'mo V. Oskotskogo v redaktsiiu zhurnala "Novyi mir," 1953; ibid., op. 6, d. 72, ll. 15–16.

4. Pis'mo E. Beliaevoi v redaktsiiu zhurnala "Novyi mir," 1953; ibid., op. 4, d. 318, l. 40.

5. Ibid.

6. Pis'mo V. Boitsova v redaktsiiu zhurnala "Novyi mir," 1953; ibid., l. 60.

7. Pis'mo A. Ostapenko v redaktsiiu zhurnala "Novyi mir," 1953; ibid., d. 317, l. 33.

8. Pis'mo Iu. Golovtsova v redaktsiiu zhurnala "Novyi mir," 1953; ibid. d. 318, l. 104.

9. *Vtoroi Vsesoiuznyi s''ezd sovetskikh pisatelei, 15–26 dekabria 1954 g.: Stenograficheskii otchet* (Moscow, 1956), 102.

10. Ibid.

11. Ibid., 102–03.

12. Ibid., 27–28.
13. Cited in *Pravda,* 4 February 1987.
14. Vladimir Pomerantsev, "Ob iskrennosti v literature," in S.I. Chuprinin, ed., *Ottepel',* *1953–1956: Stranitsy russkoi sovetskoi literatury* (Moscow, 1989), 52.
15. Stenogramma chitatel'skoi konferentsii po obsuzhdeniiu stat'i V. Pomerantseva "Ob iskrennosti v literature," 12 February 1954; RGALI, f. 1702, op. 6, d. 77, ll. 56–57.

Chapter 18: The Cult of Personality and Its Social Impact

1. Cited in N.A. Barsukov, "Mart 1953–go," *Pravda,* 27 October 1989.
2. Ibid.
3. "Plenum TsK KPSS, 2–7 iiulia 1953 g.: Stenograficheskii otchet," *Izvestia TsK KPSS,* 1991, No. 2: 195.
4. Ibid.
5. Ibid., 196.
6. Ibid., No. 1: 166.
7. Ibid., 188.
8. Ibid., 149.
9. Ibid., 146.
10. Ibid., 149.
11. Ibid., 165.
12. Ibid., 187.
13. *Pravda,* 15 July 1953.
14. Ibid.
15. Personal archive of G.M. Malenkov in possession of his heirs.
16. Interview with I.A. Dedkov; author's personal archive.
17. Ibid.
18. Ilia Erenburg, "Liudi, gody, zhizn'," *Ogonek,* 1987, No. 23: 22.
19. Cited in *EKO,* 1987, No. 10: 67.
20. Iz redaktsionnoi pochty zhurnala *Kommunist,* March 1956; RTsKhIDNI, f. 599, op. 1, d. 82, l. 117.
21. Ibid., d. 82, l. 119.
22. Ibid., d. 88.
23. Voprosy, zadannye dokladchiku na sobranii aktiva Sverdlovskoi gorodskoi partiinoi organizatsii, 16 March 1956; TsKhSD, f. 5, op. 32, d. 45, l. 45.
24. Voprosy, zadannye na sobraniiakh raionnykh aktivov goroda Molotova, 1956; ibid., ll. 70, 72.
25. Informatsiia otdela partiinykh organov TsK KPSS "O khode obsuzhdeniia materialov XX s''ezda v partiinykh organizatsiiakh RSFSR," 16 April 1956; ibid., l. 2.
26. Ibid., l. 4.
27. Ibid., l. 1.
28. Ibid.
29. See, for example, Informatsiia Udmurtskogo oblastnogo komiteta KPSS "O khode obsuzhdeniia itogov XX s''ezda KPSS na sobraniiakh gorodskikh, raionnykh partiinykh aktivov i pervichnykh partiinykh organizatsii," 7 April 1956; ibid., d. 46, l. 10.
30. Informatsiia otdela partiinykh organov TsK KPSS "O provedenii sobranii partiinogo aktiva po itogam XX s''ezda KPSS v raionakh Leningrada," 16 April 1956; ibid., d. 45, l. 26.
31. Spravka otdela partiinykh organov TsK KPSS po soiuznym respublikam "O faktakh nepravil'nykh, demogogicheskikh i antipartiinykh vystuplenii, imevshikh mesto na partiinykh

sobraniiakh v soiuznykh respublikakh po itogam XX s''ezda KPSS," 17 June 1956; ibid., op. 31, d. 54, l. 14.

32. Ibid., l. 15.

33. Informatsiia otdela partiinykh organov TsK KPSS po RSFSR "O khode obsuzhdeniia materialov XX s''ezda KPSS v partiinykh organizatsiiakh RSFSR," l. 5.

34. Informatsiia otdela partiinykh organov TsK KPSS po RSFSR o reagirovanii voennosluzhashchikh na doklad N.S. Khrushcheva "O kul'te lichnosti i ego posledstviiakh," 1956; ibid., op. 32, d. 46, ll. 204–05.

35. Interview with O.P. Latsis; author's personal archive.

36. Erenburg, "Liudi, gody, zhizn'," 22.

37. Stenogramma plenuma Moskovskogo gorodskogo komiteta KPSS, 26 November 1956; RTsKhIDNI, f. 556, op. 1, d. 693, l. 244.

38. Stenogramma sobraniia partiinogo aktiva goroda Moskvy, 9 March 1956; ibid., d. 705, ll. 146–47.

Chapter 19: Public Opinion and the "Hungarian Syndrome"

1. Zapiska redaktsii zhurnala *Voprosy istorii* chlenam Prezidiuma i sekretariam TsK KPSS, v redaktsiiu zhurnala *Kommunist,* August 1956; RTsKhIDNI, f. 599, op. 1, d. 81, l. 4.

2. Iz redaktsionnoi pochty zhurnala *Kommunist;* ibid., op. 3, d. 653, l. 199.

3. B.A. Grushin and V.V. Chikin, *Ispoved' pokoleniia* (Moscow, 1962), 204.

4. Vladimir Dudintsev, "Nachinat' nuzhno s khleba," *Argumenty i fakty,* 1988, No. 2.

5. *Argumenty i fakty,* 1989, No. 1.

6. Cited in S.I. Chuprinin, ed., *Ottepel', 1953–1956: Stranitsy russkoi sovetskoi literatury* (Moscow, 1989), 475.

7. Ibid., 476. [*Samizdat* was the "self-published" literature of underground dissent produced in multiple copies largely with carbon paper on typewriters and circulated from hand to hand by members of the movement.—H.R.]

8. *Izvestiia,* 2 November 1956; *Literaturnaia gazeta,* 24 November, 15 December 1956.

9. Pis'mo A. Shcherbakova v redaktsiiu *Literaturnoi gazety,* 1956; RGALI, f. 1702, op. 6, d. 245, l. 4.

10. Ibid.

11. Pis'mo bez podpisi V. Dudintsevu, 1956; ibid., l. 12.

12. Pis'mo Iu. Berezina V. Dudintsevu, 1956; idid., l. 33.

13. Stenogramma zasedaniia plenuma Leningradskogo gorkoma KPSS, 13 December 1956; RTsKhIDNI, f. 556, op. 1, d. 603, l. 307.

14. Ibid., l. 306.

15. Ibid.

16. V.N. Azhaev: Soviet writer, author of the novel *Daleko ot Moskvy* (Far from Moscow, received Stalin prize, 1949).

17. A.G. Malyshkin: Soviet Russian writer, author of the novel *Liudi iz zakholust'ia* (People from the Boondocks, about village life).

18. Iz redaktsionnoi pochty zhurnala *Novyi mir,* 1956; RGALI, f. 1702, op. 6, d. 243, l. 39.

19. Cited in Chuprinin, *Ottepel', 1953–1956,* 476.

20. Stenogramma sobraniia partiinogo aktiva Leningrada, January 1957; RTsKhIDNI, f. 556, op. 2, d. 671, l. 30.

21. Informatsiia otdela partiinykh organov TsK KPSS po RSFSR "Ob otklikakh trudiashchikhsia na sobytiia v Vengrii," 10 November 1956; TsKhSD, f. 5, op. 32, d. 39, l. 131.

22. Ibid.

23. Ibid.

24. Ibid., l. 132.

25. Ibid.

26. Zakrytoe pis'mo TsK KPSS "Ob usilenii politicheskoi raboty partiinykh organizatsii v massakh i presechenii vylazok antisovetskikh, vrazhdebnykh elementov," 19 December 1956; ibid., f. 89, perechen' 6, dokument 2.

27. Ibid.

28. Ilia Erenburg, "Liudi, gody, zhizn'," *Ogonek*, 1987, No. 24: 28. [At the Twenty-Second Party Congress in October 1961 the party passed a resolution to denounce Stalin more thoroughly and comprehensively and to expel his body from the mausoleum.—H.R.]

29. *Voprosy literatury*, 1989, No. 5: 210.

30. N.S. Khrushchev, *Za tesnuiu sviaz' literatury i iskusstva s zhizn'iu naroda (Moscow, 1957), 16.*

31. *Voprosy literatury*, 1989, No. 5: 211.

32. A.T. Tvardovskii, "Iz rabochikh tetradei," *Znamia*, 1989, No. 8: 127.

33. Interview with I.A. Dedkov; author's personal archive.

34. Cited in L.P. Talochkin and I.G. Alpatova, eds., *Drugoe iskusstvo: Moskva 1956–1976,* 2 vols. (Moscow, 1994), 1: 38.

35. Ibid., 292. Herluf Bidstrup was a Danish communist cartoonist whose work was often republished in the Soviet press.

36. L.M. Alekseeva, *Istoriia inakomysliia v SSSR* (Moscow/Vilnius, 1992), 199.

37. [In characteristically cramped Soviet apartments, the kitchen was the natural gathering place—with tea and *zakuski* (snacks)—of friends in conversation.—H.R.]

Index

Elena Zubkova is a senior research fellow at the Institute of Russian History, Russian Academy of Sciences. She received her degrees from the Moscow State Historical Archival Institute (B.A.) and the Institute of Russian History (Ph.D.) and has worked at the Moscow State Archive of the October Revolution (now GARF). Dr. Zubkova has published many essays and articles on postwar history, and the book *Society and Reforms, 1945–1964* (in Russian; Rossiia molodaia, 1993).

Hugh Ragsdale studied at the University of North Carolina (A.B.) and the University of Virginia (M.A., Ph.D.). He has done postgraduate study at Moscow State University and the Soviet/Russian Academy of Sciences and has worked in the foreign affairs archives of London, Paris, Vienna, Copenhagen, and Stockholm, as well as Moscow. His most recent book is *The Russian Tragedy: The Burden of History* (M.E. Sharpe, 1996).